# Iron Rookie

## Secrets of the Ironmen

www.iron-rookie.com

www.10races.com

CW00840129

For Olivia

Always Remember

*In Life, Anything Is Possible*

"Race day should only ever be one thing…

A celebration of all your training"

*Iron Rookie*

"Taking something that you believe to be impossible and turning it into the possible whilst being roared on by thousands of wonderful supporters who line every inch of the Ironman race circuit will be one of the most magical experiences of your life"

*Iron Rookie*

*Disclaimer*

All the information presented here and on the iron-rookie.com website is an individual account of the authors personal experiences of training for and entering events and is for resource and reference purposes only. It is not a substitute for, or an addition to, any advice given to you by your doctor or healthcare provider.

Readers of this work should understand that the author started his journey at race level 1 (See race history) and SLOWLY worked his way up.

Before making any changes to your lifestyle, diet or exercise habits and before implementing any information provided here you must consult your doctor, and consult them again before moving up from one level to the next.

By accessing this information you waive and release any and all claims for damages that may occur as a result of your following all or any part of the authors personal journey, including blog posts, race reports, training plans or advice.

Please understand that you are solely responsible for the way information is perceived and utilised and you do so at your own risk. You further certify that you have full knowledge of the risks involved in starting, partaking and completing a training plan.

If you ever feel dizzy, shortness of breath, discomfort or pain terminate the activity immediately and seek medical advice.

Never enter a swimming pool unless there is a qualified lifeguard present.

Never swim in open water unless it is a structured open water swim session organised by professional, qualified swim coaches with adequate safety measures in place..

Ensure your bike is regularly inspected and maintained by a qualified bike technician, make sure you always wear a helmet and that the front and rear lights are in full working order.

Consider carrying a mobile phone with you at all times whilst training in case of emergencies.

Wear high visibility clothing for both your cycle and run training and consider training only in well lit pedestrianised areas for the run and purpose built cycle paths for the bike wherever possible.

## Important

It is very important you understand that the author is not a coach, nor does he have any professional coaching qualifications.

His only qualifications are the medals that he proudly wears around his neck, of which there are 10, one for each race in the series.

The author is not preaching to you, or telling you that you need to do things in a certain way, he is merely sharing with you his personal experience of how he was able to go from being very overweight and very unfit, unable to swim, bike or run, to, ultimately, completing Ironman UK in Bolton, England.

Aside from group open water swim coaching at three sisters in Wigan (which was the best £5 a week the author ever spent) He has not read any books or had any professional triathlon coaching whatsoever.

All of the training plans in this book are the exact ones that the author followed for each race in the series and were 100% self generated by him.

Readers should note that the author was able to successfully train for, then complete, each and every race totally injury free. (For proof of results see www.iron-rookie.com)

In addition, much of the material in this book is written in the way that the author would talk, so please forgive the poor grammar at times, in particular during the Ironman diaries which were written 'in real time' and in order to preserve their purity have been presented to you here in their original, unedited format.

Finally, there is the distinct possibility that once this material is released, the floodgates will open and Ironman may turn into a 'mass participation' event, not dissimilar to the London marathon.

Now the author can think of nothing but positives if this were to happen.

An influx of first timers would mean a bigger prize pool, which in turn would attract even more amazing pros competing for the prize purse.

The organisers would be able to re-invest yet further funds into the event, making the race experience for all the athletes even more wonderful than what it already is.

More participants would bring more friends and family along with them and they would join the thousands of fantastic supporters who already line every inch of both the bike and run circuits, making race day an even more magical occasion for all....

But, if, as a result of this work, the floodgates do open, please let me say this....

Being able to race with some of the finest athletes in the world is an absolute honour and a privilege for all, and something that is only really possible for the 'average joe' in this truly amazing sport.

This book will get you to the Ironman start line, but by learning, understanding and applying the secrets within, you agree to show total respect for all the pro's, the elite age groupers, those chasing the Kona dream, those looking to 'PB' and ultimately, for the event itself, by remembering where you are and playing the game in the manner in which it is meant to be played at all times…..

No dressing up as a chicken or anything ridiculous like that…..

I'm serious….

No taking the piss….

You will end up on a stretcher, and it will be nothing to do with the run.

You have been warned!

# Contents…

## Overview

What you are about to read, is the amazing story of Iron-Rookie.

At the start of his journey, he was very overweight, and very, very unfit.

Unable to swim more than a single length front crawl, he hadn't ridden a bike for over 15 years and couldn't run any more than ten yards without wanting to stop....

The first time he got onto a road 'racer' bike he felt straight off it and nearly broke his leg...

At the end of his journey, he became an Ironman.

It all started when his wife challenged him to run round a lake trail near his house that was just 2.5km in length, but felt like a marathon to him at the time.

Once he conquered the lake trail, he entered a sprint triathlon, having seen an advert for it at his local sports centre. He taught himself how to swim, followed the training plan that you will find in this book and loved every second of it, but doubted he would ever be able to move any further up the levels.

The pivotal moment came when he moved back to Bolton and realised that he lived near the Ironman cycling loop, a well known circuit amongst long distance endurance athletes.

Iron Rookie began to cycle parts of it regularly and whenever another cyclist had the audacity to overtake him, he tried to interview them.

Surprisingly, most were happy to talk.

Some of these cyclists turned out to be Ironmen, some were very high ranking ones.

The secrets that they shared with him changed his life forever.

Iron Rookie then went on to complete super sprint, sprint, Olympic, 70.3 and full Ironman triathlons, together with 2.5k, 5k, 10k, 20k and marathon run races inbetween.

This book is more than just his story….

It's a complete manual of how he did it.

Once Iron's inspirational 'story' is told, the secrets that he learnt from the Ironmen are revealed for the first time.

The book then turns into a step by step guide showing the exact daily training plans that he followed, race by race, starting with a 2.5km 'fun run' and ending with an Ironman triathlon.

This book is unique, as it is aimed at both the complete novice, the triathlete looking to advance through the levels and the trainee Ironman, all at the same time.

It starts focussed firmly on the complete novice.

Iron rookie can clearly remember the thoughts, fears and questions that many first timers have before training for their first triathlon.

Entire chapters are dedicated to subjects such as; which bike to choose, what kit you will need, how to learn to swim properly, how to nail nutrition, and precisely what to expect on race day.

This book aims to address all those fears and more still, before providing the exact daily training plan that Iron Rookie followed to successfully train for, and complete, his first ever race.

As Iron advances through the levels of triathlon to Olympic and half Iron distances, so do the training plans that he followed, with the secrets that he learnt playing a bigger and bigger part in his journey.

In the final chapter, Iron Rookie trains for his first ever Ironman.

Not only can his exact, iron distance training plan be found within these pages, but he kept a unique, 28 part diary, providing real time commentary on his training as he did it, day by day, week by week, sharing the many lessons he learnt along the way.

Anyone aspiring to conquer the iron distance for the first time is certain to find this resource invaluable to their quest.

It was during this period that even more amazing Ironmen came into his life…

It all started when he met someone that had completed the iron distance 3 times so he ran a feature on them for his blog…..

Then he met someone who had done it 7 times……

Then 10, then 13, then 15….

And it ended with him 'interviewing' someone who had completed the iron distance no fewer than 150 times, including 20 in 20 days back to back!!!

Those truly inspirational interviews together with their top tips for iron distance first timers can also be found in this book.

So get yourself cosy and sort yourself a coffee…

What you are about to discover will blow your mind!

**A Message From The Author!**

Hi, I'm PK, the Iron Rookie, thank you for purchasing my book!

I still can't quite believe that I managed to do it, become an Ironman like!

Sounds pretty cool doesn't it?

'I am an Ironman' (no way lol).

It has been the most amazing adventure as Ironman UK was never just about 'becoming one' - it was all about the wonderful journey that I went on to get there.

But it also became about what happened on race day and the sensation an 'average joe' got by realising a dream in front of thousands of spectators.

Taking something that you believe to be impossible and turning it into the possible whilst being roared on by thousands and thousands of incredible supporters who line almost every inch of the Ironman race circuit will be one of the most magical experiences of your life.

The hairs on the back of my neck stand up every time I think about those brilliant supporters, but more about them later.

This is about you.

It is my wish that you will love this book and will find many things within these pages that will help you on your quest, no matter what 'level' you are currently at.

If you do, please remember that a book will only ever be as good as the reviews that it gets, so if you would kindly take 2 minutes to leave me a short review on amazon, it would mean more to me than you will ever know...

## Why I wrote this book

In a nutshell I wrote this book because I wish I would have found a book like this at the start of my journey.

I read somewhere a long time ago that the secret to getting anything you want in life is to find someone that has already done what it is that you want to do and follow in their footsteps.

On that basis, I wanted to leave a trail of Iron footprints for you to follow, no matter what your current level of fitness, and those footprints can be found right here in this book.

One of the funniest things I ever saw in my life happened when I was sat waiting to get out of a car park in Burnley town centre.

A small, young lady, in her early 20's, who was at least 5 stone overweight, walked past my car clutching a trio of fast food bags and smoking a cigarette.

She was wearing a T-shirt that I recognised as being from one of the local health clubs, this I found a little strange, but I didn't think any more of it.

As she walked past my car, nothing could have prepared me for what I saw next.

Written on the back of the T-shirt she was wearing were the words:

"Personal Trainer"

To this day I regret that I did not take a picture, but the image will stay with me for the rest of my days.

It was as hilarious as it was ridiculous.

I will also never forget the 'coach' at my first triathlon, who never actually enters the race himself?............

My point is that I have discovered on my fitness / iron journey that there is a lot of this – a lot of people giving advice about things when they haven't actually done it themselves.

This book aims to change all that....

At the opposite end of the scale, everybody you speak to seems to be an 'expert' in triathlon, I watched in awe on twitter as time after time a 'newbie' would ask a question, only to be bombarded with about 15 different, often conflicting, answers!

Iron rookie has not forgotten how confusing this can be for the first timer with everybody offering conflicting advice!

For some reason, many people also try to make triathlon far more complicated than what it actually is.

You won't find any talk of 'VO2 Max Zone 3 4 and 5 here!

The beauty of this book is that the advice is perfectly simple, on swim days you get into the water and go for a swim, on bike days you get on your bike and go for a cycle and on run days guess what?

You put your trainers on and you go for a run!

Triathlon is also filled with many serious professional athletes, awesome full timers recording truly amazing times with years and years of sports training behind them and sponsorships and bikes worth thousands of pounds etc etc etc.

These guys are awesome, and some of them have written really interesting books, but let's face it, they are on a completely different level to you and I.

What was needed was a book written by an 'average guy'

A book written by someone who started out with zero fitness and ended up doing an Ironman.

A book that isn't just a story, but shows you the 'how'.

A book that takes you by the hand from day 1 and says 'Hey, I know exactly what you are going through right now because I have been there myself!! – So here are all the secrets that I learned, here are all the training plans that I followed and here is all the information you will ever need to take you as far as you want to go in triathlon.

This is that book.

My wish is that in some small way, this work will help many people across the globe experience what I experienced on race day at Ironman UK.

I wanted to show that anyone, literally anyone can do it.

But, most importantly,

I wanted to prove to you once and for all……

**The only limits to what is possible for you, are those which you impose upon yourself**…….

# My Journey

At the time of writing this I am 40 years of age and I have just completed the world's ultimate one day endurance event, an Ironman Triathlon, in my beloved Bolton, England.

It was by far the most magical experience of my life.

But I haven't always been so fit – far from it – quite the opposite in fact.

A little over 2 years ago I was at least 4 stone overweight, I smoked 20 fags a day, I could drink ale like a fish, I ate all the wrong foods because they tasted delicious and I did zero exercise whatsoever. Exercise was a thing other people did, not me – I was far too busy.

Around the same time I:

1) Tried to swim one length of my local pool front crawl and nearly drowned
2) Got onto a bicycle for the first time in 15 years and fell straight off it, when I tried to cycle up a small hill near my house I nearly had a heart attack a third of the way up
3) Bought some new trainers and went for a run, at the end of my street I nearly collapsed from exhaustion (and I lived on a very small street)

All the above statements are 100% true.

I can remember asking myself "PK what are you good at?" and I am embarrassed to say that one of the only things I could think of was "being one of the lads and drinking beer?"

I knew something had to change, and I can clearly remember the day that it did.

At the time I lived with my amazing wife in Rossendale, Lancashire – near to our house was a beautiful lake, dunnockshaw reservoir and it had a trail path running all the way around it.

As fate would have it, that trial path is approx. 2.5km, not that I was aware of it at the time…

Every now and then, myself and the wife would take a stroll around that lake, only when the weather was really nice mind….

The path around it was full of the usual, couples, families, dog walkers, but every now and then, a jogger would whiz past…

I clearly remember the day I asked my wife **the** question.

A question that was to change everything….

"Do you think I could run around this lake?" I asked

"No chance" came the flippant and far too quick reply

And that was where it all started, right there, in that moment

I immediately burst into a jog.

30 seconds later I was doubled over, in great pain, and wanted to stop!

That is exactly what I did – stop!

At the time the thought of being able to run all the way around that 2.5km trail was so far out of my reality I didn't think it would ever be possible for me.

I have since gone on to realise that, in life, anything is possible, and the only limits to our reality are those which we impose upon ourselves, but more about that later.

After a few weeks I managed to run all the way around that lake.

Exactly how I managed to conquer it can be found in the level 1 training plan.

The amazing sense of achievement I got from doing so has stayed with me ever since, little did I know the journey that I was about to embark on.

From there I somehow ended up entering Rossendale Sprint Triathlon, I think I saw a sign for it at the local sports centre.

Again, being able to complete this was so far out of my reality I didn't think it would be possible, but again I proved to myself that it was.

I followed the base swim plan that is detailed in this book and also applied what I had learnt from running round the lake to the bike and the run elements and it (somehow) got me through.

At the time, Rossendale Triathlon was one of the most amazing things I ever did, but moving any further up the levels was never really on my radar.

Everything changed though when we moved back to Bolton.

I can't remember exactly how I discovered that I lived near the Ironman cycle loop (they do x2 50 mile loops) but somehow, I did…

I started to ride part of the course fairly regularly.

This is where I began to grill / interview anyone that would talk to me as they overtook me on the bike.

Surprisingly, most were happy to talk.

Some of these guys turned out to be Ironmen.

Some were very high ranking ones.

The secrets that they shared with me changed my life forever.

I then made the decision to become an Ironman myself by applying the secrets that I had learnt and working my way through the levels, getting stronger and stronger, race by race....

The final chapter in my journey came when I realised that other people might want to follow in my footsteps, so I began to write...

On that note, I firmly believe that writing this book was my destiny.

Sadly I lost my father not long ago.

We used to have season tickets watching Bolton Wanderers.

From our seats in the upper tier of the West stand, I could clearly see Turton tower in Rivington that sits at the top of the legendary sheep house lane climb on the Ironman UK route.

Please understand that neither the tower nor Ironman meant anything to me at the time, it was just a tower.

But many a time my eyes would be distracted from the game and drawn to the tower, I know it sounds weird, but it was almost as if this tower had a magical power, and was somehow calling me to it.

Shortly after he died, his widow gave me a painting, it was a painting of the Bolton Wanderers stadium signed by Fabrice Muwamba, my dad 'won' it at a re-union that we went to for the 'white hot 93' team.

When I looked at that painting, my eyes were drawn not to the subject, but to something in the background, it was the tower on sheep house lane, it was almost as if the artist had made a 'feature' of it.

The first time I cycled up sheep house and saw all the messages of support for the Ironmen sprayed onto the tarmac, I honesty cried.

All those individual hopes and dreams that those messages represented, I found it haunting, truly magical, it really moved me.

Little did I know that one day, those messages were going to represent my Ironman dreams too...

Whilst I was training for Ironman UK, I made a website and started a weekly blog about it.

Not long after I started this I began to meet even more truly inspirational Ironmen, you will find their remarkable stories in this book too.

I believe that we each have a destiny in life.

I am certain that writing this book was mine.

My wish is that you enjoy reading it as much as I enjoyed writing it.

Ready to get started?

Ok, let's go.....

## How to Use This Book

This is a book about my journey, and remember always where my journey started – I was very overweight and very, very unfit.

I was unable to run more than 10 yards without wanting to stop.

My journey started at level 1, conquering a 2.5km run..

You will notice in most of the plans that follow, I reached the target distances weeks before race day & continued to practice them, the term is 'training the race' and I'm a big fan of it.

When you arrive on the start line knowing that you already have the swim bike and run in the bag, guess what happens?

Race day becomes a celebration.

I am aware that readers are likely to fall into 5 main categories:

### 1) Complete newbies not only to triathlon, but to running

If this is you then great! You get to follow in my footsteps from the very beginning!

First job, book an appointment with your GP and get the all clear to proceed!

Then read the book in the order it is written, start at level 1, and slowly work your way up.

### 2) Runners looking to move into triathlon

If you are one of the many runners who are looking to move over to triathlon, then I would suggest that you start at level 2

Whilst I appreciate that you will likely find the run element 'easy' It does not follow that if you have already completed a 10k run race you should enter an Olympic distance triathlon.

The biggest message in this book is the wonderful and amazing journey you will go on by starting at the bottom and working your way up.

Training for and then completing the races in the exact order was also one of the main reasons that I was able to advance so easily through the levels.

Your fitness builds and builds as you complete each race.

Plus, you need to learn how to swim properly, which is probably the reason why you haven't done a triathlon before, right?

Get the all clear from your GP then read the book in the order that it is written, missing out one chapter and one chapter only, and that is the 2.5km run training plan.

### 3) People Returning to fitness after many months, (or years)

You can only possibly be one of two things

A runner, in which case point 2 above will apply

Or an existing triathlete that has been out of action (training or races) for many weeks – if this is you then book an appointment with your GP and get the all clear to proceed.

I would suggest reading the book in the order that it is written then pick up your training at level 2, slowly building your fitness back up to the level you were at before.

## 4) Active Triathletes that have already got their first race(s) under their belt and are looking to move up to the next level, from a Sprint to an Olympic / Olympic to a Half for example

If you do not currently visit your GP for regular check-ups, then First job, book an appointment with your GP and get the all clear to proceed!

Then read the book in the order it is written (skip the plans for any races you have completed) and pick up the plan for the level that you are looking to train for.

If you have not already mastered the transition from pool to open water don't miss the chapter dedicated to this.

Look through the 10 races (golden rule) and complete any races that you have missed out so far as part of your training.

If nothing else, doing so will be fun.

## 5) Those looking to complete their first Ironman

Congratulations, I hope that you will adore the huge sections of this publication that have been dedicated to your quest!.....

You need to decide which profile from the 4 listed above is the closest match to your current circumstances, see your GP, and away you go!.

Once you successfully complete a level, you then have 3 choices:

   1) Put your flag in the mountain and say 'I'm done'

Nothing wrong with that, just make sure that when you return you profile yourself as 'type 3' on the previous page.

   2) Stay at this level and enter more races for the same
      distance

Nothing wrong with that either, Enjoy!, just make sure you see your GP every 12 weeks for a check up

   3) Move up to the next level

Now we're talking! Everything you need is right here to help you on your quest, remember to consult your GP before moving up.

For levels 1-8 I would suggest a rest/celebration period of 7-10 days maximum before immediately picking up the training plan for the next level above. (note that the author moved through the levels in one continuous process totally injury free. Afterall, fitness is a way of life, right?)

If you rest inbetween levels for any longer than 7-10 days up to a maximum of 2-3 weeks, see your GP, then try picking up the training plan at week 10 for the distance that you recently conquered and see how you feel.

If you feel ok, proceed to the next level.

If it feels too difficult, adjust your training accordingly by dropping down to a level that feels more comfortable and working your way back up.

If there is a gap of many many weeks or even months inbetween levels, profile yourself as 'type 3' above.

# So what exactly are the 10 races? (The golden rule)

The 10 Races are the golden rule, the foundation upon which this book is based and one of the major clues to understanding how I was able to do what I did.

I asked an Ironman to give me some help with my Ironman training plan and he asked me which of the 10 levels I was currently at, when I replied "eh?" he talked me through the game.

"You have to start at level one, everybody starts at level one" he told me. "Once you have the medal for level one then and only then can you move up to level 2"

Breaking the journey down into 10 feeder levels just seemed like such common sense to me, so that is exactly what I did.

Think of it like the FA cup in football.

Of course every team would like a 'free pass' to Wembley, but that isn't how it works, you have to win the cup ties first. Besides, all the romance lies in the wonderful journey you will go on in getting to the final, as many a Manchester United fan will tell you.

Well it is exactly the same here, start at the very bottom and work your way up, celebrate your victories in each race as you conquer them and slowly build layers and layers of amazing fitness as you do so along the way.

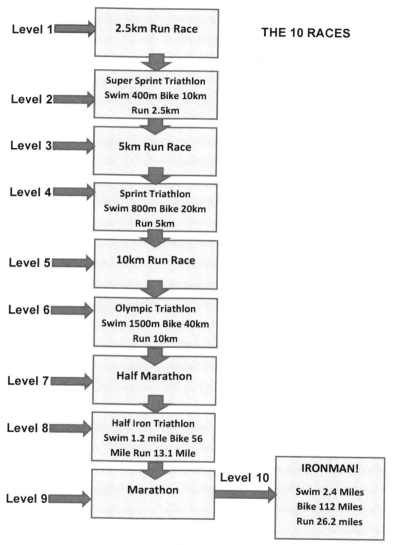

THE 10 RACES

Level 1 → 2.5km Run Race

Level 2 → Super Sprint Triathlon Swim 400m Bike 10km Run 2.5km

Level 3 → 5km Run Race

Level 4 → Sprint Triathlon Swim 800m Bike 20km Run 5km

Level 5 → 10km Run Race

Level 6 → Olympic Triathlon Swim 1500m Bike 40km Run 10km

Level 7 → Half Marathon

Level 8 → Half Iron Triathlon Swim 1.2 mile Bike 56 Mile Run 13.1 Mile

Level 9 → Marathon

Level 10 → IRONMAN! Swim 2.4 Miles Bike 112 Miles Run 26.2 miles

## Secrets from the Ironmen

So now you have a clearly defined path, what we need before we start following the training plans that will take you as far as you want to go, are the secrets.

I Guarantee that 90% of you have skipped straight to this page.

Can't say I blame you. I would have done the same. Be sure to revisit the preceeding pages though in your own time, and get with the gig.

If you are one of the 10% who didn't then congratulations, you have more willpower than I do!

As you know, I have spent many hours riding the Ironman cycle route as part of my training.

During this time I made a point of talking to every single cyclist that came past me.

Most were happy to talk and share their experiences and knowledge.

To date I have 'interviewed' many hundreds of cyclists on this route.

Every now and then a golden nugget would appear in the form of an Ironman, some very high ranking ones at that…

I was amazed at how happy these guys were to talk to me, I can't think of any other sport in the world where you would be able to do this.

Then again, I could tell that they hadn't really been asked before (not what we do in England is it? Ask questions and shut up? Let the other person talk? Try and learn from others?)

We already think we know everything, don't we?……

What these guys told me changed my life…

Here is what they said…..

(Readers should note that the secrets you are about to discover do not just apply to 'Ironman training', they apply from day 1)

## Secret Number 1 – The Great 'Iron Secret'

When I told an Ironman I wasn't sure I could ever complete the Half Iron distance never mind the full he said ah! so no-one has ever told you the 'Great Iron Secret' then?.

When I said 'Great Iron secret?' we pulled over and he showed me a youtube video which contained the key to unlock the Iron door.

The video featured a professor of sports science and nutrition who was lecturing to a group of trainee Ironmen.

The Ironman fast forwarded to the secret…

What the professor said was this….

"If you keep your heart rate low enough and your fuel level high enough then you can continue for an unlimited amount of time"

This is so profound I will repeat…

**"If you keep your heart rate low enough and your fuel level high enough, you can continue for an unlimited amount of time"**

Translated what this means is:

If you keep your pace slow enough and you eat enough food (fuel) you can continue for an unlimited amount of time.

Combine that with slowly building layers and layers of fitness by following the 'golden rule' of completing the 10 races in order as instructed in this book and you now have the great 'iron secret' that nobody wants you to know…

But wait, please expand, what food exactly? how much? and how often? And what's this about heart rates?

## Secret Number 2

What do they mean when they say Heart rate low enough?

Right,

Listen very carefully.

You can buy a watch today that will analyse your heart rate to the 'nth' degree every time you go and make a cup of tea.

The watch will do almost everything apart from complete the actual Ironman race for you!

Most coaches, many way more qualified than I, take all of this data, analyse it, then devise really complicated training plans linked to spending times in different 'heart rate zones' for maximum performance.

The average Joe looks at those training plans and immediately thinks 'Eh?'

But I have got to tell you something.

You can make this subject as complex or as simple as you like.

You are in control!

Always remember that 'Compete' or 'Complete' are two different things.

This book is all about how I took something that I didn't believe would be possible (completing an Ironman) and absolutely made it possible!

I did so by keeping everything ridiculously simple!

Think of it like this.

There is being able to swim/cycle/run fast

And then there is being able to swim/cycle/run for a long period of time.

Most coaches will tell you that the two are 'not mutually exclusive'.

But I found that the two are very different.

Linford Christie was the fastest runner over 100 metres of his time.

But If Linford tried to run 10,000 metres at his 100 metre pace he would probably either collapse after a few kilometres or end up withdrawing from the race.

It's the same for you.

One of the 'keys' to being able to complete the longer distance is to slow your pace right down.

But what do most people do?

They set off like a steam train, thinking that they have to PB every session!

No!

You do the exact opposite.

What they are talking about when they say keep your heart rate low enough from our perspective (completing the 10 races) is to stay in the 'aerobic zone' which is 60% to 80% of your max heart rate capacity with the 'sweet spot' being around the 70% mark.

Translated into English, what this means is you should be at a pace that is slow enough so you can still hold a conversation whilst doing your long, slow, run or bike and feel like you could continue at this pace 'all day long'.

I like to call it 'cruise control' - think of a car on the motorway cruising at 70mph, it's got plenty in reserve but it certainly isn't going slow, it's 'cruising!' – well it's the same here.

I was very rarely out of breath when I finished my training sessions and some people would say that I was not pushing myself hard enough.

On the contrary, I would say I was training my body to keep going at this pace 'all day' and that is exactly what I was looking to achieve.

Focus on the wonderful sensation of feeling 'strong' instead of feeling 'fast'. (I also like the 'effort' scale – think 7 out of 10)

A very rough guide to working out your max heart rate is 220-age.

So I am 40 years of age.

220-40 = 180 max heart rate.

60%-80% of 180 is 108-144 - I spent the majority of my training at around the 120 mark (67%) so bang inbetween the two.

Now many coaches will say that if you stay in this zone this you will become an expert at going 'slow'.

I personally found two things in this regard.

First, science says that the more you do something, the better you get at it.

I found this to be true of my fitness training also.

Let's say my time for my first ever attempt at the 5km distance was 35 minutes.

Simply by running that distance on a regular basis I found that my time naturally came down the more that I did it.

It then 'peaked' to my current PB of about 23 minutes.

Not a heart rate monitor in sight.

It was the same with the Ironman bike loop.

When I first cycled that loop it took me around 4 hours.

I practiced it over and over again and eventually took my time down to a PB of 2:38.

No heart rate training.

No different training 'zones'

Simple science.

The more you do something, the better you get at it.

Second, I found that increasing the distance then dropping back down meant I was able to do the shorter distance quicker so training turned into an ace version of a 'vicious circle'.

For example:

1) You are used to doing a 'long' ride of 40km on a Saturday in 'cruise control' (67% of max heart rate)
2) You drop that down to 20km for your midweek session & because the shorter distance feels much easier by comparison, you are able to ride at a faster pace (eg 75%)
3) The following weekend, when you take the distance back up again & return to 'cruise control' it feels easier versus when you 'smashed it' in the week (so slight + in pace)

Point 1 seems to benefit Point 2 and vice versa, it's almost like it's a universal truth similar to pi (π) or something.

I found that this tactic of doing a long, slow weekend bike then a shorter 'faster' (because I found it easier) session in the week seemed to work very well at every race level.

Whilst I was training for Ironman I would regularly do 100 mile rides & when I dropped down to 50 I had a lot of fun with them.

Most coaches will teach a mix of long slow sessions at a low heart rate, shorter speed drills at a higher heart rate, then throw in some hill work and in a way that is what I was doing without really realising it.

It's important to note that I didn't 'mix it up' with running. I stuck to one long, slow weekend run focusing on completing the distance instead of 'time' and staying at my 'all day long' stride.

I am convinced that this approach to running was one of the major reasons I avoided injury throughout the entire process.

My advice to you would be to get checked by your GP then get a heart rate monitor so you can keep an eye on it as you train and make sure you are staying in the 'aerobic zone' (60-80% of max for your long slow work with the sweet spot being around 70) but do not worry yourself with complicated heart rate training plans first time round each level, learn to focus instead on what 'cruise control' feels like and keep hitting it, mixing in the shorter 'faster' days to keep it fun.

Many people get their knickers in a twist about this subject (google it – your head will explode) but I would point out that this simple strategy got me a medal for **every** race in the series and for the record my 'time' was usually 'above average' at the lower levels and well inside the cut-offs at the higher ones.

## Secret Number 3 : Fuel

So now we know the great iron secret and we understand about heart rate, but what is this about fuel?

Somebody once told me that you should never exercise on a full stomach as doing so will give you a stitch. (I'm sure it was my dad!)

That thought process stayed ingrained in me for about 20 years.

As for eating whilst you train?

Are you mad?

I will also never forget taking an energy gel at Rossendale Triathlon and dismissing them as 'useless' because it didn't instantly turn me into Superman.

I have since gone on to realise that when you are training, your body is like a car.

It needs fuel. (food)

Before we talk about which foods we need to eat, we need to know **how much** food we should be eating, what is the correct amount?

The professor in the video immediately went on to say…

Your body can only process around 60-80g of fuel (carbohydrate) per hour.

On that basis, there is no point taking in much more fuel (carbohydrate) than that.

So now I knew the secret to Ironman and I knew how much fuel my body can process each hour but exactly what fuel should I take and how often and what works best??

Before I could ask more questions the Ironman had said his goodbyes and whizzed off into the distance!

From that moment on I made a point of asking every single cyclist I ever saw what their fuel strategy was and 85% of them would give me a blank look - it was obvious that they did not have one (included in this are some people that had entered Ironman which I was amazed at)

10% would say something vague like "I brought some sandwiches and an apple"

5% knew what they were talking about and had some form of strategy in place which I then went on to try out for myself with varying degrees of success.

Then one day I met an Ironman who had completed IMUK many times over.

He told me exactly what his fuel strategy was so I tried it and it changed my life forever.

I still use it to this day, no matter what distance I am training or racing and it has served me extremely well, as it will you..

## Onto Secret Number 4

Here is exactly what the Ironman's fuel strategy was:

Before I go out on a long ride I will always take a 25g protein shake and drink it before I set off.

I break my training rides down into 1 hour slots.

After 15 minutes I will suck on a shot block (energy chews)

After 30 minutes I will take an energy gel.

After 45 minutes I will suck on a shot block

After 1 hour I will eat a chia charge flapjack

I repeat this for every hour that I am out on the bike in training. It's exactly the same for my run drills but here I will only use gels. This is also the precise strategy I use for races, I take my first flapjack immediately after the swim and I only ever eat one thing for breakfast and that's porridge.

Every 15 minutes during training I will sip on my electrolyte drink to keep me hydrated (further source of carbs)

I thanked him for his advice and on my next ride copied his strategy to the letter as it matched what the professor had preached in the video.

It was a defining moment.

The effects were explosive.

I felt full of energy throughout my whole ride, I made sure I kept my pace slow and literally felt like I could continue riding forever - that feeling of 'running on empty' had left me for good!

My nutrition strategy was finally nailed!

I still apply this fuel strategy today to any training/races of 30 minutes plus (both bike and run) although I am not religious with the shot blocks and I too only use gels on the run. (but love the alternate flapjack/gel combo on the bike!)

Different types of food/gels/bars (fuel) work for different people, experiment yourself with different things in training to find what works best for you, I have tried all sorts. Literally all sorts. Read the label and look for the carbs content.

The key thing that transformed my ability to cycle/run for longer distances was the amount (30-40g carbs) and the frequency (every 30 mins).

For reference a typical gel/flapjack will have 30g carbs in it, 2 of those per hour gives you 60g plus the carbs in your electrolyte drink will easily get you into the 60-80g per hour zone.

It's important you understand that this fuel strategy applies throughout all of your training, not just on race day.

## Secret Number 5

What to put in your drinks bottle

There is one thing that should be in your drinks bottle and one thing only and that is a good quality electrolyte drink (I use Science in sport Go)

Again, I am amazed how many people don't do this.

I had a conversation with a guy who had raced the Ironman just the other day and said he fell over during the run, they took him to the medical tent and gave him some electrolyte and he was raving about it to me like he had discovered a wonder drug – I asked him what was in his drinks bottle during his ride and he said vimto!

Get another cage fitted for your long rides and take 2 bottles of electrolytes with you.

Sip it every 15 minutes to keep yourself hydrated.

Just on the subject of hydration, whilst staying hydrated is very important, I need to draw your attention to the fact that it is possible to over-hydrate and this can potentially be very dangerous.

The condition is called hyponatremia – please google it and do further reading. (don't worry about it, just be aware)

The symptoms are similar to dehydration: confusion, fatigue, nausea, vomiting and changes to the colour of your urine.

If you ever experience any of these symptoms or any changes to the colour of your urine (especially darker) either during, or in the days immediately following, your event, please consult a medic immediately.

## Secret Number 6

You already know the sixth secret as I have shared it with you earlier.

But it is very powerful so I am going to repeat it to re-emphasise the point – it's the golden rule.

Let me ask you a question.

How do you eat an elephant?

The answer is one bite at a time.

In other words, you don't just go out and do an Ironman triathlon 'straight off the bat'.

You start at race level one and slowly work your way up, building layers and layers of fitness over a long period of time as you do so.

Never under-estimate the power of combining secrets 1-5 with the golden rule - completing the ten-races in order as instructed!

## Secret Number 7 : Compete or Complete?

Many different people said many different things to me throughout my journey, but one of the most profound was this.

**The difference between 'compete' and 'complete' is that there is one 'L' of a difference.**

Forget about 'competing' or achieving a certain 'time' to be happy, Learn to focus instead on the sheer joy of simply completing a race distance that you previously thought was impossible.

That message lies at the very core of this book, my website and my entire journey, it applies to every race level from 1-10 and is something you can only really do the first time round.

In order to demonstrate the point, let me share with you what happened at my first 10k race.

I think about 600 people entered it.

I had previously dismissed being able to complete a 10k as 'impossible' and was absolutely buzzing just to be lining up on the start line.

Looking down the start list I could see that the race was filled with club runners.

I was convinced that I was going to come last.

I started at the very back of the pack.

After a short while into the race something amazing happened.

I began to overtake people without even trying particularly hard.

In the end, I think I finished position 399 out of 600.

That 388 people finished ahead of me was completely irrelevant.

The fact was I had completed a race distance that I had previously thought impossible and not only did I not come last, I actually overtook 201 other people in the process.

201!

How amazing was that? How much did I enjoy that race?

I wasn't stressing about times, or PB's or pushing myself to the max, I was simply loving every second of being able to 'do it'!

The thing is, once you get to Ironman level, there will be thousands & thousands of supporters lining the race circuit who believe that what you are doing will never be possible for them.

Just the very fact that you are now 'one of the Ironmen' makes you a superhero as far as they are concerned and they will treat you as such.

Those wonderful supporters have been stood on their feet for hours, so give them what they want by playing up to them, having a bit of fun, pretending that you are finding it easy etc. and they will treat you like a legend.

To experience the sensation described above is the beating heart of this book and getting your head into the 'Secret 7' way of thinking is one of the major keys to understanding how you turn completing an Ironman from the impossible to the possible.

## Secret 8

"Yes Ironman is a race but it's not really a race at all – it's an endurance event"

Adopting this attitude will help you more than you know. Think of it not as a race and more as an endurance event and it changes everything from a mindset perspective. Pace pace pace is the thing that Ironmen would say to me most when I asked for their tips.

The guy who finishes in 10 hours gets called an Ironman.

So does the guy who finishes in 16:59.

Always remember that....The medal is exactly the same.

## Secret 9 - The secret to increasing your run distance

The biggest secret to distance running is that it's really simple, all you need to do is put the miles in and your body gets stronger and stronger every week.

I often feel it's like a clock face that can only turn to position 2 from position 1, position 3 from position 2 and position 4 from position 3 - In other words once you run 1km it unlocks 2km and once you run 2km it unlocks 3km and so on.

Your body really is quite a remarkable machine it will do whatever you tell it you just have to follow the rules by putting the miles in and increasing your distance bit by bit each week

Someone once said this to me, it's another one that keeps cropping up so always remember it because it's true:

If you can run 1k you can run 2k, run 2k and you can run 5k, If you can run 5k you can run 10k, run 10k and you can run 20k

And finally... If you can run 20k, you can run 40k

## Secret 10

The secret to the swim

Most swim coaches will disagree with this one but remember they are probably swim coaches not triathlon coaches.

The purpose of this book is to share what has worked for me on my journey so here goes.

I very rarely kick hard on the swim, I rotate my hips and my upper body and my arms do most of the work, my legs trail behind with only gentle kicking.

The term is more pull less kick.

I find when I get out of the water my legs are fresh for the bike as I have been using different muscle groups on the swim and this is why I found I did not need to practice swim/bike brick sessions that much.

Yes hard kicking will help you swim faster but I think of my legs as a pair of turbo boosters that can be used if required but when utilised will use up a lot of energy.

As the long distance races are all about energy conservation, I keep leg kicking to 'gentle'. I would point out that my swim split times are always in the upper percentile of races and I always feel strong after the swim so it works for me, try it.

In addition by far the best Open Water training session I ever did was at 3 sisters in Wigan.

The coach got us to pair up and practice swimming on our partners feet.

This changed my life – it made all of my Open water swims, including IMUK, easy.

Learn how to do it.

Finally, at Pennington Flash the format of the open water swim 'training' at the time of writing is that you go into the water on your own and everybody is very spread out doing their own thing with a couple of safety kayaks on hand.

At 3 sisters in Wigan they do **group** open water training drills and **group** time trail 'races'

I learnt more at those group sessions in a few weeks than I did in 6 months of swimming on my own at pennington flash.

When the time comes (level 6) find a weekly coached open water **group** training/TT session near you and join it, always swim open water in a group, do not waste time doing it on your own.

And once again, learn how to master the dark art of swimming on someone's feet.

For further reading on this, please see the section entitled 'making the transition from pool to open water' and the Specific secret to the IMUK swim later in this chapter.

**Secret 11**

The secret to getting faster.

This is not a book about speed.

This is a book about how you take something that you believe to be impossible and bring it into your reality.

However…

There are a few things that I discovered in this regard.

One of the unintentional side effects of my training was that quite a way into my journey I re-entered a super sprint distance triathlon to see what would happen and I won the race!

What I found was that if I trained at a higher level then dropped down to the shorter event I would return faster to the target race.

For example, let's say that you wanted to improve your 5k time. If you trained at the Half Mara level before dropping back down I absolutely guarantee that you will return stronger and will smash your time versus your first attempt at the 5k.

You can have a lot of fun with this especially at the 'lower' levels, but be aware it only really works once! (second time round).

In addition, doing 1 Hour interval sessions where you warm up for 10 minutes, do 2 minute blasts as fast as you can followed immediately by two minutes recovery (x10) then a 10 minute cool down also helped me increase my speed for all 3 elements.

Learning how to swim on other people's feet in open water helped my swim times no end (see above).

Caffeine laced gels definitely gave me a turbo, but also a headache, so I ditched them. Try, but always read the label.

Many runners swear by short sharp track work.

Regarding the bike, here is how I PB'd the Ironman loop in training. (I took it from 4 hours down to 2:38)

No heart rate zones, no vo2 max.

I simply practiced the loop over and over again and gradually got quicker BUT:

Cycling with someone slightly faster than you, getting on their back wheel and asking them to push you will improve your time.

It's called 'drafting' and some class it as cheating – why? Because it works (don't do this on race day unless drafting is allowed and don't even think about doing it at Ironman)

My PB for the loop was just under 17mph average and had been for a while so I found a guy who was 18mph average, got on his back wheel and asked him to push me round the route.

Doing this took 10 minutes off my previous PB.

But I repeat, do this in training to improve your speed by all means, but don't even think about doing this at Ironman, you will get a DQ. (and probably a slap).

What you need to realise is, unless your name is Joe Skipper (current British iron distance record holder), there will always be someone faster than you, deal with it.

The training plans that I created got me a medal for every race in the series and took me all the way to Ironman, which, at the end of the day, is the objective of this book.

I managed to record a 'decent' time at some of the lower levels by revisiting them later in my journey, 'average' times at the mid levels and was well within the cut offs at the higher levels (which was all that mattered!)

If at any point speed, 'times' or 'competing' become really important to you, I suggest you read the interviews with the speed demons at the back of this book and give them a shout!

## Secret 12 : A 20 minute gain on the bike can potentially destroy your run

This one would come up time and time again from the Ironmen.

They would always say things like 'I smashed half an hour off my bike time on race day but I went to pieces on the run and lost hours'

When you are feeling strong on the bike it is very easy to 'go for it' but it's equally as easy to forget that you have the little matter of the marathon waiting for you at the end!

Pace, strategy and discipline are key at all levels but especially iron distance!

## Secret 13

Practice the Bike loop in the correct order

You need to get out onto the Ironman bike and run loops and practice the **actual** circuits as often as you can.

But more than that, I wasted a lot of time cycling the route in the wrong order, picking up the circuit 40 odd miles in near to my house.

All that happened was I got really good at cycling the Ironman bike route in the wrong order but when it came to cycling it in the correct order, I was stuffed!

If you are going to practice the bike loop, it is essential that you ride the loop in the exact order as you will on race day.

Now before you start thinking 'it's alright for you' bear in mind that both Pennington flash, Babylon Lane (start of the IMUK bike loop) and Chorley New Road (IMUK Run route) where all at least a 90 minute return car journey from my house.

I appreciate you may live much further afield than this but you need to find a way to get up/down here as part of your training.

If there is just absolutely no-way that this can be possible for you then go onto the organisers website, study the route, and create your own 'loop' of similar mileage with similar elevations at similar points, like a 100 mile bike circuit with monster climbs at miles 15, 45, 60 and 90 for example and practice this instead.

I would go as far as to say that, when training for Ironman, any 'long' ride on a circuit that isn't either the actual Ironman loop, or a similar replica of it, is a waste of your time. (same for the run)

## Secret 14

Master the bike cut offs

Once you get to Ironman level there are quite rightly cut offs in place throughout the course and amongst other things these help to maintain the purity of the sensational achievement and prevent the event from turning into a farce.

You need to know exactly where these cut offs are, when they are and where you need to be by when.

They are readily available on the organisers website, get out onto the loop and practice them.

You should have a couple of race strategy's in place before the event, a best case scenario and a worst case scenario.

If you plan your 'worse case' scenario around these cut-offs, you will enjoy your race day experience so much more when you realise that you are 'way ahead of time' at the various points, which is exactly what happened to me on my big day!

## Secret 15 : Ignore everyone else, Race your own Race

This applies from level 1 up!

Never, ever, get into a race with anyone, ever.

How many times have you been in this situation:

You are out on a training ride and someone comes stomping past you, immediately your ego kicks in and you go after them.

You then spend the next half an hour in a 'duel' and just as you get to the bottom of that monster climb they peel off and go in the other direction leaving you knackered and you have still got 4 hours left to do.

I must admit I am still guilty of this sometimes but why do we do it? All we end up doing is blowing ourselves up and depleting our energy levels for later in the race! Don't do it, not ever, especially not on race day

It's the same in the pool, you are 40 lengths into a drill and a guy gets into your lane then starts swimming like Michael Phelps.

You feel he is making you look slow so you start racing him – why? Stick to what you are here to do and that is train your body to continue forever - after 6 lengths he will invariably stop anyway!

I used to race too but now I look at these guys as 'energy vampires'.

Loads of people will always come stomping past you but you must learn to resist the temptation to react!

Race your own Race!

## Secret 16 Don't chase a PB on your long training days.

I know its tempting but don't do it, leave the PB chasing for another day, remember the long drills are there for you to get miles under your belt and train your body to continue forever, not chase the PB's!

## Secret 17 Run race strategy

I have one strategy when it comes to run races and one strategy only – start at the very back.

Run races can usually be split into 3 categories.

1) 5% will be The serious runners that are looking to win
2) 45% will be club runners and decent amateurs
3) 50% will be everybody else, including you.

Follow these training plans, Start at the very back of the grid and I guarantee you will overtake the majority of the people in bracket 3.

At Southport half marathon 1200 people entered and I overtook nearly 600 of them starting from the very back. Not a single one came past me – not a single one.

Compare that to if I started at the front and 600 came past me!

Do you see the difference!

Start the race slow – really slow, the same pace as those around you, notice how strong you feel, increase your pace slightly as the race goes on but resist the urge to put your foot down half way round despite the fact you are feeling strong.

Sit on people's shoulders for a bit and steal their energy before passing them.

Continue at your training pace and you will notice that you are still overtaking as most people start too fast and begin to struggle later on - if you still feel there is plenty left in the tank 3 miles out by all means go for it!

## Secret Number 18– Trainers!

When I first started running I used to run in a pair of trainers that I felt comfortable in but my toe nails started to go black and then fall off.

I did some research into this, even spoke to an 'expert' and was told this is what happens to most runners when you start increasing your distance so I just put it down to 'one of those things'

One day, an Ironman asked me if I had ever had a professional shoe fit, where they video you running, make you some in-soles and then sell you a proper pair of running shoes to suit your running style.

Of course I had never done this……

Omg please go and do it! you will feel like you are running on air. Black toes are a thing of the past – I used to hate running but now I love it! A decent pair of running shoes and tailored in soles will change your life. Get proper run 'ankle' socks too.

Also on the run - Changing your socks half way through the marathon/half will make your feet feel like they are in heaven – do it!.

## Secret Number 19

The Superfood that is scientifically proven to make you last longer

An Ironman recommended I watch a programme whereby they did lots of clinical trials with ordinary members of the public and asked them to run on a treadmill for as long as they could without stopping and recorded their results.

Two weeks later they got them back in, gave them the superfood and repeated the test. On average they were able to stay on the treadmill for 20% longer after taking the superfood.

That superfood was beetroot. Something to do with the nitrates in it.

I am lucky I love beetroot, I can't get enough of the stuff, make it your friend and eat loads of it as often as you can.

You can now also buy beetroot juice in a little shot bottle – I will always drink one of these with my porridge on race day. Some races will even put them in their goody bags!

## Secret Number 20

The Energy superfood that should be 10 times its price!

Did you know that the average banana has nearly 30g of carbs in it? Not only that but those carbs are rapidly absorbed into your system? It's no wonder they give these out at the Ironman fuel stops.

Bananas are a great way to supplement your fuel intake at a fraction of the cost of an energy gel with similar carbs – I have drafted these bad boys into my fuel strategy in place of a gel as I find they work just as well and save me a fortune in the process.

Experimenting with different things in training as a cheaper alternative to gels will help keep your costs down.

Bananas, fig rolls, Soreen malt loaf (love the banana version), cooked pasta (with sauce) and jacket potatoes are 5 things I would regularly combine with gels in training to reduce the cost in this regard!

But I have to admit I found gels combined with chia charge flapjacks (alternate on the bike, just gels for the run) and SIS electrolyte 'Go' drink worked the best for me.

The key thing is the amount of carbs and the frequency (see earlier secret)

## Secret Number 21

How to sort out cramps

Cramps often happen because you have lost essential salts that your body needs like magnesium via sweat but guess what?

You can replace them?

Guess how? There is a great product available called Saltstick.

If you suffer from this, try one tablet an hour during training to keep cramps at bay for good! (always read the label)

But again, safety first, if you keep getting cramps, go and see your GP.

## Secret 22

When I first started I wasn't using clip in pedals and I didn't have aero bars. An Ironman took one look at my bike and said you want my top tips? Get clip in pedals fitted and learn how to use them.

I did this and immediately felt stronger, my bike felt much more responsive and I could tell that my energy was being used way more effectively. My times began to come down.

He also said once you have done that get aero bars fitted and learn how to use them too.

These changed my life, especially on the flat and the descents.

Often I will freewheel past people who are pedalling because of these bars – they shaved big chunks off my time. Get them full stop. You might also want to consider having a proper bike fit – another one that kept coming up from the Ironmen.

But for goodness sake learn how to use the aero bars and the clip in pedals in a traffic free environment first, like a park or a purpose built cycle path for example – do not venture out onto the open roads until you are fully confident using them.

## Secret 23

Don't look at it as a 25km run, or a 100 mile ride, break it down into 30 minute slots and say to your body – in 30 minutes you will get food.

I find breaking it down this way has a massive psychological benefit, I never think about the distance I always think "in 30 minutes I can have a gel" the time seems to pass quicker and my body seems to respond very well to this –the distance almost becomes irrelevant.

But in order for this to work you must make sure you give your body  the food that you promised it on time every time!

## Secret 24

Hills

I spent a lot of time asking the Ironmen about hills.

On more than one occasion, the strategy on the run seemed to be walk the hills on the basis that they can do so at 75% of the pace that you can (badly) run up it, but will expand far less energy in the process. This made sense to me so I tried it and now I will never do anything else, I find it works very well.

Cycling up Hills seemed to follow a similar theme with the exception of one or two animals. One guy said to me 'u gotta make love to the hill' and again I find if I take it really slow, almost an over exaggerated slow this is the secret to maintaining energy levels. Yes people will stomp up the hill past you but I guarantee you will pass 80% of them at some point later in the race.

Remember guys, we are not chasing no 'king of the mountain' prize here, our goal is to conserve as much energy as we can and hills are another energy vampire waiting to relive us of it so treat them with the respect they deserve!

## Secret 25

Wind.

We all dream of a perfectly clear and still day with the only wind being a strong tailwind as we are cycle up hills but the reality is it's never like that, especially in Bolton when the wind only ever seems to blow one way and that is straight at you.

Wind can make a huge difference to your bike times, huge.

Never get into a fight with the wind, it's an energy vampire coming to test you.

If you try and take on the wind there will only ever be one winner and it will not be you.

Get down low on your aero bars, batton down the hatches, dig in and concentrate on a slow steady rhythm then ride out the storm!

Whilst on the subject of the elements, do not become a fair weather cyclist, I remember asking an Ironman if he ever checked the weather and he said 'why? I am going out anyway.'

Dig in and get used to going out in all conditions – it is great prep for race day and when the nice days finally land you will feel stronger than ever.

I spent the majority of the winter riding the Ironman bike course, when summer finally came round it felt like a completely different circuit and my times came down dramatically. Use the poor weather as practice for getting the miles in.

That said don't keep beating yourself up week after week if the weather is constantly bad, in hindsight I would have been better doing a turbo session at times, find a balance between the two.

## Secret 26 Brick Sessions

This is the term given to training sets of a bike immediately followed by a run to simulate race day.

The reason they are called brick sessions is because your legs feel like a ton of bricks when you first start running off the bike.

The secret to dealing with this is to first, practice them in training but second, understand that your body needs time to kick into 'run' mode. For me this can be anything from ten minutes to half an hour.

Guess what the secret is whilst you are waiting for your body to kick in? slow down!

I will literally over exaggerate my pace to about 50% when first running off the bike.

You will be able to tell when your body has switched over to run mode because you will get that nice warm fuzzy feeling in your leg muscles – you want to maintain this feeling for as long as possible and guess how you do that? Keep the pace nice and slow!

The more brick sessions you practice the better, simple as that, but they don't have to be long ones, just 15 mins off the bike on a regular basis served me extremely well at all levels.

Also, in hindsight, I learnt that you don't ever need to do any more than 1 hour maximum straight off the bike, even at level 10.

**Secret 27**

Transition.

It can be like you see on the telly with everybody stressed out to the max charging around like headless chickens, but it really doesn't need to be!

I will chill out and take my time in transition, there really is no rush.

Relax, take 5 (15 in my case!) sort yourself out and start the next element feeling strong!

**Secret 28**

Once you go beyond 20k on the run it's largely a mental battle.

This has come up time and time again when asking for tips. The common school of thought seems to be once you have trained at 20k for a period of weeks your body will be able to complete 40k if you apply the same pace and fuel strategy, your body is now strong enough to do this, so moving up from level 8 to 9 is largely a psychological battle not a physical one.

**Secret 29**

When you don't feel like it – go anyway.

I have often regretted **not** going for a run, but I have never regretted *going* for that run.

Point is sometimes you will not be in the mood but get your trainers on and get out there – the amount of times I have been in this position and after 10 minutes my mood changes dramatically for the better once I get cracking.

**Secret 30**

I know it's a pain in the arse but you have got to learn how to change a tyre.

Practice this until you master it and always take some decent tyre levers, a small pump and a couple of innertubes with you on your rides. Seriously you need to sort this if you haven't already.

That said, gator skin tyres combined with the expensive 'slime' innertubes served me extremely well and I managed to complete every single race in the series without a single puncture on race day including IMUK (thanks also to the iron gods!).

## Secret 31

A significant percentage of Ironmen walk large parts of the marathon, in fact many actively train this way. I didn't realise this but it's true, so don't be too precious about that marathon, you can always walk large chunks of it - no one said you have to run all of it without stopping!  (see later IMUK secret)

## Secret 32

Whilst on your journey, when you are stood on the start line, and during the event, particularly at run races, look around, say 'Hi' to the person next to you, talk to people, ask them about their journey, make friends – some of the most wonderful people you will ever meet will be at these races and many of them will become friends for life.

At Southport half marathon there was a guy stood next to me on a lead and at first I thought "what the hell" but it turned out he was completely blind and was running 20k with a guide – how amazing is that? – It doesn't half make you count your blessings.

Have a look at the start list pre race to see who has entered - At Rossendale I noticed there was a guy in his 70's in it, after the race most people were fussing over the "pro's" but I knew who the real hero was – the guy in his 70's and I went on a mission to find him.

I noticed there were 3 blokes in the 70+ category at the Bolton Ironman this year – how awesome is that? An Ironman at 70!

Then there are legends like Steve Cook, who I had the absolute honour of riding the IMUK bike route with in training. He raced Ironman UK this year using a hand cycle - he was paralysed from the waist down following a horrific road accident. Doctors told him he would never be able to walk again yet here he is lining up at IMUK (see blog).

Meeting truly inspirational people like this, they just instantly knock down all of your barriers…What was your excuse again?

## Secret 33

Use the treadmill.

I did all my running outdoors until I got to level 5 where I used the treadmill to increase my distance from 5k to 10k – I set the treadmill at my 5k pace and gradually increased the distance week by week until I got to 10k, it worked. Try it.

(note other than that I did all my running in the open air and 100% of my bike work was done outside, mainly on the IMUK loop!)

## Secret 34

Another one that keeps coming up – especially from the high rankers, "above all else be grateful for your blessings, train with a happy heart and a big smile on your face, think of all the people that would love to be able to do what you are doing right now but cannot due to illness or some other misfortune, don't over think things, don't ever put too much pressure on yourself, just get out there, make it fun and enjoy every single second of it."

## Secret 35

You don't need a posh watch

You can spend hundreds of pounds on a watch today that will do absolutely everything apart from complete the actual Ironman for you.

But you don't need to do this.

My £9.99 argos special took me all the way from level 1 to completing an Ironman triathlon – always remember that!

## Secret 36

On your long slow runs, take a 5 minute stop and stretch every 10k.

During my Ironman training I went for a 30k run without stopping and it took me 3:40.

The following week I did 3 x 10k runs back to back with a 5 minute stop and stretch inbetween and I took my time down to 3:10.

Try it.

## Secret 37

Double hat

When you are training in a group but certainly on race day and time trial days, wear two swim hats with your goggles sandwiched inbetween.

If you get a whack in the face those goggles are going no-where!

**Secret 38**

The IMUK Swim

An Iron distance swim is 2.4 miles.

But, at the time of writing it is not 2.4 miles straight at IMUK.

It is 2 laps of 1.2 miles with a short break (walk) inbetween.

Not a lot of people realise this.

They think it is 2.4 miles straight.

Now in my opinion, there is a massive difference between swimming 140 odd lengths of a pool non stop (almost 2.4 miles) and 2 x 70 odd lengths with a rest inbetween.

Huge.

Go and do it and you will soon see what I mean.

For me, Splitting it makes it a piece of cake by comparison.

In addition, I found my ironman swim on race day to be miles easier than my training sessions down at the flash, miles easier.

Why?

1) In training down at the flash whilst there are other people in the water with you, you are mostly swimming on your own and therefore you are 100% responsible for your own sighting so you end up worrying about where the buoy marker is all the time instead of concentrating on your rhythm and technique.

On race day, there are 2,000 other people in the water with you so if you keep them on the side that you breathe you do not need to worry about sighting, you can use the other people as your guide – so long as you can see the pack, then you are doing perfectly fine.

2) There are a handful of safety kayaks in the water in your training due to limited resources, this can make you feel uneasy, as it did me.

On race day there are hundreds of safety kayaks in the water spaced every few hundred metres with loads of people keeping an eye on you, this is far more re-assuring from a safety element leaving you free to focus on your swim.

3) In training at pennington flash the buoy markers are the size of a football, painted white, and spaced far apart so are very difficult to see.

On race day the buoy markers are the size of Blackpool tower, fluorescent yellow and spaced every few hundred yards so are very easy to see – this makes race day a completely different experience versus training.

4) There are 2,000 other pairs of feet in the water with you on race day. Learn how to get on peoples feet, learn how to draft, pick your partner carefully and get them to 'tow' you all the way round.

**Secret 39**

The IMUK Marathon

At the time of writing the IMUK marathon can be broken down into 2 parts. (many iron distance races have a similar 'lap' structure)

First part – 9km (ish) run from the Bolton Wanderers stadium round to the main 'lap circuit'

2nd part – Main 'lap circuit' : Chorley New Road : 4.5km (ish) downhill all the way to the town centre then 4.5km (ish) back uphill to your entry point x3. (then your 'victory parade')

Now, even if you took the maximum time allowed for the swim then the maximum time allowed for the bike and arrived in T2 right on the cut-offs, you would still have 6.5 hours to complete this marathon.

Once you get to Ironman level, you will easily be able to run the first bit (9km) in 1 hour.

This leaves you 5.5 hours to complete the 3.5 lap circuit.

Let me tell you something.

You could walk 3.5 laps up and down Chorley new road in 5.5 hours.

Easily.

Also, I found this.

Running 4.5km downhill into Bolton town centre is easy.

Running back the other way is not easy – far from it - however....

Let's say I could run the uphill part of Chorley New Rd in 20 mins.

I found that I could **walk** it in 40 mins.

You will find that plenty of people are walking this bit!

So why not run the first bit (9km) then when you get onto the main 'lap' circuit run the 'easy' 4.5km into town, run the 'flat' 1km (ish) back to Chorley Street Hill but then from there walk all the way back up Chorley New Road?

Repeat this 3 times and the medal is virtually yours!

Easy!

Told you - the mara is not what you think!

## Secret 40 - The Final Secret

There can only be one final secret.

The Ironman mantra is 'Anything is Possible'

When I first started I couldn't run up the stairs without gasping for breath yet I went on to do a marathon and then conquered an Ironman.

I have realised that the Ironman mantra is true.

Not just for triathlon....

But for your life.

**The only limits to what is possible are those which you impose upon yourself.**

Those secrets, the 10 races (golden rule) and the training plans you are about to discover helped me successfully complete levels 1-10 of my journey and if you learn them, apply them, then follow the plans, they will help you do likewise.

But wait…

You want more secrets?

Ok…..

When I was training for IMUK I met even more amazing Ironmen who kindly shared with me their personal secrets and tips, particularly for Ironmen first timers.

These can be found in the interviews towards the rear of this book.

****IMPORTANT****

Now that you know the secrets, please do not presume that you can dive straight in and begin training for you first Ironman straight away!

This is not how it works!

I have shared the secrets with you from the outset because they will help oil the wheels of your journey from the very beginning!

Always remember the golden rule! – You have to combine the secrets with completing the races in the correct order as instructed in the beginning of this book!

## Prepare For Your Amazing Journey!

Now you have a clearly defined path and know the secrets, all you need now are the training plans!

You are about to discover the exact daily training plans that I created and followed in order to complete each race in the series together with things I learnt about other key elements like strava, diet, strength training, which bike to choose, how I mastered the swim and precisely what to expect on race day.

If you choose to follow the plans (see disclaimer!) I would recommend getting yourself a good quality photo album and asking someone to take a picture of you right now. Your body is going to change (in a good way!).

Once you start entering and completing races, you want to be taking as many photographs as possible for your album, race by race, trust me on that.

If you can get someone to take a picture of you as you cross the finish line, great, but many races will have someone that do this for you to buy after the race, check with the organiser before you enter and also check that every finisher gets a medal (no medal = no entry).

ALWAYS keep your race number and staple it to your medal.

Also, I personally only like to enter races that publish results as proof (most do online) but again you might want to check this.

You need to give some thought as to where you are going to display your medals as you collect them.

Mine take pride of place in my hallway and every visitor to my house gets a 20 minute lecture as they enter, race by race.

Needless to say I don't get many visitors anymore.

Buy yourself a wall planner from Amazon right now, you can buy them there any time of the year. My preference is the Sasco compact year planner, put it somewhere you will see it every day, they are perfect for recording your training plans, weight, race dates etc and make excellent reading looking back at them.

I have learnt more from looking back at these planners to review what I actually did in training versus what I should have done than I have any other material.

You will need access to a computer. Be careful with things like Strava and facebook. They are great but dangerous, I understand that many people get motivation by sharing their journey with friends and I get that but the trouble with these things is that everyone can see them, including your boss, so be careful.

Personally I prefer mapometer.com to plan my routes but have a play and see which one suits you best.

Some people may be quite happy just completing level one, (I was for a while) others may want to go all the way, how far you progress is entirely up to you, however all the information you will ever need is waiting for you in the pages ahead, when you are ready.

Right, I think you are pretty much good to go..

I just want to cover off two more things, Strava and diet, and then we can get stuck into the first training plan!

## Strava

I never really discovered Strava until I started my Ironman training.

For those of you who do not know what Strava is, it's a free app that you can download onto your phone and 'record' your swim, rides and runs onto it for the world to see.

There are now a lot of similar apps out there, but Strava is my personal favourite.

You can also buy a posh watch that does it for you, but I always used my mobile phone.

The idea is that before you start your ride, or run, you log in to strava via your phone, hit record and away you go.

Once you have finished, lots of valuable information is then displayed for your review.

Time taken, distance travelled, average speed and calories burnt as standard.

But the greatest feature of Strava is also the most dangerous.

At the end of your workout, a league table appears and you can compare your time to every other person that has ever ridden the same route as you.

This is seriously addictive.

You then spend the rest of your days trying to move up the rankings of your chosen route.

It's like a real life computer game and you are player one.

But this is not book about how to move up the strava leaderboards, it's a book about how to advance through the different levels of triathlon.

Going out and spanking all your energy trying to move 2 places up the strava leaderboard is not conducive to that, as you will soon discover.

But used properly Strava can be a fantastic tool.

It provides an excellent way for you to keep an accurate record of all your training, the amount of useful free information is superb, you can build a following who will give kudos and motivate and you can analyse other peoples times to see which parts of the route are likely to offer you the most improvement.

Strava isn't perfect, many a time I have been waiting ages for the GPS signal to 'be found' which can be frustrating, and if it ever doesn't record your ride on a day that you PB it, you will be spitting feathers for weeks.

That said, I very much recommend you consider Strava, just make sure you use it properly, and take heed of the warnings within this chapter.

Don't forget that the whole idea of Strava is that the world can see your activity.

Not least your boss.

Be sure to remember that the next time you are tempted to go for 'that ride' when you have phoned in sick!

## Diet

People have written entire books about diet for triathlon - This isn't one of them.

I am quite certain you will already know exactly what you should be doing in this regard, a balanced plate (google it), loads of fresh fruit and vegetables, cut out the fast food and the saturated fat, no alcohol, no smoking, no chips, no chocolate, sweets, crisps, ice cream, biscuits etc etc etc.

All the stuff that people have repeated over and over a thousand times but nobody listens so they repeat it again a thousand times.

At the end of the day, always remember this:

If you burn more calories than you consume, you will lose weight.

If you eat more calories than you burn, you will put on weight.

One of the positive side effects of regular exercise and a decent diet is that your body will change shape for the better and if you consume fewer calories than you burn, you will lose weight.

When I first started, I was very overweight.

By being sensible with what I was eating (you all know what to do) I found that I was able to lose a small amount of weight each week, no more than one or two pounds.

When I was not sensible with what I was eating I either put on weight or it stayed the same.

The key thing was that by applying the fuel strategy I shared with you in the secrets, and eating carb rich foods like pasta the night before my long rides/runs, I found I had plenty of energy during my training and at the end of the day energy for training is how we should view food (how anal does that sound).

Do not put too much pressure on yourself on the diet front, try and do all the things you know you should, but don't overly stress about it.

During my Ironman training in particular I literally ate whatever I wanted and usually my weight would stay the same due to the amount of cardio I was doing.

One thing I would point out though is this - I found when I ate lean I felt lean and when I ate crap I felt crap!

If you can try and get into the mindset of 'food is fuel' then this will serve you extremely well!

But make no mistake, I was no saint! I have a sweet tooth like everybody else!

Also, sorry to end with this one, but drinking alcohol was a definite no-no for me during my training blocks - it's a very slippery slope as we all know!

More importantly, I noticed I was way sharper without it. OK I would celebrate after my races, but avoided it like the devil once training re-started!

If you need any help with your diet then make an appointment with your GP and tell them your plans, Monitor your weight each week and if you notice any dramatic changes from one week to the next, go and see your GP.

## Level 1 Training Plan : 2.5km Run

Note:

The level one plan is aimed at people who are at the very beginning of their fitness journey and have done very little previous exercise (exactly as I was).

The whole purpose of this book is to share the exact path that I followed.

I know there will be people already at a higher fitness level than this who can already run at least 2.5km without stopping.

If this is you then please turn the chapter entitled 'how to use this book'

Things you will need to complete this level:

A cap (optional)

Sunglasses (optional lol)

A stopwatch (I bought the cheapest one available in argos and used it all the way to Ironman)

Access to strava (free via mobile phone)

A Running T-Shirt or Vest

A lightweight waterproof jacket

A snood (optional) (its kind of like a scarf – google it)

Running Shorts

Leggings or man tights (optional)

A Pair of running socks

A pair of decent running trainers (you don't need to spend a fortune)

Just a note on the trainers

Going to a specialist running shop, getting my run analysed and buying a proper pair of running shoes with insoles tailored to my needs – (see secrets) was without doubt one of the best things I ever did, but bear in mind I was at level 4 by this point.

If you are starting at this chapter then you must be a complete beginner and the last thing I want you to do is go out and buy a really expensive pair of trainers right now.

Pretty much any pair of trainers will be fine to complete level 1, just make sure they are trainers designed for running in.

I would hold off splashing the cash until you can run at least 2.5km without stopping.

Before we go any further, have you seen your GP?

If not book an appointment and go and see them before you begin!

Also, have you got your year planner? If not go and get one NOW! I don't care what time of year it Is you will find one on amazon right now, get one it will change your life..

Use mapometer to map your route and walk it 3 times in your pre training week.

Make sure your route starts straight outside your front door, if you have to drive somewhere to begin then you are less likely to do this on the days that you don't feel like training (we all have them)

Record your actual effort versus your plan on your wall planner at the end of each day.

Don't worry too much about nutrition, a bottle of water and a banana will be fine for your sessions.

Before you start you need to sign up for your first race!

A simple internet search for 2.5km runs in your local area should bring up lots of races for you, pick one that suits.

I also love www.racecheck.com, it's a global race directory with real reviews by real people that have already taken part in the event you are interested in! use it!

Read the next chapter before race day – 'what to expect at your first race.'

You need to find a race that will be in roughly 12 weeks from now.

Sometimes these short races can be a little thin on the ground.

If you can't find one search again on racecheck and then again on google for 'fun' runs in your area 12 weeks from now.

If you still can't find one, don't worry about it, make your own 'mock race' and return to the event when it takes place at a later date when you are operating at a higher level to collect the medal and smash it. (trust me, this will be lots of fun for you).

This plan takes it real slow, and is the exact one that I followed. (I hadn't done any running at all since school!)

If you find that you are able to complete this level in far less time than has been allowed, feel free to move up to the next level but don't forget to drop back down to race it and collect your medal on race day!

Stretch your legs before and after each session.

Take the Jog pace real slow, do not try to sprint, be conscious of really over emphasising the easy pace.

Do not be concerned about the other runners, especially when walking - we all started somewhere, they are on their own journey and you are on yours – it will not be long before you are the one doing the overtaking!

Enjoy your training, remember you will never forget your first race and get thinking about where you are going to put that medal.

Go on to mapometer.com and map out a 1.25km run circuit from your front door.

Remember you will have to come back! So make sure you only map out 1.25km, to give a total route of 2.5km!

You need to break your training route down into 12 equal sections, as in the diagram on the next page.

Give each section a number, in order, 1 to 12.

Look for a landmark for each section, a tree / bin / sign etc.

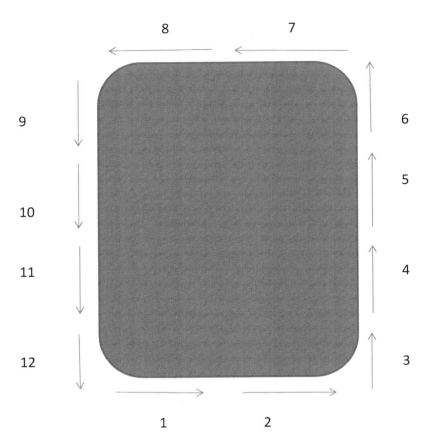

# Level 1 training schedule 2.5km Run

| Week | Mon | Tues | Weds | Thurs | Fri | Sat | sun |
|------|-----|------|------|-------|-----|-----|-----|
| 1 | | JOG 1 | | JOG 1 | | | JOG 1 |
| 2 | | JOG 2 | | JOG 2 | | | JOG 2 |
| 3 | | JOG 3 | | JOG 3 | | | JOG 3 |
| 4 | | JOG 4 | | JOG 4 | | | JOG 4 |
| 5 | | JOG 5 | | JOG 5 | | | JOG 5 |
| 6 | | JOG 6 | | JOG 6 | | | JOG 6 |
| 7 | | JOG 7 | | JOG 7 | | | JOG 7 |
| 8 | | JOG 8 | | JOG 8 | | | JOG 8 |
| 9 | | JOG 9 | | JOG 9 | | | JOG 9 |
| 10 | | JOG 10 | | JOG10 | | | JOG10 |
| 11 | | JOG 11 | | JOG11 | | | JOG11 |
| 12 | | JOG 12 | | JOG12 | | | **RACE!** |

Key : Jog 1 = jog section 1 only walk the rest

Jog 2 = jog section 1 & 12 only walk the gaps

Jog 3 = joh section 1, 6 & 12 only walk the gaps

Jog 4 = jog section 1, 4 6 & 12 only walk the gaps

Jog 5 = jog section 1 4 6 8 12 walk gaps

Jog 6 = jog section 1  4 6 8 10 12 walk gaps

Jog 7 = jog sections 1 2 4 6 8 10 12 walk gaps

Jog 8 = jog sections 1 2 4 5 6 8 10 12 walk gaps

Jog 9 = jog sections 1 2 4 5 6 8 9 10 12 walk gaps

Jog 10 = jog sections 1 2 3 4 5 6 8 9 10 12 walk gaps

Jog 11 = jog sections 1 2 3 4 5 6 8 9 10 11 12  walk 7……
**JOG12 = Jog all!**

## What to expect on your first 'run' race day

Once you have registered and paid for your chosen race online, you will usually get some sort of confirmation e-mail from the race organiser.

If you do not get this within 24 hours of registering I would contact them either by e-mail or phone to confirm they have received your registration.

Within the welcome e-mail there is usually loads of helpful stuff about times and where to park etc.

Most races now will have at least a facebook page so join in the pre race party and get yourself involved!

The race organisers will either post your race number to you, but for most races at this level you will collect it on the day.

I like to make a checklist of all the stuff I am going to need on race day and have this laid out and packed the night before along with my confirmation e-mail and directions to race registration.

On race day itself arrive a good hour before race start and look for the registration tent.

Here you just give your name and show your confirmation e-mail and they will give you your race number, sometimes in an envelope full of fitness related flyers and on the odd occasion – a free gift!

You always wear your race number on your front for run races so you have two choices – you can either pin it on using safety pins, or you can treat yourself to race belt (which I recommend as they are ace for triathlon) – you will find these at any decent running shop.

If the race does electronic chip timing there may also be a timing chip.

Sometimes this is attached to the race number or sometimes it is a bracelet that you put on your arm or leg.

If it is on your race number, then you do not have to do anything with it after the race.

If it is a bracelet then make sure you put it on now and don't forget to hand it back after the race!

One thing to note, If the race does offer chip timing (unusual for level 1) the way this works is that they put a long strip on the start line, one on the finish line (sometimes others at various points of the course) and the chip automatically starts and stops as you run over the strips.

I personally like to stay well away from these strips until the race begins as you don't want your time to be affected by you aimlessly wandering over the strips pre-race so watch out for this.

There may also be a bag drop and if so this is great – make sure you take full advantage as it allows you to get changed race side without having to go back and forth to the car – usually you just give your number as you hand your bag in and then show your number after the race to collect.

Once all that is out of the way you can just relax, warm up and wait for either the announcer to call you forward or follow the masses as they make their way to the start line a few minutes before the race is due to begin!

Don't forget, line up at the very back of the pack and off you go!

When you cross the finish line you will usually be presented with a medal.

If you can see them giving medals out but for some reason they do not give you one – make sure you go and claim your prize!

Some races have t-shirts, goodie bags, free drinks, bananas etc, so make sure you claim whatever you are entitled to.

Once you have been through the finishers area – that's it – you are free to go!

It's all a bit of an anti climax!

Personally I like to stay around and clap a few of the final finishers etc so you might want to consider doing this too.

When you get home the race results will usually be uploaded to the organisers website either later that day or the following day and there is often a buzz about their facebook page with everyone uploading pictures etc.

Do not look at how many finished in front of you, focus instead on people that you managed to overtake, If you have followed my plan, I guarantee you will not have come last.

You will cherish your first medal forever!

Don't forget to staple your race number to it, proudly hang them somewhere where you will see them often and wallow in the fact that you have just done something truly amazing – you have completed your first ever race!

## Base Swim Plan

Before we move onto the first triathlon phase we need to cover off three things, the swim, strength conditioning, and getting a bike.

Lets start with the swim.

The thing that people say to me most when I talk to them about my journey is "I would love to do triathlon but I just can't swim"

Now when they say this what they really mean is one of 3 things:

a) They literally cannot swim, meaning if I threw you in some deep water right now you would not know what to do and would most probably drown. If this is you then you need to learn to swim. Do it now, you never know it might just save your life or someone else's one day. Go down to your local leisure centre and book yourself in for adult swim lessons on either a 121 or group basis. The great thing about starting from scratch is you can learn to do it properly straight away - Tell them you are only interested in learning front crawl. Incorporate your lessons into the plan that follows.

b) They can swim but what they mean is they cannot swim front crawl just breaststroke. Now, let me tell you, it is possible to go through all the levels just swimming breaststroke and many people do, even at level 10. But if I was you I would learn to swim front crawl. When I first tried to swim front crawl I managed half a length and nearly drowned. I can now swim 150 lengths front crawl without stopping and tumble turn every lap.

I say this not to brag but to assure you that Learning to swim properly is a fun mini journey and the sense of achievement as you advance is awesome. It's like everything else in life, the more you practice the better you get.

c) They can swim but not in open water
   If this is you then you do not need to worry about this until at least level 6 as nearly all level 2 and 4 races will be pool based. (only enter ones that are) However it will do you no harm to have a read of the open water swim chapter, 'Making the progression from pool to open water'.

Most people will likely fall into category b) above, so with that in mind, My top tips for learning to swim front crawl would be as follows:

First off, You need to go and get the right gear for this.

The amount of people I see down at the pool trying to swim front crawl without goggles and in knee length, really thick Bermuda shorts is frankly ridiculous.

Get a tight pair of speedos (no one is looking trust me plus you are there to do one thing only and that is swim not parade around poolside) a swim cap, a decent pair of goggles and a nose clip.

Do not even get in the pool until you have got all of these things. they are not expensive. £20 for the lot, look after them and they will last ages.

Pick a nice quiet section of the pool to practice, do not get into a busy lane full of decent swimmers!

Most people when they get in the water will try and swim like Michael Phelps for the first lap and attempt to set a new world record, then spend the next 10 minutes wheezing against the wall.

Your goal is to do the exact opposite. Focus on swimming as slow as you possibly can, really over exaggerate your stroke, almost as if you are taking the micky, focus on your breathing instead of trying to swim fast.

Take a deep breath then lie flat on your stomach  with your head in the water looking at the floor and then slowly breathe out, Relax, notice how

 1) You will float without really moving and

2) You can stay in that position for ages.

Get comfortable being in this position and practice it often because it will help with your breathing and make you realise you can relax with your head in the water. Now all you need to do is slowly move your arms and I mean slowly.

At the bottom of the pool they very helpfully painted a blue line - this is to keep you straight. You do not need to look anywhere else other than down at the blue line when your head is in the water.

Do not worry too much about kicking your legs really hard. I only every gently kick my legs, I more rotate my body into each stroke and my upper body does most of the work.

This will go against what most swim coaches will tell you but I find hard kicking of legs yes makes me swim faster but also uses up loads of valuable energy and that is not the gig here as you will find out later.

All I can tell you is this strategy of not kicking the legs has stood me in excellent standing for increasing the distance..

Do not worry about anyone else in the pool ever – they are on your journey and you are on yours. Smile to yourself and keep your ego at the door.

Follow the plan on the next page, its identical to the run plan you just followed.

Read the notes for the level 2 training plan and factor the swim drills into your swim training days. If you are having swim lessons do likewise and make sure you complete the drills that follow as part of your lesson.

**Remember do not worry about the time it takes you to swim the lengths , in a way the longer the better at this stage, relax, slow right down and focus more on your breathing not speed and take it real real slow - have as many breaks as you want inbetween lengths**

**You will be swimming in a pool only at this stage and there should  be a lifeguard on duty at all times. if there is no lifeguard report this to reception and do not get into the pool until they arrive.**

One final thing – do not get pool rage! Play nicely! Believe me, I have seen it all, people walking/dancing/playing ball in my lane etc but be nice to people, make friends, you are likely to keep seeing them in the weeks ahead and once you advance you will find most people will stay out of your way.

The base swim plan, to be used in conjunction with the level 2 super sprint triathlon training plan, follows on the next page.

## Take a break inbetween sets

Personally I found that once I was able to do crawl once every third length I very quickly went to once every other length and then all of a sudden it just clicked and it will for you too!

Remember! Nice and slow is key! There is no rush!

Just a note about tumble turning, don't even think about this yet, tumble turning is the cherry on the cake but first we need to learn how to bake the actual cake!!

85% of people will not be tumble turning on race day at levels 2 and 4!

I didn't master the tumble until way into my journey, I have written a blog post all about this which you will find on my website and it will be waiting for you when the time comes (Think level 6 at least!)

# Base swim Plan   16 x 25m x2 sets (32 lengths total)

**This is not a Stand Alone Plan! Use it in Conjunction with the level 2 Super Sprint Triathlon Training Plan!**

| Week | Mon | Tues | Weds | Thurs | Fri | Sat | sun |
|------|-----|------|------|-------|-----|-----|-----|
| 1 | S1 | | | S1 | | | |
| 2 | S2 | | | S2 | | | |
| 3 | S3 | | | S3 | | | |
| 4 | S4 | | | S4 | | | |
| 5 | S5 | | | S5 | | | |
| 6 | S6 | | | S6 | | | |
| 7 | S7 | | | S7 | | | |
| 8 | S8 | | | S8 | | | |
| 9 | S9 | | | S9 | | | |
| 10 | S10 | | | S10 | | | |
| 11 | S11 | | | S11 | | | |
| 12 | S12 | | | S12 | | | |

Key : (Do 2 sets of 16 lengths)

S1 = swim front crawl length 1 only breaststroke the other 15

S2= swim crawl lengths  1 & 16 only breaststroke the rest

S3 = swim crawl 1, 8 & 16 only breaststroke the rest

S4= swim crawl 1, 4,8,12, & 16 only breaststroke the rest

S5 = swim crawl 1,4,7,10,13,16 only breaststroke the rest

S6 = swim crawl  1,4,7,10,13,16 only breaststroke the rest

S7 = swim crawl 1,3,5,7,9,11,13,15 only breaststroke the rest

S8 = swim crawl 1,3,5,7,9,11,13,15 breaststroke the rest

S9 = swim crawl 1 2 3 4 5 6  8 9 10 11 12 breaststroke the rest

S10 = swim crawl 1 2 3 4 5 6  8 9 10 11 12 13 breaststroke the rest

S11 = swim crawl 1 2 3 4 5 6 7 8 9 10 11 12 13 14   breaststroke the rest

**S12=SWIM ALL 16 FRONT CRAWL!**

## Weights Routine

I am a big fan of strength conditioning for triathlon.

You will notice that twice a week throughout the plans that follow, strength conditioning was factored in as part of my training.

This is something that I did from the very beginning and stuck with it from level 1 all the way to level 10.

My goal was not to get good at lifting heavy weights, my goal was to maintain my strength as I lost weight throughout the process.

So if I could do x10 Dumbell rows @ 20kg when I weighed 16 stone, my goal was to still be able to do that when I weighed 12 stone.

In addition, I would always take time to relax in the sauna afterwards which, in my opinion, was important for my muscles.

I would always feel a million dollars as I made my way back to the car after my twice weekly gym sessions, and that's an ace feeling.

You might want to find your own routine (loads of free strength routines online), hire a Personal trainer, or follow mine.

Whatever you go with, do it twice a week.

Here is my routine:

The first step was to find my 'level'.

For each exercise, find a weight where you are able to do 3 sets of 10 reps.

If you are not able to do 3 sets of 10 reps then the weight is too high.

If, halfway through the third set for example, you find yourself having to stop, then the weight is too high and you need to drop down.

Once you are able to do 3 sets of 10 reps for each exercise, then you have found your current strength level.

Your goal is to maintain this strength as you lose bodyweight.

You do this by keeping the weight you lift the same throughout your training.

I do subscribe to the idea of building muscle, particularly in your legs, feel free to do further reading on this and seek specialist muscle building advice from a PT, but be careful, the last thing you want to do as a triathlete is get injured trying to lift heavy weights.

I did the same routine for 2 years:

Here it is:

Protein shake with breakfast on weights day (25g)

Warm up – 1,000 metres on the rower

Dumbbell Rows 3 sets of 10 reps

Dumbbell Chest press 3 sets of 10 reps

Shoulder Press 3 sets of 10 reps

Lat Pull Down - rear – 3 sets of 10 reps

Lat Pull Down using triangle to front 3 sets of 10 reps

Bicep Curl 3 sets of 10 reps

Overhead extension 3 sets of 10 reps

'Row' pull (sit on floor legs in front pull triangle to stomach) 3 sets of 10 reps

Leg extension 3 sets of 10 reps

Leg press 3 sets of ten reps

Relax in Sauna

25g Protein shake to finish

## What Bike?

Now we have covered off the swim, the other thing you are going to need for your first triathlon is obviously, a bike.

Remember, you are about to train for your first ever triathlon, a super sprint.

Whatever you do, Please do not go and spend thousands of pounds on a top of the range bike!

That old mountain bike gathering dust in the garage will be perfectly fine for your first triathlon.

If the above is not your reality, I guarantee your mate will have one gathering dust in his garage that he will let you have for free.

If you don't have any mates, then buy a second hand one off E-bay for £50.

As long as it is in good working order and the tyres, gears and brakes are in decent condition, it will be fine.

Do not think that everyone will be laughing at you when you rock up at your first triathlon – they will not, you will see all manner of bikes there, with many first timers in precisely the same boat as yourself.

What did I do?

I learned to cycle on an old mountain bike gathering dust in the back of my garage.

Once I was certain that I was going to stick at this, I treated myself to a new Viking racer for £160.

I bought it because it looked nice (lol) and it had the 'click' gear changers on the handlebars, but It weighed a ton!

That bike got me round my first triathlon absolutely fine.

Once I knew I was hooked on triathlon I then did loads and loads and loads of research about buying a full carbon bike.

I became aware of Planet X who are (at the time of writing) an online retailer with stores in South Yorkshire only.

I printed off their Pro Carbon bike that was on sale for £999 at the time and showed it to every single bike shop owner that I could find.

They would always have a very similar spec of bike for sale at £500 more expensive than the Planet X one.

I asked them to tell me the difference between the bike in their shop and the Planet X pro-carbon, except £500.

I was not satisfied with any of their answers.

I took the plunge and bought the Planet X Pro Carbon and it was the best thing I ever did.

After owning the Pro Carbon for about 18 months I took it into the Planet X store for a service and ended up buying an RT-90 with aero bars for £1200.

That bike was even better still, and is the one I used for IM 70.3 Dublin and IMUK Bolton.

At Ironman 70.3 Dublin a fellow competitor complimented me on my bike, and said he used to have one himself.

He told me that whilst he had since gone on to spend several thousand pounds on a new, 'upgraded' bike, he could not really tell much of a difference between that and his Planet X one.

I have always wanted to ride the IMUK loop on one of those bikes worth £6k to see for myself what difference they actually make.

Unfortunately, owning a bike at the level was way out of my league!

Planet X has served me very well, you seem to get a lot of bike for the money whilst the prices remain sensible.

So there you go, that is what I did.

I very much recommend you go through a similar process to mine, start with any old bike, then, once you get into it, move to a budget racer for no more than a couple of hundred quid..

When you finally get a decent bike you will appreciate it so much more.

Keep an eye on my website, there may be discounts from Planet X for you lucky readers on there!

Also, find a really good local bike technician and make friends with them, they are worth their weight in gold.

Ian at Wigan bike tech is my 'go to guy' for any issues/repairs (recommended if you are in the NW) and he always gave me a sterling service.

So now we have got both the swim and the bike sorted, its time to start training!

**Level 2:**

## Super Sprint Triathlon : 400m swim, 10k bike, 2.5km run

Congratulations on completing level 1 – its an amazing feeling right? Hold onto that sense of achievement you are feeling because it will stay with you forever.

It's time to move into your first triathlon! The run for this one is 2.5k and guess what – you have already nailed it in the previous level! So it's just a question of maintaining that & bringing the swim and bike into play.

Things you will need:

A swim cap

Nose Clip (optional)

Swim Goggles

Stopwatch (nothing fancy)

Budget tri suit (amazon)

Trunks

Bike Helmet, cycling shorts, bike shoes, socks

Sunglasses

Cycling Jacket (cheap, lightweight waterproof - amazon)

Snood (Optional) Race Belt (optional but recommended)

Gloves, bum bag, puncture kit

Bike, drinks bottles, electrolytes, gels

Running Cap (optional)

Running Shorts, Running Trainers, ankle support socks

Please re-read the swim section and make sure you have the proper swim gear.

We are now introducing brick sessions where you go for a short run immediately after getting off the bike. Have your trainers set out ready for when you return and the tri suit will help with quick transition but take your time there is no rush. (I often take 10-15 minutes – it's not like you see on the telly in real life!)

As previously discussed, I did a swim/bike brick only a handful of times during my journey, largely due to the fact that because I didn't really kick my legs I was using different muscle groups so my legs always felt fresh once I got on the bike.

However please practice this for yourself at week 6 and see how you feel. If you need to incorporate more of these swim bike/brick sessions then factor more in as required. .

You can also bring the nutrition strategy you learned to this level, its time to invest in a box of gel's!, amazon rock for these.

Regarding the bike, at this stage any roadworthy bike you can get your hands on will be sufficient, do not go out splash the cash on a new bike, re-read the 'what bike' chapter.

Never get on the bike without wearing your helmet and ensure working lights front and rear.

Go online to www.racecheck.com or google and research super sprint triathlons in your area taking place 12 weeks from now and book yourself in!

I very much recommend you wear your tri suit throughout your training – this is what I did from day one.

I have factored in gym sessions for strength conditioning, (and the all important sauna). (see previous chapter)

At week 6 you will see the word ''EASY' this is an optional recovery week, you can take the week off if you want. I prefer light training but it's up to you – see how you feel.

The plan for level 2 follows on the next page

Remember the secrets! – Pace pace pace! , we want to be training at our 'all day' pace, 60-80% MHR. Keep it slow and steady!.

For the pool sessions you have 2 choices.

If you can already swim 16 lengths from crawl then this is what you will do. (x2 sets).

If not, incorporate the base swim plan/lessons into these days.

Now you might struggle to find a super-sprint event that has a 10km bike element, many feature a 20km which is the distance for a sprint! (the next level up)

My advice would be to only enter an event where the bike is 10km. If you cannot find one, then I suggest you make your own 'DIY' race (its fun and the beauty of them is you choose the course and the date!).

Leave your bike in the boot of your car and create your own bike and run routes using mapometer.com that start and finish at the pool.

I have done this many times.

Then, whilst you are training for level 4, the sprint, drop back down to this level and collect the medal for the super-sprint event that you saw! (You will smash it)

Read the next chapter, 'what to expect at your first triathlon' before the race.

Enjoy your training and best of luck!

**Level 2 :**

**Super Sprint Distance Triathlon Plan**

| Week | Mon | Tues | Weds | Thurs | Fri | Sat | sun |
|------|-----|------|------|-------|-----|-----|-----|
| 1 | Pool 16 | gym | Bike 5km | Pool 16 | gym | Bike 5km | R 2.5k |
| 2 | Pool 16 | gym | Bike 5km | Pool 16 | gym | Bike 6km | R 2.5k |
| 3 | Pool 16 | gym | Bike 5km | Pool 16 | gym | Brick 7/0.5 | R 2.5k |
| 4 | Pool 16 | gym | Bike 5km | Pool 16 | gym | Brick 8/0.5 | R 2.5k |
| 5 | Pool 16* | gym | Bike 6km | Pool 16 | gym | Brick 9/1 | R 2.5k |
| 6 EASY | Pool 16 | gym | Bike 7km | Pool 16 | gym | Brick 10/0.5 | R 2.5k |
| 7 | Pool 16* | gym | Bike 7km | Pool 16 | gym | Brick 10/1 | R 2.5k |
| 8 | Pool 16 | gym | Bike 10km | Pool 16 | gym | Brick 10/1.5 | R 2.5k |
| 9 | Pool 16* | gym | Bike 10km | Pool 16 | gym | Brick 10/2 | R 2.5k |
| 10 | Pool 16 | gym | Bike 10km | Pool 16 | gym | Brick 10/2 | R 2.5k |
| 11 | Pool 16 | gym | Bike 11km | Pool 16 | gym | Brick 11/2 | R 2.5k |
| 12 | Pool 16 | gym | Rest | Pool 16 | 2.5k run | Rest | RACE! TRI |

**Key :**

Pool 16 = 16 x 25m pool swim (do 2 sets!) (see base swim plan)

Gym = gym session as per plan

Run = Run in km

Bike = Bike in km

Brick = Brick session bike & run in km

*= Factor in some short bike work straight after your pool session (5km max) and notice how easy this is if you don't kick your legs in the pool! Take your time in transition, get showered and changed first (add more of these if you find it difficult)

Now you might find that the super sprint requires you to do less than 16 lengths – if so great! You will smash it training at the higher level!

Read the next page before your race which goes into detail about what to expect at your first triathlon

## What to Expect on Race day at your first triathlon

Once you have registered for your first triathlon, you will usually get some sort of confirmation / welcome e-mail straight away.

If you do not get this within 24 hours, contact the event organisers to ask why.

Usually attached to your confirmation e-mail will be lots of information about the race so be sure to read it.

Check the event organisers website and facebook page  as there will be lots of 'noise' going on in the weeks leading up to the event, feel free to join in and get involved!

I will talk you through what happened at my first ever triathlon as I found pretty much every triathlon followed suit except Ironman (amazing).

Once I registered I got a welcome e-mail and one of the things it told me was to keep an eye on their website for my start time.

About 3 weeks before race day, my swim start time appeared on the organisers website.

In my case, my swim time was 12pm, and it said I needed to register at least one hour before.

Do not get confused with the start time of the actual race or registration opening time!

The first swimmer was due to start at 8am meaning he had to register by 7am so registration opened at 6.30am.

There was absolutely no point me going down to register at 6.30am when I wasn't due to start until 12pm!

I would have been hanging around for nearly 6 hours!!!

Personally I like to give myself a good hour and a half to park and do everything I need to do.

I like to have everything I will need laid out and ready for me the night before the race as there is nothing worse than running round trying to find stuff on race day.

When you arrive at race start, the first thing you need to do is register.

Take your confirmation e-mail to the registration tent and give your name.

They will then hand you an envelope which will contain the following things:

Your Race number

Race number stickers

Timing chip (if they are doing this)

Swim Cap (although not always)

Freebies

Leaflets

If the event is doing chip timing in the form of a bracelet – make sure you put this on straight away, you don't want to lose this!

The first thing you need to do is attach your race number to your race belt.

Then you need to put your race number stickers on, usually there are 3 for the helmet – front and either side, 2 for the bike (front and seat post) and one for your kit bag.

Some events have number tattoos that you fix to your arms and legs which is ace.

The key to these is to put them on then soak them wet through before you remove them.

If they don't have stickers they will usually have a lady with a marker pen in registration who's job it is to write your number on your arm – make sure you go and see her!

Next job is to rack your bike.

Usually the bike bays are numbered and at the end of each row there should be big signs with 1-49 – 50-99 – 100-149 etc.

Find your row and rack your bike.

Make a mental note of where you will exit the pool (normally through fire exit lol) and gauge which row you are on relative to the pool, 1$^{st}$, 2$^{nd}$ 3$^{rd}$ etc.

If the bike stands are not numbered, and they often aren't, I would pick somewhere that is easy to remember, like end of a row for example.

There should be marshalls in the bike area and they will check that your brakes work on your bike and make sure your helmet fastens so make sure your helmet is fastened as you enter the bike area.

Be careful as you are walking around as the race is likely to be in full flow and the last thing you want to do is get in another athletes way.

Once you have racked your bike it is time to lay all your gear out.

There are boxes that you can buy for this, some events allow them others don't.

I personally like to put all the stuff I will need for my bike in one pile head to toe and then all the stuff I will need for the run in a separate, smaller pile, but experiment with laying your stuff out in training.

I found it helped to have a written checklist of everything I needed so I can tick it off. (don't forget vaseline!)

You can't spend too much time in this area checking, double checking and triple checking that you have everything you need.

Make sure you have your water bottles attached to your bike and that your fuel is waiting for you somewhere safe. (In a sock for example).

Once this is done you get to chill for a bit and soak up all the atmosphere before your race briefing.

There will usually be a compulsory race briefing.

At this level it is often done 15 minutes before your swim start by the side of the pool but some have them the day before etc-check with the organisers as you need to make sure you attend this.

If you did not get given a swim cap at registration you need to go and get one now.

Go and find a marshal pool side and ask where you get them from, they will often reply 'me'.

All that remains is for you to attend the race briefing if you have not already done so.

As I said at my first tri this was done poolside 15 mins before my start.

Make your way there as instructed by the organisers and you will notice other people with similar numbers to yours milling around.

Keep an eye out for the marshals and listen to what they tell you to do.

At mine we all got into the water about a minute before we were due to start and then someone counted us down from 10!

Normally there is a marshal sat at the end of your lane counting your lengths, the signal for your final length is that they will put a coloured paddle into the water for you to see – keep an eye out for this.

When you get out you usually have to shout your race number to the marshal so they know you are done and then its off to T1!

Transition is fairly straightforward, just take your time.

In an ideal world you would have ridden the bike route beforehand in your training but keep an eye out for the other athletes, signs and marshals as you make your way round.

T2 again should be relatively straightforward, make sure you dismount where the marshal tells you to and keep your helmet on at all times until you get to your bay.

Get changed into your running gear and off you go!

Once you finish collect your medal and whatever other goodies the organiser has in store for you!

Don't forget keep your race number but hand your timing chip back if you need to do so!

Other than that you are free to go!

Staple your race number to your medal and proudly hang it pride of place as you wallow in the glory of your amazing achievement!

The race results are usually uploaded later that day or within 24 hours on the organisers website and don't forget to join all the post race 'noise' on their facebook page if they have one!

## Levels 3&4

### 5k Run / Sprint Triathlon: Swim 800m Bike 20km Run 5km

Ok, because this plan is triathlon focused, it is time to merge to two levels into one training plan on the basis that you will be covering this distance as part of your plan anyway so you can incorporate the run race element into one of your training days.

You should follow the nutrition strategy you learned earlier throughout your training and of course on race day.

You may want to start contemplating and researching a new bike, dependant on what your current arrangements are in this regard. (see 'what bike' chapter)

Even though many sprint tri swims are only 400m or 16 lengths, in this schedule the swim distances start to ramp up on the basis that you could easily complete 16 lengths in 10 minutes and it is unlikely you will go to the pool for such a short length of time.

You should now be able to swim at least 16 lengths in a pool front crawl non stop – if you cannot do this please get swimming lessons by a qualified swim coach or incorporate the base swim plan into your swim days.

Training at a higher swim level will make you stronger for race day and will set you up nicely should you wish to progress at a later stage.

Again go online to www.racecheck.com read the reviews and enter a sprint tri that is scheduled roughly 12 weeks from now and a 5k run race roughly 8 weeks away! Also try a Google search of events in your area i.e. search '5km run in (nearby towns).' & Remember, train at 60-80% MHR – your 'all day' pace for the longer sessions!!

**Level 3 & 4 :**

**5K Run race and sprint Triathlon**

| Week | Mon | Tues | Weds | Thurs | Fri | Sat | sun |
|------|-----|------|------|-------|-----|-----|-----|
| 1 | Pool 16 | gym | Bike 10km | Pool 16 | gym | Brick 10/2.5 | R 3k |
| 2 | Pool 18 | gym | Bike 10km | Pool 18 | gym | Brick 12/2.5 | R 3k |
| 3 | Pool 20 | gym | Bike 10km | Pool 20 | gym | Brick 14/2.5 | R 4k |
| 4 | Pool 22 | gym | Bike 10km | Pool 22 | gym | Brick 16/2.5 | R 4k |
| 5 | Pool 24* | gym | Bike 10km | Pool 24 | gym | Brick 18/2.5 | R 5k |
| 6 EASY | Pool 26 | gym | Bike 10km | Pool 26 | gym | Brick 20/2.5 | R 5k |
| 7 | Pool 28* | gym | Bike 10km | Pool 28 | gym | Brick 20/2.5 | R 5k |
| 8 | Pool 30 | gym | Bike 10km | Pool 30 | gym | Bike 20 | R 5k race |
| 9 | Pool 32* | gym | Bike 10km | Pool 32 | gym | Brick 20/2.5 | R 5k |
| 10 | Pool 34 | gym | Bike 10km | Pool 34 | gym | Brick 20/2.5 | R 5k |
| 11 | Pool 36 | gym | Bike 10km | Pool 36 | gym | Brick 20/2.5 | R 2.5k |
| 12 | Pool 40 | gym | Bike 10km | Pool 40 | 2.5k run | Rest | RACE! TRI |

**\*Enter a 5k run race as part of your training for week 8**

**If you can't find races within your timeline then create your own! But be sure to return to collect the medal!**

**Key** : R= run in km / 5km run race at week 8

Pool = x 25 metre lengths (all day pace)

Gym = gym session as per plan

Bike = Bike in km

Brick = Brick session bike & run in km

*Pool – short bike work after pool session, no more than 10km

Use the shorter bike in the week to put your foot down and have a bit of fun but remember to return to your 'all day' pace at weekend!

You will notice that in all of these plans, they are not running intense.

It is the authors experience that running is the area where athletes are most likely to become injured so he found that one simple long, slow run each week coupled with a separate brick session directly off the bike served him extremely well throughout the entire process including full iron distance.

However feel free to add an additional shorter run (50% of your Sunday distance) midweek, if you feel up to it, maybe at the opposite end of the day to one of your gym pool or bike sessions perhaps, but do no more than 3 running sessions per week (the brick run and the long slow run count as 2).

Your long slow Sunday runs should be exactly that, SLOW at your 'all day' pace (see secrets)

Recce the bike route and ride it before the race on your 20k bike days if you can – if not create a replica with similar climbs at similar points.

## The Transition from pool to open water swimming

Now that we are moving into the Olympic triathlon level it is time to make the transition from pool to open water as most races from now on will feature an open water swim instead of a pool based swim, either in a lake, reservoir or ocean.

Let me tell you the way that I did it and then, with the benefit of hindsight, let me tell you the way I would recommend that you do it.

I will never forget the first time I went for a swim in open water.

By this stage I classed the swim as one of my strongest disciplines. I was regularly swimming 60 lengths front crawl in the pool without stopping and averaged around 30 seconds a length, my swim splits were always way above average in my previous races so I was very confident with the swim element.

This was soon all to change.

Organised open water swim sessions were being held at Leigh sailing club on Pennington flash a few times a week which is where the IMUK swim takes place. (I would point out that these are nothing to do with the race organisers).

Now I say 'organised swim session' basically you paid a fiver and got in on your own with a couple of safety kayaks on hand, All the other swimmers were very spread out all over the huge reservoir and this is a very significant point as you will soon find out.

I hired a wetsuit, and in I went.

OMG…

Talk about being taken way out of your comfort zone!

I didn't like it one bit. It just felt so open and so deep. I have always had a fear of deep water and I longed for the security of the pool. I didn't feel comfortable getting my head down and found it impossible to swim in a straight line.

I spent the entire first session swimming about 10 yards from the shore where I could still stand up - zig zagging all over the place!

Being able to swim the course seemed light years away and I got out depressed thinking I am going to need at least 6 months training to master the open water swim element as it is a completely different animal to what I was expecting.

It turns out 90% of people go through the exact same experience but everyone ends up falling in love with it in the end. (well, kind of).

When I got home from that first session I did lots and lots and lots of reading about it online and found hundreds of people were in the same boat with the usual endless opinions and advice.

The 2 best tips I read were this:

1) Swimming is swimming, if you can swim in a pool you can swim in the sea. Slow down, try to relax and have faith in all the training you have been doing in the pool, this training will serve you well, relax and find your pool rhythm, it's exactly the same, there is just no blue line on the floor.

But by far the best was:

2) "Just bloody get in the water"

I love 2, it says it all, just get in and practice, practice, practice!

Our mind likes to play cruel tricks on us and we run all sorts of ridiculous scenarios in our head but I was determined to crack this element and the second my mind began to wander I reminded myself of the two things above.

I went back down there week in week out to battle my demons with it and slowly but surely, my confidence began to improve.

In the end, after many many weeks, I got to the point where I was able to swim the 'short course' in a relatively straight line, a 450 metre 'circuit' comprising of 3 small buoys the size of a football in a huge triangle.

Readers should note that (other than one occasion when I was feeling particularly brave) I never swam any further out than the short course throughout my entire Ironman training as doing so was frankly dangerous in my opinion, yet I managed to record a 1:30 swim at IMUK on race day and was nearly an hour within the cut off.

Not only that, but I found my races at Olympic level (in a lake) the 70.3 Dublin (in the North Sea!) and IMUK itself a piece of cake by comparison to these training sessions, a piece of cake.

A couple of observations, and then I will tell you what I would do differently if I was going through this process again for the first time:

First, the two things that most people struggle with most are pace and sighting. What has this book been about from the first page? Pace Pace Pace! Relax, Slow down, it is not a race! find your pool rhythm and replicate this, have faith in all the training that you have been doing, it is there to serve you!

Second, It's better to swim straight and slower than fast and all over the place as you will only end up swimming a much greater distance than you need to by swimming off course and expanding miles more energy in the process.

One of my bug bears is that on race day the buoys are usually bright yellow and the size of Blackpool tower whereas the buoys in my local club are miles apart and the size of a football – Race day is miles easier on this front!

By the way, don't make the mistake I did in my first year by going charging down to the OW swim sessions in winter, you are making it ten times harder for yourself – wait for the water to warm up in spring, it's a completely different experience.

But here is the biggest thing that I learned about open water swimming.

About 4 months into my Ironman training, I went down to a coached group open water swimming session at 3 sisters in Wigan. (they wait for the water to warm up!)

The format was that once a week you would split into three groups, novice, intermediate, advanced and then each group would have a one hour training drill swimming in a **big group of people**.

Then, every 3 weeks, there would be 'Time trials' over various distances where once again you picked your distance and swam in a **big group** in a mock race environment.

I learnt more by going to these sessions in 6 weeks than I did in 6 months going down to penny flash on my own. In hindsight I wasted a lot of time swimming solo in Pennington flash. Swimming in a big group or pack is far better training, far better, as it is a simulation of what actually happens on race day.

As a general rule, if you can see other people when you are swimming in a big pack, then you do not need to worry about 'sighting' – keep the pack on the side that you breathe and so long as you can see them, all you need to worry about is your technique.

In addition, learning how to swim on someone else's feet changed my life!

Ask the coach to teach you not only how to do this, but how to pick your 'partner' as you need to choose them carefully (avoid the aggressive kickers – it's the gentle ones that you are looking for! and u need to make sure they are taking you where you want to go!)

If the coach does not know what you are talking about when you ask them this, find a different coach.

Now there is some truth to the statement that by learning to swim in the flash in a straight line on my own I went on to find race day very very easy by comparison, it's a bit like practicing kicking a football into one of those kiddies nets when on matchday the goalposts are huge, but if I had my time again, I would definitely do all my open water training in a coached, group training environment.

But guys, please…..

Swimming in the open water does not need to be dangerous but it can be, so please always follow these safety tips:

**Never go for an open water swim on your own**

Look on the internet and find organised, structured open water group swim sessions for beginners run by qualified open water swim instructors and go down to these sessions for as long as it takes for you to get comfortable

**Never go for an open water swim on your own outside of these organised sessions**

Always wear a full wetsuit (you can usually hire them – I bought an ex-hire one for £40 – fine for IMUK) goggle masks designed for open water and a bright coloured swim cap.

As you progress, Make sure the swim sessions have plenty of safety boats and kayak's out there to help you if you get stuck, swallow your ego and ask these guys to look out for you – they will totally understand your situation and will appreciate you telling them.

If you get in to trouble try not to panic, lie on your back with your arm in the air (the wetsuit will help keep you afloat) and have faith, the safety boat will come and get you.

Always try to swim in 2's if possible

In the plan that follows, don't worry too much about the distances early on just keep going to the structured, organised open water novice swim sessions at your local club as often as you can and I promise you the distance will come much sooner than you think.

Get some bodyglide and use it before each session on your neck.

Oh, and learn how to swim on someone else's feet, it will change your life!

Learning how to breathe every 4 strokes helped me massively, I then increased this to every 6 and eventually every 8. I would train in the pool at 8 then race in open water at 4, this made race day feel very easy.

## Level 5 & 6 Olympic Triathlon & 10k road race

## Swim 1500 metres, Bike 40km, Run 10km

If you have reached this level you may now want to treat yourself to a new bike if you have not already done so.

You should have a decent pair of running shoes bought from a specialist running shop that have been tailored to your needs.

You should be wearing clip in pedals by now, if not start practicing with them, same with aero bars. (but be careful – see secret!)

Feel free to invest in some decent clothing for your bike sessions.

Did you read the preceding chapter 'Making the transition from pool to open water'? if not, please do so.

Make sure you continue to follow the nutrition strategy you learned, consider experimenting with different foods just make sure you keep to the max carbs per hour of 60-80g and eat every 30 mins whilst training.

Sip a good quality electrolyte drink throughout your training to keep you hydrated.

Other than that go smash it!

10k race at week 8 and Olympic tri at week 12, research events on www.racecheck.com or google search '10k races / olympic triathlons in (nearby towns)'

Reece the bike route and ride it beforehand if possible towards the end of your plan. If not create a replica of the race loop with similar climbs at similar points using mapometer.com.

Enjoy!

## Level 5 & 6

## 10K Run race and Olympic Triathlon

| Week | Mon | Tues | Weds | Thurs | Fri | Sat | sun |
|---|---|---|---|---|---|---|---|
| 1 | Pool 40 | gym | Bike 10km | Ows 1hr | gym | Brick 22/2.5 | R 6k |
| 2 | Pool 42 | gym | Bike 12km | Ows 1hr | gym | Brick 24/2.5 | R 7k |
| 3 | Pool 44 | gym | Bike 14km | Ows 1hr | gym | Brick 28/2.5 | R 8k |
| 4 | Pool 46* | gym | Bike 16km | Ows 1hr | gym | Brick 32/2.5 | R 9k |
| 5 | Pool 48 | gym | Bike 18km | Ows 1hr | gym | Brick 36/5 | R 10k |
| 6 EASY | Pool 50 | gym | Bike 20km | Ows 1hr | gym | Brick 40/2.5 | R 10k |
| 7 | Pool 52 | gym | Bike 20km | Ows 1hr | gym | Brick 40/7.5 | R 10k |
| 8 | Pool 54 | gym | Bike 20km | Ows 1hr | gym | Bike 40 | R 10k race |
| 9 | Pool 56* | gym | Bike 20km | Ows 1hr | gym | Brick 40/2.5 | R 10k |
| 10 | Pool 60 | gym | Bike 20km | Ows 1hr | gym | Brick 40/7.5 | R 10k |
| 11 | Pool 60* | gym | Bike 20km | Ows 1hr | gym | Brick 40/2.5 | R 5k |
| 12 | Pool 60 | gym | Bike 10km | Ows 1hr | 5k run | Rest | RACE! TRI |

Key : R= run in km / 10km run race at week 8

Pool = x 25m pool swim (all day pace)

Bike in Km

Gym = gym session as per plan

Brick = Brick session bike / run in km

Take a break at week 6 if you want

*pool/bike brick no more than 15km on bike

OWS = Open water swim

For the open water session, find a group open water session near to you that does **group** open water swim training for around 1 hour each week.

Move one of your other training days around to suit if required but always try to leave at least one day gap between the same discipline (ie not 2 gym days back to back etc)

The best open water training I did was down at 3 sisters in Wigan, each week they would do group training drills for one hour and then every 3rd week it was a time trial 'mock race' for various distances – this is ideal – for the time trials you want to be peaking at 1500 metres maximum but do not worry too much about your distance initially, just keep going to the coached sessions and the distance will come

Do not waste time going to open water swim sessions where you are not in a group and never go for an open water swim on your own.

You are very unlikely to be able to go straight down to open water and begin swimming for 1 hour straight away. Do not worry about this, everyone is the same.

Cover the distance in your pool sets and keep going down to the weekly group open water training sessions.

Explain you are a novice to open water, listen to the coach, do what the coach tells you to do and bit by bit, each week you will improve!

In addition, you will notice that in all of these plans, they are not running intense.

It is the authors experience that running is the area where athletes are most likely to become injured so he found that one simple long, slow run each week coupled with a separate brick session directly off the bike served him extremely well throughout the entire process including full iron distance.

However feel free to add an additional shorter run (50% of your Sunday distance) midweek, if you feel up to it, maybe at the opposite end of the day to one of your gym pool or bike sessions perhaps, but do no more than 3 running sessions per week (the brick run and the long slow run count as 2).

Your long slow Sunday runs should be exactly that, SLOW at your 'all day' pace (see secrets)

Use the shorter bike in the week to put your foot down and have a bit of fun but remember to return to your 'all day' pace at weekend!

## Levels 7 & 8 Half Marathon and Half Iron triathlon (70.3)

### Swim : 1.2 miles (just over 70 x 25m lengths) Bike 90km: Run 21km

If you have made it this far all the way from level 1 then well done! That is an awesome achievement!

You should be fairly confident with the open water swim element now and I bet your first open water race went way better than you expected!

You have your nutrition strategy nailed, you know what you are doing, it's just a case of following a training plan and the medals will come!!

This time, no 'rest' at week 6, we are in Ironman territory now!

On the subject of rest I found it worked for me to have a 5 min rest, an energy gel and a stretch at 10k on the run, try it for yourself in training and see how you get on.

Half marathon run race factored in for week 8 training day (you will be able to run these all day long!)

In hindsight I realised there is little need to run any longer than 1 hour straight off the bike in a brick session so the max bike/run brick is 10km with the majority being 2.5km (these served me perfectly well for the full Ironman never mind the half!)

Levels 7 & 8 plan follows on the next page as does my race report from the 70.3 (half Ironman) in Dublin.

You are now playing in the Ironman zone so get onto their website and pick a 70.3! use google or racecheck to find your half mara at week 8.

# Level 7 & 8 Half Marathon & Half Iron Training Plan

| Week | Mon | Tues | Weds | Thurs | Fri | Sat | sun |
|------|-----|------|------|-------|-----|-----|-----|
| 1 | Pool 60 | gym | Bike 1hr | Ows | gym | Brick 45/2.5 | R12k |
| 2 | Pool 60 | gym | Bike 1hr | Ows | gym | Brick 55/5 | R14k |
| 3 | Pool 60 | 7k/am gym/pm | Bike 1hr | Ows | gym | Brick 65/2.5 | R 16k |
| 4 | Pool 60* | gym | Bike 1hr | Ows | gym | Brick 75/7.5 | R 18k |
| 5 | Pool 62 | 9k/am gym/pm | Bike 1hr | Ows | gym | Brick 85/2.5 | R 20k |
| 6 | Pool 64 | gym | Bike 1hr | Ows | gym | Brick 90/10 | R 10k |
| 7 | Pool 66* | 10k/am gym/pm | Bike 1hr | Ows | gym | Brick 90/2.5 | 20k |
| 8 | Pool 70 | gym | Bike 1hr | Ows | gym | Rest | R 20k race |
| 9 | Pool 70 | gym | Bike 1hr | Ows | gym | Brick 90/10 | R 10k |
| 10 | Pool 70* | 10k/am gym/pm | Bike 1hr | Ows | gym | Brick 90/2.5 | R 20k |
| 11 | Pool 70 | gym | Bike 1hr | Ows | gym | Brick 90/2.5 | R 10k |
| 12 | Pool 70 | gym | Bike 10km | Ows | 5k run | Rest | RACE! TRI |

Key : R= run in km / 20km run race at week 8

Pool = x 25m pool swim (all day pace)

Bike in Km

Gym = gym session as per plan

Brick = Brick session bike / run in km

Pool*= pool/bike brick no more than 30km on bike

OWS = Open water swim – Group open water training session for one hour / 1 hour Group Time trial (see notes on level 5&6 plan)

My 70.3 race report follows on the next page, please read for inspiration before starting your training for this level.

In addition, you will notice that in all of these plans, they are not running intense.

It is the authors experience that running is the area where athletes are most likely to become injured so he found that one simple long, slow run each week coupled with a separate brick session directly off the bike served him extremely well throughout the entire process including full iron distance.

However feel free to add an additional shorter run (50% of your Sunday distance) midweek, if you feel up to it, maybe at the opposite end of the day to one of your gym, pool or bike sessions perhaps, but do no more than 3 running sessions per week (the brick run and the long slow run count as 2). (Midweek example as above)

Your long, slow Sunday runs should be exactly that, SLOW at your 'all day' pace (see secrets) Fuel is key (see secrets).

Take a 5 minute stop and stretch after 10k on the run.

Use the shorter bike in the week to put your foot down and have a bit of fun but remember to return to your 'all day' pace at weekend!

## Ironman 70.3 Dublin Race Report

So despite a (very) early night last night on the eve of my first Ironman 70.3 I finally drifted off to sleep at around 9pm and managed to have a deep quality sleep until 1.30am at which point I woke up needing a pee.

I knew if I got up that would be it.

This was to prove true as I was to spend the next 4 hours wide awake and unable to get back to sleep, I was just so excited and constantly thinking about my first ironman 70.3 race, I clearly remember thinking to myself that I hadn't felt like this since I was 10 years old on xmas eve, ridiculous given that I am now nearly 40.

Anyhow at 5am I hears the guy from brazil rattling around and I really wanted to meet the mysterious fellow Ironman athlete that had eluded me up until this point.

I got up to find his door open and his wetsuit laid out neatly on the floor, I introduced myself and we had a great chat about our journey thus far which was to prove a little too enthusiastic for the B&B owner… "shush!!!! It's 5am and other people are asleep!" he said with a bemused look on his face as if he could not understand how anyone could be so full of beans at such an early hour….but we were both buzzing.

Our chat continued over breakfast, it turns out that the guy from Brazil travels all over the world racing the Ironman events and he was half decent too – he was to rank top 30 in this race, naturally I quizzed him for his secrets, which I have added to my book. – "Do not start like the lion" he was to say before wishing me all the best, he seemed more in a hurry than I was – maybe he just wanted to get away from the crazy guy at the B&B asking him all the questions!

So, having finished my breakfast, I got changed into my wetsuit and I was good to go.

I felt quite relaxed walking down to the Ironman start tent, but a few things were playing on my mind. 3 in particular:

1. For some unexplained reason I kept thinking that something would have mysteriously gone wrong with my bike overnight like a tyre burst on its own, for example, why, I do not know, but I did
2. That I would not be able to access my bike bag and put my gels /tool in it
3. That I would not complete the swim / make the swim cut off time of 1.10

On arriving in T1 I was delighted to observe that first of all, the bike was fine, and second, when you went into the transition tent, there was a team of ladies waiting to put extra things into your bike bag for you.

I noticed that a lot of people seemed stressed out, running around like headless chickens, but I really couldn't understand why, afterall, surely that was the whole point of doing everything yesterday? No, Not me, as far as I was concerned, everything was perfect, and the lady even complimented me on how relaxed I was looking, which I very much appreciated

. I was just buzzing to be part of the whole thing.....and I was ready to race .

I had been training well for the Ironman Dublin race and knew I easily had the distance in me for both the bike and the run. Despite the swim practice going well yesterday I was still concerned abut the swim element, but I knew if I could complete it the medal would be mine, save technical problems on the bike.

The buoys were out clearly marking the swim course and a helpful local pointed out exactly the route, "keep all the buoys on your left until the last one" he  said, sounds easy right?

I could hear the announcer saying that the pros were about to get in the water so I made my way over to the swim start which was a fair walk from the tents, I had bought some cheap slip on beach shoes which came in very handy for the walk. On the way down I was on such a high and was babbling rubbish to anyone that would iisten…. I found that either:

1. People  thought I was a lunatic and ignored me / didn't play along
2. People fed / bounced off my enthusiasm and joined in

I had learnt by now to surround myself with as many of type 2 above as possible and that is exactly what I did.

I also found that there are broadly 2 types of people at an Ironman branded event,

1.  serious athletes taking everything hyper serious
2.  those that are on their first ironman and are  just buzzing to be a part of the whole thing,

I was certainly a champion for the latter group and I wanted to savour every second. I must say that the way Ironman itself embraces the latter group is one of the things that makes an Ironman event so special..

Our swim time was based on our age group with a 15 minute gap between each one with my swim time being 7.15am. it was only 6.45, so plenty of time to observe the other age groupers starting their swim.

I was clear on my swim strategy, I would be  starting at the very back of the pack.

However when I got to the start line and observed one of the earlier age groups getting into the water, I noticed 2 things:

1. there was no warm up / acclimatise time in the water- you were straight in
2. 200-300 athletes formed an orderly queue to get down the ramp with the strongest at the front and it took easily 10 minutes for everyone to get into the water once the starter hooter went

Starting at the back I was concerned about getting stuck in slow moving traffic ahead as it was, but in addition I realised if I did this I was now certain to be caught up by a large chunk of the strong swimmers in the group behind.

In light of the above I switched strategy on the basis that I would rather be in the water for a few minutes getting used to the cold rather than stood in a big queue waiting to get in it and I naturally wanted to reduce my chances of getting swamped from behind.

I positioned myself at the front only to be surrounded by out and out animals so I shuffled slightly further back in the pack.

There is something magical about being stood in the start pen of your first Ironman event, I shook hands with the guys around me, we chit chatted with big smiles on our faces waiting for the hooter, the adrenaline was pumping and it felt like we were off to fight a war. I wasn't nervous, I was ready to fight.

The roar that went up once the hooter sounded will give me goosebumps for the rest of my days.

I made my way down the ramp and into the water and every other athlete burst straight into a swim. Not me, I spent a good few minutes acclimatising to the water, dunking myself at least 3 or 4 times. I must have looked like a certain DNF to the crowd on the bank but I didn't care, I was doing my own thing.

This was to pay off handsomely as when I eventually sets off (approx. 85% down the pack) I took to it like a duck to water, I didn't get the initial 'shock' of the water you get when diving straight in and instead settled straight into my 4 stroke rhythm.

Within 10 minutes I knew the swim was mine.

I am going to write a separate article about this but open water swimming on race day is just so much easier than practice for 2 major reasons

1. Instead of the buoy markers being the  size of a small white football bobbing on the surface a mile apart like they are in training, the buoy markers on race day are the size of blackpool tower,  illuminous yellow, and spaced every few hundred yards apart – this makes sighting on race day way easier than practice
2. Keeping a bunch of fellow swimmers on the side that you breathe on means you never have to look up and can concentrate instead on your rhythm

10 minutes into the swim and I was feeling very strong, my swim training had put me in great shape. I clearly remember feeling angry at myself for stressing so much about it  pre race.

30 minutes into the swim I noticed that the caps around me were a different colour, it was at this moment I realised that rather than  the group behind catching me up, as was my big fear, it was  I that had caught up the group ahead!

Never again will I fear an open water swim.

A swim 'expert' had told me that by only breathing on one side I would end up swallowing loads of water – this turned out to be bollokcs – breathing on one side was perfectly fine.

With regard to the horror stories of other swimmers crashing and banging into you, this is nowhere near as frequent as you think it will be, remember you are not in a pool you are in a big wide ocean so there is plenty of room for everyone! In my experience when it does occur one of two things will happen in this situation.

1. the person behind/side will try and trample straight over you
2. the person behind/side will swim round you/ stop

I have found that thankfully the vast majority fall into the second category, afterall they don't want you to kick them in the face anymore than you want them to try and swim over you.

With regard to those in group 1, I have also found that 95% of the time, if you hold your line, keep strong and don't stop, the vast majority  will just 'bounce' off you and if I am  honest I actually love it when this happens,  it makes me laugh. it really does.

A great example of this was when one of the leaders from the group behind tried to swim over me at the last buoy and he just bounced between me and the buoy like a pinball.

Can I be really honest and say I secretely enjoy the fight? The biggest thing  I have learnt  about my journey is that despite the 'nice boy' persona, deep down, I am a fighter at heart. Discovering this inner warrior is worth the Ironman entry fee tenfold.

One guy did swim straight over me on the final leg and I remember thinking to myself 'how rude' but honestly, it is no big deal, you just take a few seconds to settle yourself and regroup  before getting on with it and settling back onto your rhythm.

Making that final turn into the home straight was an awesome feeling.

Swim exit is an interesting experience for a first timer, I literally swam right up onto the exit mat and some hands came from no-where and yanked me out of the water with a resounding 'well done' – for a minute it felt like this 'yanking' pulled a muscle in my leg but no I was fine.

My swimtime was a very respectable 40 minutes which  was slightly faster than my training drills and well within the 70 minute cut off – I was literally buzzing.

I came out of the water on such a high, I knew that the medal was now mine, save technical problems on the bike but that was now in the hands of the iron gods and I was  celebrating with the crowd who played along as I made my way to the transition tent.

I spent a laughable 11.30 minutes in T1, .but I didn't care, it felt like everyone else was stressing and rushing around to get changed but not me, I was still on such a high having completed the swim and I was taking my time and laughing and joking with anyone that would join in.

One guy was going on at me about how he got stung by a jellyfish showing me a big red mark on his hand and was asking for my advice like I was some sort of expert?  I told him to go see the medic for some cream – he seemed fine to continue bless him, I had heard talk  about these pre-race but quickly changed the subject!- thankfully they never came knocking at my door!

I finally gets out of T1, got my bike and made my way to the bike start line, still high as a kite from completing the swim. I was shouting 'lets have it' to the crowd as I ran past and they once again responded to me which I loved.

I was clumsy getting onto the bike on the start line which was a bit embarrassing in front of the large crowd, but we shared a smile and I shouted, 'thank you for your support, you are all f**** amazing" before finally setting off, still buzzing.

This outburst was to come back to haunt me as when I passed the first bike timing mat I could clearly hear the alarm going off and I convinced myself that I had been disqualified for swearing at the bike start..

I then spent the next hour and a half worrying about this until a fellow athlete kindly set my mind at ease by telling me that the alrams went off for everyone – not just me!

The bike course was nothing too exciting, fairly flat with some steady climbs and a couple of fairly steep hills but nothing like sheep house lane in Bolton.

I had been practicing the Bolton loop in training and this served me extremely well. There wasn't really any fun bits in Dublin, just more long consistent peddaling and going through the motions. The Bolton loop is way more fun.

I made a point of waving to every single person who was out supporting us on the course and it was very well supported in parts, this gave me such a buzz and kept me going.

I played cat and mouse with a couple of other athletes to keep me entertained and tried to keep myself under reign as I knew the half marathon was waiting for me and would bite on the arse if I pushed it too hard on the bike.

I was a bit disappointed to notice that there wasn't any distance markers which unsettled me as I had no idea how far I had left,

In hindsight the feed stations made excellent distance markers but still the odd km board would have been appreciated as I kept having to ask other athletes with the posh watches how far we had gone.

Large stretches of the course had full length speed bumps in it which was very annoying and a puncture waiting to happen in my opinion. Also I nearly took myself out on one of the corners near the end, it was a fairly fast approach to a very sharp left turn, the steward on this bend was useless and it wasn't just me that nearly ended up in the hedge on the opposite side of the road!

I was feeling strong toward the end and was relieved to enter the gates of phoenix park with no technical issues, the bike had once again served me well.

I got round the bike course in 3.04 which I was very pleased with as 3 hours is my PB for the 48 mile loop in Bolton so to do 55 mile in 3.04 was awesome as far as I am concerned.

More importantly I knew I now had at least 4 hours 30 to do the 20k which was only taking me 2 hr in training so at this point I knew my medal was certain.

I then spent a laughable 15 minutes in T2. but I didn't care, I knew the medal was mine. I needed a dump and that took a while, and I just took my time getting changed and gave my muscles a break, chatting rubbish to anyone that would listen but most were stressed out rushing to get changed which I can't be doing with, my performance thus far had bought me the luxury of taking my time in transition as far as I was concerned and that is exactly what I did.

I am becoming very aware of how relaxed and chilled out I am on race days, this was even more evident at the Ironman as I would say 80% of the fellow athletes seemed stressed out in transition which I don't understand. Someone said to me recently that the race day is a celebration of all your training and that is exactly what it felt like to me, a celebration, and I was savouring every moment, including transition, but I know that spending a total of 27 minutes in T1&2 is ridiculous and an easy win from a time improvement perspective going forward.

Onto the half marathon and once you got off the initial grass area you are onto fairly flat tarmac road /path, which was very much appreciated as I hate trail runs, tarmac is heaven.

I saw a couple of guys withdrawing themselves from the run with the stewards and whilst I felt sorry for them this only made me feel stronger as I was ready.

The crowds were out in force again for the run and were shouting my name as I went by which again I very much appreciated this gives you such a lift..

The crowd near the finish line that we would run past 3 times gave me goosebumps every lap..

My strategy on the run is always to take it super easy at the start, let everyone overtake me whilst I wait for my body to click into run mode and then get slowly stronger as the distance goes on, I have noticed with my runs to date that this strategy seems to be the polar opposite to the majority, who I end up overtaking later in the race and this makes me buzz.

I understood that we were to do 3 laps of the run course and would get a band after each lap. It felt like I had been running for ages without getting a band so I began to quiz the other athletes about this only to be told that bands were not being issued which I found annoying.

The other thing that annoyed me was that there were no distance markers on the run course which I was very disappointed about and I expected better from an ironman event. again I had to ask the people with the posh watches how far we had travelled which was not ideal.

I enjoyed tagging on to a couple of the other athletes and swapping stories which helped pass the time.

The run went well, I followed the nutrition strategy I had learnt from the experts and I was feeling strong.

I felt like I was going to get a blister so a quick stop at the st johns ambulance for a plaster sorted that out.

On my final lap I could hear the announcer and the crowd getting closer and this made me very emotional.

When the finish tower appeared in the distance I even had a little cry, thank goodness for my sunglasses.

The final turn into the finish straight and I found myself in a race with 2 other lads, I let them go as I didn't want them ruining my finish line photo!

The run down the finish straight with that amazing crowd was awesome, very emotional and by far the best experience of my fitness life.

I high fived the announcer then ran down the finish straight with my arms in the air shouting 'yeeeeeeessssssss!' the crowd played along and it was honestly amazing, just the best feeling ever.

If you are thinking about doing an Ironman event you simply must do it just to experience this sensation, it will certainly stay with me forever.

The run took me 2:10, giving a total race time of 5hr 56min but when you add in the transition this becomes an official finish time of 6hr.23min. Anything under 7 I was happy with, I suspected it might begin with a 6 and was secretely hoping for it to start with a 5 but hey, 1900 entered and I ranked 1198 so I am over the moon with this.

I finally got my hands on the medal I had wanted so badly and it felt great.

Into the athletes 'after party' area and I was shocked to see they were giving out free beer – that was the last thing I fancied but the majority did not appear be of the same mindset and were taking full advantage.

Into the finisher tent and if you don't want to look like a novice like I did remember to take your timing chip off your ankle and give it to the dude on the door.

Inside we got given our finisher t-shirt, which is awesome, a slice of dominos pizza, a cup of hot chocolate which I passed on and asked for coffee instead but they said there was none, and a glass of cola. I always wondered why they gave cola out at these events and now I know why -it tastes amazing after a race! honestly its like a magic drink and I couldn't get enough of the stuff.

I was on such a high and was once again babbling on to the people round me with mixed reactions..

Pizza went down well and I passed on the offer of engraving my medal.

I went over to the finish line to watch a few of the other athletes come in and then it was a case of going getting my bike back.

At this point my attention turned to getting back to Dun Leerie to pick up my bike box. I sounded out some of the locals about the best route back and they were like what you are going to cycle back there now? they gave me a look which made me buzz even more before giving me directions first to Dublin and then to the coast road. getting to Dublin seemed fairly straightforward and I knew once I got to the coast road it was just a case of following it all the way round to Dun Leerie, approx. 20km in total.

Time was tight as I had to be at the airport for 5 with a flight at 7 and its now about 3pm.

There was a big queue to get our transition bags but once we had these we could collect our bike and we were good to go.

Cycling back was not ideal, I had a big red ironman bag on one side of my tri bars and a big blue ironman bag on the other and I was naturally tired after the event,some of the looks I got from people leaving the park were hilarious but nothing compared to those I got when I finally arrived back in Dun Leerie after about 40 mins or so.....

I passed the ironman tent where the swim had started from all them hours ago and a couple of guys were in the process of taking it down, when they saw me cycling past with my big blue and red ironman bags on the front of my bike they both double took, put down their tools and just stared at me open mouthed as I went by, this made me feel like some sort of legend. .

This feeling was to continue in the taxi back to the airport.

"How did you get back from Phoenix Park to Dun Leerie?", asked the driver

"Cycled" I replied

"You did the Ironman then cycled back with all your kit?"

"Yep"

"Jesus, You are a fucking Ironman!" said the taxi driver.

Those words will ring in my ear every day of training until my new mate the Ironman announcer shouts it out for the whole of Bolton to hear on July 16th, 2017.

## Levels 9 & 10 – the final chapter!

Congratulations!

You now have 2 choices dependant on how far in the future your Ironman race will be.

1) You can merge levels 9 & 10 and complete the marathon as part of your iron distance triathlon
2) You can complete the marathon first.

I chose option 2, purely because I never believed I would ever be able to run a marathon and wanted to get the medal, plus I had plenty of time before the ultimate race, the Ironman..

My marathon was October and Ironman was the following July.

This meant I could drop the bike for the mara training.

When I did this I felt very strong.

'What no bike or brick sessions?' my body said – just run?

Easy peasy!

I really enjoyed conquering the marathon.

Once I did it I felt certain the Ironman would be mine.

I have included the race report for your review.

Here is the training plan that I followed for the mara, I purposely didn't increase my distance until later on because a) I didn't see the point and b) I was petrified of getting injured in training!

Managed to get the medal and got round fine but above all stayed injury free!

# Level 9 Marathon Training Plan

| Week | Mon | Tues | Weds | Thurs | Fri | Sat | sun |
|------|-----|------|------|-------|-----|-----|-----|
| 1 | SWIM 60 | Gym | R 10K | Gym | SWIM 60 | Off | 20km |
| 2 | SWIM 60 | Gym | R 10K | Gym | SWIM 60 | Off | 10km |
| 3 | SWIM 60 | Gym | R 10K | Gym | SWIM 60 | Off | 20km |
| 4 | SWIM 60 | Gym | R 10K | Gym | SWIM 60 | Off | 10km |
| 5 | SWIM 60 | Gym | R 10K | Gym | SWIM 60 | Off | 20km |
| 6 | SWIM 60 | Gym | R 10K | Gym | SWIM 60 | Off | 20km |
| 7 | SWIM 60 | Gym | R 10K | Gym | SWIM 60 | Off | 25km |
| 8 | SWIM 60 | Gym | R 10K | Gym | SWIM 60 | Off | 25km |
| 9 | SWIM 60 | Gym | R 10K | Gym | SWIM 60 | Off | 30km |
| 10 | SWIM 60 | Gym | R 10K | Gym | SWIM 60 | Off | 30km |
| 11 | SWIM 60 | Gym | R 10K | Gym | SWIM 60 | Off | 35km |
| 12 | SWIM 60 | Gym | R 10K | Gym | SWIM 60 | Off | RACE! |

Key : Pool = x25m lengths

Gym : Gym session as per plan

Run = Run in km

Race report follows on the next page

3-5 min stop and stretch every hour (with fuel as per nutrition strategy – see secret)

Use **www.racecheck.com** or a google search to find your mara!

## Level 9 : My First Marathon : Chester Mara

I had chosen Chester as my first marathon because it was fairly local, described by the organisers as 'relatively flat' (can I have a word with whoever was responsible for writing that please?) and the date of the event fitted nicely in to my plan.

The organisers had sent my race number and programme by post a good 3 weeks before race day so everything was already sorted in this regard.

I had made the decision to stay over the night before in Chester to remove any stress on the morning of the race.

I know chester fairly well and opted for the Village hotel at St David's Park, approx. a 15 minute drive from race HQ which starts at the quaint Chester racecourse right in the city centre..

I arrived at the hotel at about 9.30pm on the Saturday evening and cheked in using their 'self check in print your own key' service which was certainly a first for me.

I starts making my way over to my room and came to a junction in the corridor, rooms 1-100 turn left, rooms 100-150 turn right.

To the left there was silence...

To the right there was a Charity ball going off in full swing with the guests in fine voice making merry and the music pumping out at maximum  volume.....

Guess which way my room was....

As I made my way past all the party goers getting pissed the reality of the path I had now chosen dawned on me.

It wasn't long ago that I would be the one stood at the bar having 'fun' at this time on a Saturday night, but now I find myself on a very different road.

There is something tragic about the lone athlete making his way to a hotel room for an early night whilst the rest of the masses party the night away, although it is equally beautiful and tragic at the same time...

The devil came and knocked at the door and for a split second I thought about dumping the bags and joining them, but no, the marathon medal was the one thing I wanted more than anything in the world right now, so a pint was the last thing that I fancied.

As I walked up the stairs to the sound of raucous laughter ringing out from the party I reminded myself that come the morning, when they are making their way home from the night before, nursing a hangover and no doubt cursing the marathon runners because of all the road closures, I would have the last laugh, and he who laughs last ,laughs loudest.

A member of staff that I had seen in the lobby passed me on the stairs, gave me a big smile and said good-night, I am sad to admit that rather than returning the compliment, I scowled at her and said 'if I can hear all that in my room you will be seeing me again in a couple of minutes'...but she just smiled at me...

As it transpired it was so quiet I could hear a pin drop in my room....

I set my alarm for 6.30am and managed to drift off into a deep sleep at 10.30pm.

At 12.30am I wakes up 'ping' wide awake.

I was simply unable to get back to sleep until 4.30am, Whilst I was aware that my body was resting in that it was just lying there, My mind was whirling at a million miles an hour with a mixture of nerves and excitement and I was just so excited about the day ahead that I simply couldn't wait to get up.

I have found that in every race so far this happens to me and the higher I advance up the levels, the earlier I wake up.

Its so annoying as its the mental strength you need more than anything on race day and only having 2 hours sleep on race eve is far from ideal.

I finally managed to get a good hour in 4-5 and was very thankfull for that as I am sure it made all the difference.

At 6.20 I walked down to the breakfast area, first challenge of the day, see if the chef will put my poridege  and milk in the microwave for 90 seconds for me.

I have had a bad  experience of this in the past where the chef refused to do it because of 'health and safety'..... seriously??? stress you just don't need.

Anyway I managed to find the chef and not only did he oblige but we had a lovely chat as he seemed very interested in the marathon, asking me all about it.

As I walked out of the kitchen a fellow athlete was coming in to do likewise, he was a decent runner and had prior experience of the course at Chester which he shared with me and I lapped it all up.

"Big Hill at mile 16 and then again at 24 he said but make it to 24 and then you are all downhill to the finish! "

"Those hills are getting walked up" I said...he laughed and we wished eachother all the best for the race...

I arrived atChester in good time, 7.30 to be precise, I was aware the carpark on the racecourse was to shut at 8 to allow roads to close for race start at 9.

Driving onto the racecourse itself there must have been a couple of thousand cars on that field, the morning mist had not yet lifted and the sun was streaming down, it really was a beautiful sight.

Despite my lack of sleep earlier I was feeling strong and was ready for the race.

I could see the start line which was on the racecourse itself! to the left there was a huge marquee with a few mobile cafes dotted around outside.

I treated myself to a coffee and made my way inside the big tent which was accessible to members of the public, not just the athletes.

On the door a helpful marshall gave me some overshoes to stop the grass getting on my running trainers once I put them on - at this point I was still fully clothed and was flattered that he recognised me as 'an athlete'!

It was very busy inside the tent with all the fellow athletes and their families buzzing around.

, I have to say I was quite impressed with how nice everybody was, my experience in the build up had given me the impression that Chester was a bit of an elite race for some reason.

Whilst Chester does seem to attract lots of very serious runners, I found everyone I spoke to to be very friendly, which is great for a first timer.

Inside there was a big café, late registration, bag drop, sponsors stands and lots of stalls selling all the usual clothes and gels.

Around the parade ring (remember we are on a racecourse) there was lots of different rooms and here you could find the massage room, a kids room and the 'elite' racers room which I was very tempted to walk into and just nod at people to see what would happen, but thankfully I managed to resist.

I went and collected some free goodies for the little one (hand clappers, balloons etc) and made my way back to the car.

Time for the customary pre race dump and there must have been about 100 portoloos in a long line and whilst we still had 45 mins to go to race start there was already fairly big queues.

I went and joined it and watched in awe as many of the fellow athletes were jogging on the spot whilst they waited and then when one became free they would sprint up to it with the person leaving holding the door open for them before sprinting off themselves!

I have never seen anything like this before! another measure of how far my journey has taken me! i'm now rubbing shoulders with some serious runners here!

With that out of the way I just milled around for a bit taking some shots and once again the start crept up on me.

The announcer on the mike said '5 minutes to go so please come and make your way to the start' - I waited to take some last shots of everyone lining up which I shouldn't have done really as it didn't leave me much time.

Thankfully the car was not far away and I quickly stripped down to my trusty tri suit that has been with me since level 5, put on my running shoes and makes my way to the start., note there were still queues for the toilets!

At every race level so far I have started from the very back of the pack and I didn't intend to change that now.

In total 2,200 lined up at race start on the racecourse itself and the line certainly went back a few furlongs!

On arrival at the back I starts giving everyone around me a high 5, it was obvious I was just buzzing to be there and before long I found myself surrounded by a couple of others who were clearly of the same mindset so we started our own little pre race 'bounce off each others energy' party which was just the best!

Going into the race I had 4 main objectives:

   i.  To make the first cut off point - half way by 3 hours
  ii.  To collect the medal
 iii.  To  make the finish within 5 hours to fall in line with my target for Ironman
 iv.  To make the official results board on the Chester website (6 hours)

All of the above would be just amazing, secretly I was hoping for a 4:30 finish, so my strategy was nailed...

I would run the first 2 miles at 11 minute mile pace, and the other 24 miles at 10 minute mile pace, with a 2 minute stop and stretch every hour -this, by my calculations, would bring me dead on 4:30.

I had not done any mile pacing in my training, but could remember from my half races that both 11 and 10 minute miles felt relatively comfortable for me, so this was the plan.

Lets just pause for a second here, a 4:30 marathon would be considered by many competitive marathon runners as slow. but google the average marathon time globally and you will get the reply 4:21,....So, my goodness, to come in just over the global average will do me very nicely thank you very much!

Whilst I salute all those that were to finish ahead of me, remember that I am just totally over the moon to be lining up at the start line, and let's not forget, at the end of the day my goal is ironman, not getting fast at running marathons!

Also, get this- estimates suggest that only 1% of the population will complete a marathon in their lifetime.....,1%,. ....think about that for a second..... complete a marathon and you will have achieved something amazing that 99% of the population will never do in their life!

How fantasic is that?

I remember being stood on the start line feeling totally relaxed, I was once again  in that magical place where just getting round and collecting the medal would be enough for me.

I was confident my legs had the miles from the training I had done, I could now relax and enjoy it, soak everything in, and just take the race at a nice steady pace.

I wasn't as emotional  at the start as what I thought I would be ,I was more just buzzing to be a part of the whole thing and ready for the longest race of my life.

It wasn't long before the countdown began.

As the claxton sounded I let out my trademark scream of 'COOOOMEEEE ONNNNN!" at the top of my voice.

As always this produces one of 3 reactions from fellow athletes:

i.   they will join in
ii.  they will turn round and smile at me
iii. They will turn round and look at me as if I am a psycho

The reaction in chester was an mainly 2's and 3's above, with an approx. 80/20 split in favour of 3.

This surprised me.

I am trying to emulate what happened in Dublin where 2,000 athletes joined in at the mass start and the roar that went up will stay with me for the rest of my days, it still gives me goosebumps every time I think of it.

I continue in my quest to replicate it at races with varying degrees of success, however something tells me that the response is likely to remain largely muted until july 17th...

I would add at this point that I was also quite surprised by the lack of fancy dress here at Chester.

I spotted one snowman and one spaceman and that was about it out of 2000 runners, the rest all had the proper running gar on and many had a dead serious 'club runner' look on their face.

Nothing wrong with that of course, its great to run with so many talented athletes it really is and I wasn't quite expecting the London marathon, full of people dressed as a chicken etc, I just thought there would me more 'fancy dressers' for some reason.

Anyhow race finally gets underway and I noticed it took me only 3 minutes to cross the start line which I was shocked about as I was expecting it to take much longer than that.

I crossed the start line dead last.

For the first few hundred yards (furlongs lol) you are running on the actual race circuit which is good fun.

I stayed behind the Snowman and had a laugh with the other runnersaround me at the back of the pack.

Once you get off the racecourse you are out into the city itself and there were plenty of members of the public stopping to clap and waving at us from bridges as we whizzed by.

Out onto the closed open roads and almost straight away you run up a fairly steep hill, I had left snowman behind at this point and up ahead I could see the 5 hour pacers which I was really pleased about, I had caught up with them much quicker than I thought I would.

I joined them and almost immediately saw the one mile marker, I passed it at 10:45 so pretty much bang on schedule, and getting that first mile out of the way felt good.

I stayed with the 5 hour pacers until mile 2, there was a large group of runners with them and the pacer somehow had the music pumping out as he ran.

Mile 2 and I was now at 22 minutes so bang on plan, the 11 minute pace felt too easy for me and as the road started going downhill I took full advantage and set about increasing my pace to 10 minute miles.

As I accelerated away from the 5 hour guys I heard one of them say 'see people go way too soon' - words which  I could have done without hearing to be fair, at least wait until I am out of earshot pal!

Mile 2 to 3 and I was getting  closer to my target 10 minute mile pace.

I really appreciated running on fully closed roads, it makes such a massive difference, and I just wallowed in this luxury for a while. with the course still 'undulating' at this point (I hate that word by the way- what does it even mean?).

I have since discovered that the word 'undulating' means not flat, i.e. up and down.....

Or 'hills' to you and me, but the organisers can't put that otherwise no-one would enter so they use the word 'undulating' instead.

There was a water station at around 5k which I took advantage of as my mouth was dry from the start  with all the adrenaline.

A note on the water and feed stations at Chester, they were approx. every 3 miles, not that it mattered to me, save the water.

I can not over emphasise enough how important race day nutrition is, One of the biggest secrets that I learned from the Ironmen was about this subject, and unless you can say that your race day fuel strategy is 100% nailed on then this chapter alone will be worth the cost of the book tenfold.

I caught up the 4:45 pacer group which was busy. I passed them fairly quickly as at this point I viewed running with the pacers as cheating on the basis that there will be no pacers at Ironman so I wanted to replicate this.

I  spent the next couple of miles chatting triathlon to a lad in a tri-suit. The road started to go very straight and gently down and at around the 10k mark I could see the 4:30 pacers up ahead.

In training I had been stopping every hour to have a 90 second stretch by the side of the road and whilst I was feeling strong the hour was upon us so I forced myself to stop.

Many other runners overtook me at this point and gave me a bemused look as if they couldn't understand what I was doing or they were thinking jeez, if this guy is stopping now what's he going to be like later. but I had my plan and I was sticking to it.

Energised from my power break I sets back off in a quest to catch the 4:30 guys.

The next 10k went by smoothly. and fairly flat, 6 weeks ago, I had been knocking out 20k 'long' runs on a Sunday for fun, and this distance came easy to me now.

I was playing cat and mouse with the 4:45 pacers, Every time I went ahead they kept catching me up, so I kept telling them to piss off and thankfully they saw the funny side. (the pacers at Chester are ace by the way).

I said 'whilst I am on a quest to catch the 4:30 guys if I see you on the hill at mile 24 I will be a very happy man!'

One of the most wonderful things about running a marathon is the people that you will meet whilst running.

At Chester you are out running on the roads surrounded by beautiful countryside and there is not much going on so it gets a bit boring.

The organisers get round this by putting bands on at various points but more on them later.

I passed the time by catching people up and chatting to them until we were both bored of eachother before moving on to the next victim.

One of the most interesting guys I met was wearing a t-shirt for the '100 club' - it transpires there is a club for people that can prove they have run over 100 marathons! this guy was in his fifties and on number 162! He had travelled all over the world running them.

Meeting someone like this, he's knocked out 162 marathons and I'm making such a big deal about completing one, there is something mentally awakening about it...

I asked which one of all was his favourite 'Loch Ness' came the reply.

I remember that getting to mile 9 seemed fairly straightforward but getting to mile10 seemed to take ages, I paused between the 2 to take my second hour power break.

It transpired that the mile 10  marker had gone awol, as confirmed by a friendly marshall, so the next marker we saw was at mile 11.

Here the course doubles back on itself and I looked to see what the mile marker said on the other side of the road .

It said mile 15, meaning the guys crossing us were 4 miles ahead.

There were just as many runners going into mile 11 as there was coming the other way into mile 15, with long lines either side.

The ones that were 4 miles ahead gave us that smug 'I'm kicking your arse' look but I didn't let that phase me, I was interested to see  how many would still be on the other side when I got to mile 15 though!

I got round the next 4 miles which were flat and pretty uninteresting as we were out in the middle of no-where, the field now very spread out.

I was running about 6 minutes behind plan and my minutes per mile had droped down to around 10:30.

I remember hitting the 13.1 mile half way point at about 2:20 and the reality of how far this race was began to hit home, but at least I had made the half way cut off time of 3 hours.

It was now my turn to hit the 15 mile marker and look back at those approaching mile 11 at the cross over.

There was now just a slow trickle of runners approaching the mile 11 point and instead of giving them 'the look', the people on our side clapped them and shouted encouragement as we crossed.

One of the guys approaching the 11mile marker at this point was the snowman! he was still in full costume and I have total respectfor this guy.

Onto the dreaded mile 16 and what a stonker of a hill this is.

I knew from the outset that this was getting walked up and walk I did, annoyingly someone took my picture on this section and I joked with him that he could have took it at mile 5 when I was in full flow!

As you got to the top of the hill you enetered a small village, Holt if I remember right, and the hill was lined with people shouting encouragement at you which was very much appreciated.

As you got to the top and turned the corner there must have been 1,000 people packed onto the street at either side, it felt like the whole village had come out to support the runners.

The course was now flat at this point so I started to run again and shouted 'COOOMMMEEE ONNNN!" at the crowd - this was like lighting the blue touchpaper of the best firework in the world and the crowd erupted and started going mad.

The noise they made gave me such an amazing burst of energy at exactly the point in the race when I needed it most and it is worth running the Chester marathon just to experience this sensation.

People of Holt - thank you! you rock!

I rode the adrellaline wave from the crowd for the next 2 miles, and before I knew it I was at mile 18 although I remember feeling a little bit dis-orientated at this point.

Here there was a further water station with a brass band.

I stopped for a loo break and for some reason I tried to get the top off the water whilst still in the portoloo as I wanted to put my electrolyte sachet in it but the water eneded up going everywhere! Why I attempted to do this whilst still locked in the portoloo I will never know.

I apologised to the next in line for the loo and returned to the water station where a helpful marshall opened a new bottle for me.

If you are taking electrolyte don't take the powder satchets like I did they go everywhere, invest instead in the tablets.

Shortly after I took my 3rd power break.

Miles 18-22 were the hardest bit of the race for me as it flet like this was one long, continuous slight climb that never ended save a short respite at mile 20..

Many people were walking by this point but I was still managing to keep going, albeit slowly, but I hate these long slow steady slight climbs that go on for ages, there is just no let up for the legs.,.

I have heard a lot of talk about 'the wall' in marathon, and was wondering when I was going to hit it, stupidly, I half wanted to experience what it was like, but as yet , I was still OK.

My 4:30 dream had pretty much gone out of the window by this point however I was still ahead of the 4:45 boys as they had not come past me for what would be the hundreth time!.

The army had come out to support the event and at mile 20 I loved the sergent major shouting '6 miles to go, lets get moving' as if the previous 20 miles were just some kind of warm up  and this gave me a lift..

Around mile 22 it was time for my next power break, this I now badly needed, but I took comfort in the fact that the long slow climb appeared to be nearly over.

I felt energised by how far I had come, and by the fact that I knew in just 2 more miles we would be downhill.

We passed another band and I clapped them as I ran by because they were ace, but the lead singer just looked at me with a look on his face as if to say 'you are the one doing all the running son'

A note on the bands at Chester, every 4 miles or so there is a different band playing as you run by.

There is something magical about these bands that I can't put my funger on, the way they look at you, the mutual repsect of you appreciating them and them appreciating you, there is something haunting about them.

It was almost  as if when you run by you do so in slow motion and really savour the moment, it's beautiful, it really is.

The next 2 miles I got through, I think passing mile 20 gives you such a psychological boost, I said to myself in 10 minutes i'll be at mile 23, then another 10 minutes 24 and then I'm nearly done.

It was weird, miles 18-22 were harder for me than miles 22-24!

I remember seeing a road sign that said 'city centre 2.5' so at this point I knew the medal was mine and this gave me such a lift..

Before long we hit the dreaded hill at mile 24 and this was another stonker.

It didn't phase me though as it was getting walked up and I knew once I got to the top I was done. Half way up and who catches me? the 4:45 pacer, but this time I was pleased to see him and we high 5'd..

Once at the top the hill went down but what was waiting at the bottom? another stonking hill!

This got walked up too but thankfully the guy in the hotel was right and once you got up this you sailed all the way down into the city centre.

Into the last mile and it was a joy running along the river with the streets  lined with supporters. (still no sign of 'the wall!')

It felt like it took me ages to get onto the racecourse but I finally makes it onto the hallowed turf and you run the final few furlongs like a racehorse and round to the finish.

The run down the home straight was very well supported with everyone clapping you, the announcer on the mike calls your name as you approach so I high 5'd him and one of the organisers was there to welcome you home with a big smile and a well done, so he got high 5'd too.

I was buzzing to cross the finish line in 4:46, which I am elated with as it hit all of my pre race goals and placed #1744 / 2896 on the official results board.

But, when you look closer, over 700 either entered the race but did not turn up (kerching for the organisers!) or started the race but did not finish it.

So my 'real' position out of the people that actually finished the race was:

1744/2135

Yes, 1,743 people finished in front of me.

But that is irrelevant.

Don't forget - I started the race at the very back of the pack and I crossed the start line dead last.

Remember also that this race was filled with dead serious 'club runners'

And do you recall the girl in the video?

I was fully expecting to come last.

Not only did I **not** come last, but I actually overtook 391 people - **Three Hundred and Ninety One!!!**

How awesome Is that?

Offer me that at the start of the race and I would have snatched your hand off!

Remember always that it's your perception of what is good that becomes your reality - have you seen Alice through the looking glass?

Finally, never forget that it's all about joining the 1%.

I had done it, I had completed a marathon, (no way lol) more importantly, I knew Ironman was now surely mine. as this marathon was the final piece of the jigsaw in the ironman puzzle.

At the finish I got presented with a medal and yet another kiss! (Iam on a lucky streak in this regard) a goodie bag containing jelly babies, a kit kat chunky, a snood which will be ideal for cycling, some energy gels and a satchet of porridge.

I also got given a long sleeve t-shirt with Chester marathon written on it.

So I had got round without meeting the dreaded and eagerly anticipated 'wall'... maybe that was him flirting with me at mile 18, although I am convinced the power breaks & fuel strategy kept him at bay..

I chilled for a bit to let it all sink in before walking over to the bridge where I clapped the other finishers (including snowman) before making my way back to the hotel for a well earned bowl of pasta and to go sit in the Sauna for at least a week!

I have to tell you, collecting that medal was a fantastic experience, very emotional, and one that I will never forget in my life.

I never imagined at the start of my journey that one day I would be collecting a medal at the finish line of a marathon, it was so far out of my reality there was more chance of me going to the moon..

It still feels like it's all not real, and I'm just having some amazing dream.

But, I have to let you into a little secret....

Something the 1% would rather you didn't know about.....................

A Marathon is a sheep in wolf's clothing- it's all bark and no bite you know....

The word 'marathon' has this mysterious magical power about it, and many people put it on a 'not possible for me' pedastol, way up in the clouds somewhere, completely out of reach.

Yet at the end of the day, what is a marathon?

A marathon is just one big run, exactly like all the others, but longer!

And once you learn and apply certain secrets, then follow a plan, you will realise something magical......

That the only limits to what is possible, are those which we impose upon ourselves....

To your amazing journey!......

# Ironman Training Plan and the Ironman Diaries

Once I completed the marathon in October I did some light training at Olympic level and a few loops of the IMUK circuit but nothing too serious – I certainly made sure I enjoyed myself over Christmas!

On the 1 January, that is when my Ironman training began.

What follows is the actual 28 week training plan that I created and followed for Ironman UK.

Furthermore, I also wrote a 28 part diary to provide 'real time' commentary as I went through the process.

This started as a 'blog' on my website, but I soon realised that the quality of the content was becoming extremely powerful, so I locked it down!

What you are about to read are not only the weekly training plans, but also my thoughts, feelings and emotions as I did it.

I bring you these in their original, un-edited form.

Looking back over my training with the benefit of hindsight, I would change only 3 things:

1) There is no need to do all of the monthly 'race simulations' – the brick runs straight off the bike don't need to be any longer than 1 hour maximum. I would substitute the monthly race simulations for a long bike then a 1 hour run. You will notice however that the vast majority of brick sessions are just 2.5km in length and these worked perfectly.

2) I would not be too precious about going out onto the bike in horrendous weather like I did, join a gym that has watt bikes and ask the people that work at the gym to show you how to use them properly and go do that for an hour instead. Or get a turbo trainer and learn how to use it indoors. – be careful though, the weather is always horrendous in England and you still need to get out onto the loop!!

3) Some weeks, especially early on, I did 2 'long bikes' in a week. In hindsight I would have done just one long ride and then on my other bike day a shorter, faster, 1hr speed session that looked like this:

10 min warm up

2 minute fast as you can followed by 2 min rest x10

10 min cool down

Other than the 3 points above, I would not change a single thing.

I trained for 6 months solid without a single injury but when you look at the training 4 days out of 7 were gym and swim work which felt like days off to me and they will to you as well at some point (if not already!)

I loved every second of this process (well, almost!!) and met many wonderful people along the way.

The training that I did served me extremely well and I felt very strong throughout race day which was to become one of the most magical experiences of my life.

You will notice that I did a fair few long bike sessions on a Wednesday, this is because I created circumstances that allowed this to happen.

I understand that may not be an option for many people however I would recommend you consider using some of your holidays during the latter part of your training to take advantage of the (hopefully) finer weather.

If that is not possible for you simply do your long bike at the weekend and the shorter work during the week (see point 3 above).

Most people will easily be able to fit this training in before or after work and then do the longer stuff at weekends, my plan averages only around 10 hours most weeks.

If you are still struggling for time then draw your inspiration from the amazing lady that I interviewed which can be found at the rear of this book.

Finally, make sure your family know what is involved and are prepared to support you throughout this process.

'Support' doesn't mean holding up a placard on the finish boulevard with your name on it come race day.

It means supporting you from day 1.

Right, now all that is out of the way, let me ask you a question......

Are you sitting comfortably?

Then the story can begin....

Enjoy!

# Ironman Training Week 1 of 28

Monday : Rest

Tuesday : Rest

Wednesday : Rest

Thursday : Pool Swim 1 mile

Friday : Gym S&C Session (see chapter)

Saturday : 47 Mile bike (IMUK loop)

Sunday : 10k run

And Here is my commentary from week 1 of training:

So, 2017 brought the beginning of my 28 week IRONMAN plan, the sasco year planner is firmly on the wall, and my IMUK training schedule has been duly inked upon it .

Exciting right?

I promised you a 'warts and all' account every week, so here goes.

My first week got off to the worst possible start!

After enjoying the xmas festivities and everything that brings to the full throughout december, 1/1/17 was meant to be mark the re-birth of the pre marathon iron-rookie, no drinking, no smoking, eating right and diving head first into my IMUK training plan..

Sunday the 1st started well enough, I awoke feeling excited about the new me,  I even managed to get down to the local pool that morning and bang out 64 lengths.

However on my return the wife announced that instead of driving home that day as we initially planned, we would be staying with friends for a further night.

On came the football and out came the beers! (as did pretty much everything else that I really shouldn't be partaking in)

This debaunchery spilled over to Monday & Tuesday and I didn't train as planned on either of these days !

I was looking forward to getting out on the bike Wednesday but didn't as I ended up writing the car off! don't worry I am fine, but the car isn't! Basically I skidded on some ice on a roundabout and the car is now history! thankfully no-one else was involved.

Life has a habbit of getting in the way of your training, and it can easily consume you, however writing this blog has given me an unexpected yet welcome degree of accountability, so I made sure I trained as planned thurs, fri, sat & sun.

My diet has been poor throughout December and this continued pretty much all week this week, I still had some beers left over in the house from xmas and these got polished off, as did pretty much all the left over xmas treats.

No surprise then that when I got on the scales for the first time in 2017, I had put on a good half a stone over xmas and am now a full stone heavier than my pre marathon weight  which is frankly unacceptable and needs to be sorted out…

I am feeling the extra weight and I ain't liking it…..it's messing with my 'zen'……

Thankfully I know precisely what I need to do in this regard!

One of the things I will be closely monitoring over the next 28 weeks is my weight, and my body fat %, my goal being to get down to pre-mara/70.3 weight as a minimum before IRONMAN.

I have discovered that at my gym they have a bodytrax machine which not only weighs you but gives you hundreds of various health related measurements and is apparently 99% accurate.

I am very keen to observe the effect of my training on these stats, and will record them for all to see here, but I will continue to use my own scales as a back up!

December wasn't all bad though, I managed to maintain regular mile swims and a few 50 mile bike loops, but I dropped my runs right down to 10k, as I saw little point in running any further than this.

Readers should not be under the illusion that I am going into this 28 week Ironman thing straight 'off the bat', the exact opposite in fact!!

Getting to this point in the journey was the training if that makes sense. (see training plans)

My present level of fitness is such that I would feel very comfortable tackling an Olympic triathlon tomorrow and could possibly even stretch to a 70.3.

So, in summary, a mixed bag this week, a poor start but a strong finish.

**Swim**

When I first started swimming I was unable to swim more than a single length front crawl but 64 lengths comes very easy to me now,

After each pool session i'm like what? i'm literally not even drawing breath here! This was very much the case once again this week and feeling like I could still fight a lion **after** my swim sets is precisely the feeling that I am looking for..

I enjoy my swim sets loads I really do but I must admit swimming against the clock so I can post my time on here is agitating me, its upsetting my rhythm.

My mile time this week was just over 38 minutes which I am cool with. I will talk more about times next week.

**Bike**

Similar to the swim, when I first started I hadn't ridden a bike for over 15 years but the training plans that I have been following mean that I am now totally comfortable riding 50 mile IMUK loops.

The biggest challenge out on the course for me is the weather, certainly at this time of year, and this week virtually the entire circuit was shrouded in thick fog, cold and very, very wet......not exactly the cycling conditions we dream of!

My chain appears to be slipping so I must get this looked at before it snaps and at times I felt a few of the climbs this week but I felt strong towards the end of the ride which is always good!

Despite the poor weather it felt great to get my  first loop of 2017 under my belt and I recorded a time for the 50 mile circuit of 3:23 which I am very happy with given the conditions, but more on times next week!

**Run**

Run training is run training, I still wake up on run days looking forward to it and I do love entering run races! especially given that when I first started, I was unable to run more than 10 yards without wanting to stop!

My first 10k of 2017 certainly blew away the cobwebs!  It felt as though I didn't warm up until 5/6k!

I am going to enter a 10k race at the end of Jan to see how I get on as I always seem to be much faster in races than in training, why I do not know but it always seems to be the case.

My 10k time this  week was 1:02 which was my regular 10k training time last year,so I am pleased with this! Don't forget that my goal is not to get fast @10k's, but to feel strong after  them, like I could do it again and again (and again!)

**Brick**

Short brick run after the 50 mile loop, all good, used to these now!

**Strength Training**

Weights are easy when compared to the above , right?

However I must say, I always feel a million dollars after my gym sets.

Looking forward to going 'all in' and getting fully 'on board' week 2, with the big priority being to sort out diet once and for all!

## Ironman Training Week 2 of 28

Monday : Pool swim 1 mile (64 lengths non stop)

Tuesday : S&C @ Gym (see chapter)

Wednesday : 47 mile bike (IMUK Loop) + 15 min Brick

Thursday : Pool Swim 1 mile

Friday : S&C @ Gym

Saturday : 47 Mile Bike (IMUK Loop)

Sunday : 10k run

So the big priority from week 1 was to sort my diet out and I was literally buzzing this week when I got on the scales Sunday and discovered that I have lost almost half a stone versus my start of year weight.

Not only that but my mojo is back and I am waking up each morning full of beans and genuinely looking forward to getting stuck into the training that the day brings.

I find the whole 'health kick' thing relatively straightforward until night time, where I appear to become possesed, sweet things being my kryptonite, but so far I am managing to keep everything under control.

I am closely monitoring my food intake and am trying to eat as many of the things we all know we should be eating and none of the things we all know we shouldn't.

I said last week that the biggest challenge out on the bike course is not only the course itself but the weather, and never was this more apt than week 2.

I had either Wednesday or weekend available for my bike loop session this week..

Looking at the weather forecast I had a choice of dry and warmer but 28mph winds or cold and freezing with lots of rain and potentially snow.

This is a little like being asked which you would prefer to be hit over the head with, a shovel or a baseball bat, but I chose the wind as weekend snow had the potential to wipe out a loop session completely this week.

This week was very much a tale of two rides, as you will soon see below!

**Swim**

I am loving my swim sessions.

I always feel strong on swim day and 64 lengths comes very easy to me now. (it wasn't always like this)

The fun will begin once the open water swim season starts but there is ages before that yet.

In the meantime I am quite content banging out my 64 for the rest of this month and my two separate pool mile sets this week were 37 & 38 mins.

I must admit my second session later in the week felt a little more 'stiff' than the first, didn't really get into the zone so to speak despite feeling well up for it pre-session, will be keeping an eye on this!

## Bike

As mentioned above, google forecast 28mph winds for this weeks 50 mile IMUK loop session which were already in full flow by the time I set off.

The first 25 miles went by straightforward enough,  whilst I could hear the carnage going off all around me, I floated along unaffected in my own little bubble, the hedgerows either side acting as excellent windshields.

I even had the wind behind me for both the Hunters Hill and Sheephouse lane climbs, which was most welcome and certainly a first, 'loving this', I thought to myself.

However, Once I got over Sheephouse, which marks the half way point the way I ride the route, the Lion was waiting for me, and boy did it gave me one hell of a mauling.

As I made my way from Rivington over towards abbey village, and for pretty much all of the next 25 miles, a 30mph gale was blowing straight at me.

It felt as if I had two huge millstones attached to either side of the bike, and every now and then someone would come along and hit me a few times with a baseball bat for good measure.

Cycling for 20 odd miles into a relentless 30mph headwind is not fun, and one of the most energy sapping things I have ever experienced out on this loop.

On more than one occasion I felt certain that the wind was going to pick me up and throw me into a hedge, but thankfully I just about managed to stay upright.

For large sections it felt like I was cycling but not getting anywhere, even some of the downhill parts felt like I was cyling up Hunters hill such was the force of the headwind.

Bu hey, at least it wasn't raining! (much!)

I was relieved to finish the loop still in one piece, recording a time for the 50 mile circuit of 3:31.

Whilst I returned to base exhausted, still being battered by the relentless gales, I know deep down that it's these training days that make you stronger.

Cycling in these conditions, whilst far from ideal, serve as excellent bike strength conditioning, and I know that my reward will be waiting for me come the warm, calm sunny days, (if such a thing exists in Bolton) where the loop will feel a good few notches easier by comparison.

Case in point I awoke on Saturday feeling amazing and full of energy, the weather, despite what Michael fish had predicted earlier in the week, was beautiful, sunny, calm and little wind.

I was meant to be doing some simple hill work today as I had already ridden the loop midweek but I found it impossible to resist getting out and doing another!

Whilst the first half of the ride started well, The conditions further into the course were still far from ideal, the circuit was cold and wet, and the wind was around 12mph according to google which once again I felt on the second half of the circuit, but hey, it was a warm summers day compared to Wednesday.

For large periods I was feeling strong and even thought I was going to PB the loop 2 weeks in, but in the end I ended up recording a time of 3:09.

On the subject of time……

Remember always where I started, unable to swim a length, not ridden a bike for 15 years, unable to run more than 10 yards….

My goal is plain and simple, to get the IRONMAN medal.

Offer me a guaranteed finish and a time of 15 hours right now and I will snatch your hand off.

My plan, which I will go into next week, allows 3 and a half hours for each bike loop.

So, 2 weeks in, why am I chasing some ridiculous end of the rainbow PB?

This is one of the biggest things I have learnt on my journey, to reign it in, the ego.

Returning to base after that 2nd bike loop Saturday (which I shouldn't even have been doing) did I feel like could go and do another 50 mile circuit?

No!

Run a marathon?

No chance!

Was my body telling me that I had pushed it a bit too much on that bike session?

You bet!......And I have learnt to listen to my body!

I am happy to let myself off the leash and scratch the PB itch every now and then as a special treat, but weekly PB chasing stops, **right now!**

The big bike test is coming, at the end of the month.......

# Run

Now that I am bringing brick sessions back in, even though they are short ones, when I wake up on run day and all I have to do is run, I find it very easy, especially at my pace.

Not being funny but when you are used to starting a run having first cycled for 50 odd miles and then all of a sudden you get to run on fresh legs, it feels like heaven!

However, please do not mis-understand, I approach my runs with the total respect that they deserve, as I am fully aware that the run is the place where I am most likely to become injured.

I am keeping my run distance at 10k for the rest of this month, not least for the point above.

Loved this weeks 10k, I changed my shorts to blue and got more 'honks' than I ever had, they are most certainly coming out again next week! (If you wonder what I mean about 'honks' I mean honks of the horn from cars – I got one of those 'IRONMAN in training tops' see which I seriously recommend, believe me when I say this, the 'honks' give you energy!)

Having just returned from today's 10k, therein was another firm lesson.

At 7.5km I was feeling totally in control and very strong, I was in the magical land of 'I could run all day at this pace'

A quick look at the watch and I noticed I was at 45 min, the sub hour was firmly on plus I had the wind on my back, so I couldn't resist 'going for it.'

I returned to base with the watch showing 57:59, my best training 10k for ages.

What did I just say about chasing end of the rainbow PB'S?

That applies to the run too you know iron-rookie!

Whilst it felt great to land the sub hour training 10k, The point I am making is this.

The biggest thing I have learnt on my journey is that there is a big difference between running 'fast' / chasing short distance PB's and running longer distances.

The 'sweet spot' for running longer is to get into the 'I could run all day at this pace' zone.

The trick is to feel strong, as if you could keep going forever, not run fast, exactly like I was feeling @ 7.5km on todays run.

I should have continued in the 'strong all day zone,' not started chasing rainbows!

Seriously Iron-rookie what is wrong with you? PB chasing stops, **NOW**!

**Brick**

Short 15 minute brick after 50 mile bike loop midweek, certainly 'felt it' after! Hot bath, tea bed!

The big brick test is waiting for me at month end! more on this at the end of Jan!

**Strength Training**

Sad but true, relaxing in the sauna drinking my protein shake after my weekly weight training sessions is the highlight of my week!

## Ironman Training Week 3 of 28

Monday : Pool Swim 1 Mile

Tuesday : S&C @ Gym

Wednesday : 47 Mile IMUK loop + 15 min brick

Thursay : Pool Swim 1 Mile

Friday : S&C @ Gym

Saturday : 47 Mile IMUK Loop + 15 min brick

Sunday : 10k Run

Why aren't you on Strava Iron', asked one of my twitter followers this week.

He made a good point.

'Why ain't I on Strava?' I asked myself'

For those that don't know what Strava is, it's a free app that you  download onto your phone and record your rides & runs onto it as you do them for the world to see.

But the greatest feature of  Strava is also one of the main reasons that I wasn't on it.

Once you complete your bike, or run, a 'leaderboard' is then displayed and you can compare your times with everyone else that has ever done the same route as you.

You then spend the rest of your days trying to move up the leaderboard of your chosen circuit!.

This is very addictive.

Its like a real life computer game and you are 'Player 1'.

But this ain't the gig here....

As I touched on last week, Chasing rainbows and trying to PB the bike loop/move up leaderboards is my kryptonite and my ticket to an Ironman DNF!

But I understand that some of my followers and readers of this blog may like to see my training as I do it, so I was happy to oblige.

From now on I will post links to my training runs & rides each week in the stats section at the bottom of the page, thanks to Paul for pointing it out.

Having duly signed up I was itching to get out onto the loop again Wednesday and take Strava for a spin.

I'm sure you can guess what happened next....

I defy anyone to wire themselves up to strava for the first time, go out onto a route they know well, press record, and then not attempt to 'smash' the hell out it.

This is exactly what I did. (tut tut tut Iron, really, how long is this going to go on for?)

But before I started the loop on this weeks session I remembered another reason why I wasn't on Strava.

As I sit by the side of the road in the freezing cold and the pissing rain, trying in vain to get Strava to work, I gets the error message...

'No GPS signal being received'

I swear I nearly threw the damn phone into the river at one point.

I need to be starting my 50mile IMUK loops totally relaxed and in a happy, harmonious place....

Not stressed, vexed and wanting to throttle someone because I cant get bloody Strava to work.

As it turned out, it worked perfectly, and I was literally buzzing when everything 'synced' just as it should as I finished my loop.

For the stats lovers amongst you, a total of 1,339 people have recorded their IMUK loop time on Strava.

This weeks effort of 3:10 ranked 993, which, believe me, I am totally over the moon with! – remember I am still just buzzing that I can actually 'do it' & not come last.

1st place did it in 2:02 (but you are in IMUK legend Joe Skipper territoty here, british IM record holder lol) and last took 4:19.

Interstingly the average time is around 2.55, if I can find 15 minutes this would move me up 300 places to the 'half way' marker.......

And this is where Strava becomes dangerous for my IMUK plan.

As I keep saying, moving up PB leaderboards / chasing pot's of gold at the end of rainbows really isn't what I am trying to achieve here.

I vowed last week that I would stop chasing PB's once and for all..

Strava wasn't exactly condusive to that this week, 'Ok, one last go at chasing the rainbow', I said to myself on Wednesday, 'but then that is definitely it'.

My first big test is coming at the end of January and we are nearly there…

All was well on this front until I awoke Saturday full of energy, with the sun streaming through the curtains……...

Here Is how I got on this week:

## Swim

2 x 64 length sets, separate days, time of 39 mins & 38 respectively.

My time is not going anywhere but this doesn't phase me.

My goal as always is to finish the session feeling strong like I could  go and **fight** a lion, not feeling weak like I have just **fought** a lion by spanking all my energy trying to PB a mile swim.

## Bike

Again I had Wednesday or Weekend available for my 50 mile IMUK circuit and with higher temperatures (8 degrees lol) 2mph wind and little rain forecast for Wednesday, midweek it was!

Wired up to Strava for the first time (see above) I couldn't help put my foot down, and the first half of the circuit sailed by.

I kept seeing a group of cyclists up ahead at various points and I finally caught up with them just before Babylon lane.

Turned out it was a local tri coach, we had a quick chat and he very kindly invited me out with his group, whilst I really appreciated the invitation, I have been a lone wolf my entire journey up until this point, and I don't intend to change that now! maybe later in the year, once the final chapter comes to a close.

The second half of the loop was once again much windier than the first, certainly felt much breezier than 2mph, but totally tropical compared to last week.

In the end I didn't PB despite going for it, but I recorded a decent time of 3:10.

Just like last week I was meant to be taking it easy on Saturday and doing some hill work but once again awoke full of energy with the sun literally beaming through the curtains.

'How can you not go and do the loop on a day like this?' I thought to myself, and off I went.

Duly wired up to Strava, here we go again! my focus was firmly on the leaderboard!!!!

There were many more cyclists out today and it was an absolute joy to see Sheephouse Lane literally full of helmets making their way up.

It was here that I met Patrick, another IMUK first timer, and me and Patrick spent the entire 2nd half of the loop playing cat and mouse with eachother.

Half way into this 'duel' and I am thinking to myself 'what the hell am I doing? I aint no Joe skipper, all I want is the Damn medal.'

Not only am I 'racing' the Strava leaderboards, but now I find myself getting into a 'duel' with another competitor, the exact thing that the Ironmen told me I should **not** be doing.

Once my loop was over, I sat by the side of the road waiting for Strava to 'sync'. Patrick pulled over and we ended up having a good chat.

Turns out we are both in precisely the same boat, Strava Leaderboards, PB's, 'duels' & ego's getting in the way of the bigger picture, the IRONMAN picture.

We laughed but this is no laughing matter. Partaking in this behaviour is my guaranteed ticket to a DNF.

This needs to stop

Thankfully, 2 things are fast approaching that are going to help me.

1. Next week will be my first of 6 Race simulations
2. February will see me begin increasing the bike mileage.

I have had my fun on the bike, now its time to get serious….

Oh and I also achieved last weeks goal of getting the bike looked at, apparently I can either stay out of a certain gear or I need a new everything………Great

## Run

Nice steady Sunday 10k @ 1:03 dropped it down a notch from last week, (penny finally dropping!!) certainly felt like I could 'go again' at the end of the run, exactly the feeling I am looking for!

Big lesson from this weeks run was to make sure I visit the loo before setting off!!! (annoyingly I already know this but didn't do it & paid the price!!)

My first big run test of the year is coming at next weeks race simulation #1 of 6!

## Brick

'Gentle' for want of a better word 15 minute jog after both 50 mile bike sets

## Strength training

As always sitting in the sauna drinking my protein shake after my weights session is the highlight of my week.

## Diet

Alcohol and smoke free since week 1, plan is to continue for the duration.

Still eating sensibly all day and closely monitoring everything that goes into my mouth

Food is fuel right?

## Focus Areas For next Week

Slow the hell down stop chasing pots of gold PB's at the end of rainbows!

Monday : Pool swim 1 mile

Tuesday : S&C Session @ gym

Wednesday : REST

Thursday : Pool swim 1 mile

Friday : S&C Session & Gym

Saturday : Race Sim #1 – See report

Sunday : Rest

So, the way I have structured my training means that, once a month, I take part in a 'race simulation'.

This week it was time for Race Simulation #1.

Exciting right?

In total there will be 6 of these 'race simulations' each one based on the distances that I have been practicing for that particular month.

The way I feel during these 'race simulations' gives me all the feedback I need about what things, if any, I need to change in my training.

More importantly, each one acts as a stepping stone to the next, and I feel sure that if I can successfully complete race simulation #6 within the forecasted time, then the Ironman medal will almost certainly be mine.

Most training plans would have me entering a sprint or Olympic triathlon, but for me, doing so would be a bit like entering a 5k or 10k run race when you are training for a maratrhon, sure they would be good fun, but really, what does it achieve?

Besides I have already completed every other triathlon distance possible  before getting to this point in my journey.

No, I would much rather play by my own rules and create my own 'races', with a course relevant to my goal and held on a date & time to suit me.

Race simulation #1 took place this week.

I opted to drop the swim element for no other reason than logistics, so January's 'race' involved one circuit of the 47 mile IMUK loop immediately followed by a 10k run, the exact things that I have been practicing all month in training….

Here is how it went:

## Race Simulation #1  47mile IMUK loop then 10k Brick Run – 'Pre' Race Week

My routine for 'race week' remained unchanged from that which I have been following all month, with one big exception.

I took Wednesday off, and Wednesday is my midweek bike day.

This meant that my week consisted of mile swim sets Monday and Thursday and gym strength training Tuesday and Friday with a complete rest day Wednesday.

I have to say, both my swim sessions and my weights sessions do not feel like training at all, they feel very easy, especially when  compared to a 50 odd mile IMUK bike slog!

I was hoping that I would feel the benefits of this 'rest' come weekend but this was not to be the case….

My little girl has been full of a cold all week and I began to start feeling a bit ropey Thursday and Friday.

By the time Saturday came this had morphed into full on man flu.

One look outside the window to discover dark skies and driving rain and I could be forgiven for thinking 'Forget it'…

Whenever I catch myself thinking like this I remind myself of the fact that 500 people will enter this amazing race but will not finish it…

I wonder how many of those said 'forget it' on a day like this…..

I sank the Ibuprofen and bravely rode into battle, but one thing is for certain, in the two weeks leading up to IMUK I will only be appearing in public wearing a full on gas mask…..

## Race Simulation #1 – 47 Mile IMUK Bike loop

The loop started well enough, wired up to Strava I felt a jolt of energy and soon settled into my rhythm.

I made a point of taking it really easy and enjoyed riding completely 'within myself' even feeling strong at times despite man flu.

The weather also appeared to settle down, which was very much appreciated.

On Hunters Hill I passed a fellow cyclist who had stopped a third of the way up.

'Are you alright?' I asked him……

'Fine – are you alright?' He replied

This I found a little strange….

'You are the one that has stopped and sorry for caring' I thought to myself, but we agreed that Hunters was a tough old climb before wishing eachother all the best.

Whilst I continued to take it easy I was aware that I was well behind my previous January 'checkpoint' times and knew I had to up the pace a little come the second half of the circuit if I was to hit my loop allowance of 3:30.

Once again though, as I got over Sheephouse lane, I was to feel the full force of mother nature.

As you make your way from Rivington over towards Abbey Village, it's like you enter some sort of 'micro climate'

It was only 2pm yet the sky was virtually black, the temperature dropped to freezing, there was howling
wind with relentless driving rain and the roads were soaking wet through (as was I).

This torture continued for pretty much the next 20 odd miles.

The Ironman UK loop almost has two courses, the Winter loop and the Summer loop, and I am not joking when I tell you that they are like two completely different circuits.

I often question the point of riding the loop on days like this, it makes such a massive differenece to your times, not least your 'zen'.

But I have my plan and I must stick to it.

Furthermore I remain convinced that whilst riding the IMUK course in conditions like this is the equivalent of 'cycling hell', I firmly believe that it **will** make me stronger, and my reward will surely be waiting for me come the warm sunny days (if such a thing actually exists in Bolton).

Besides, it wouldn't make for much of a blog if I kept writing 'couldn't be arsed' week after week would it?

In the end I finished the loop freezing, soaked wet through, and pretty miffed with a time of 3:35 – 5 minutes over my 'allowed' loop time.

I am a little disappointed as I had been peppering the 3:10 range in training, but given the sub-Siberian conditions and 'man flu' I will reluctantly take it.

## Race Simulation #1 -Transition

By the time I made it back to base my hands were so cold I was unable to open my gate. My feet also felt like they were encased in a couple of ice blocks.

I was a little apprehensive about the run that lay ahead.

I took a good 10 minutes in transition, went the loo, changed my snood as the other one was soaked, and tried in vain to warm my feet up!

## Race Simulation #1 Run – 10k Brick Run

Once I got the run underway I was a little surprised to notice how OK it felt initially.

Thankfully the weather turned once again and the sun even made an appearance! this was very much appreciated as I felt sure I was to get another soaking.

I was taking it really easy and The big challenge was my feet, which I still could not feel, and it took a good 20 minutes for them to 'thaw out'.

Running on iced feet is a very interesting experience!

Once they finally warmed up though I was feeling better than expected, even settling into it at one point..

Brick runs are a funny old business, it feels as if you are running for long periods without actually getting anywhere.

I was very surprised to notice that my 2.5k and 5k times were pretty much on par with my training runs, which I wasn't expecting, as it felt like I was running very slow.

I returned to base with the watch displaying 1:03 – I cannot begin to tell you how absolutely over the moon I am with this!

Throughout January my Sunday 10k runs have been peppering the hour mark, so if the effect of a' pre-run' 47 mile bike ride plus man flu is that it increased my 10k time by just 3 minutes, I will take this all day long!

The other thing I am pleased about is that my brick runs all month have been short at just 2.5k, which I questioned, so to achieve this result on race simulation day was exactly the answer I was looking for!

Once I returned to base I was on quite a high having completed the 'race' despite the barriers, although I have to admit once I had taken a hot bath (which felt amazing!) and eaten my tea, I wasn't up to much, so an early night it was..

Writing this blog post from the warmth of my bed Do I have any regrets about going out today despite the conditions and the 'man flu'??

No – not a single one!.

I have to say though waking up Sunday to find the sun literally beaming through the curtains was a little like being hit inbetween the legs with a cricket bat – me and google weather are going to have a serious falling out......

**Swim**

x2 mile swim sets separate days, 40 mins & 41 mins – need to keep an eye on this as drifting a little but still feeling very strong!

**Bike**

See above Race Sim #1

**Run**

See above Race Sim #1

**Brick**

See Race Sim #1!!

**Strength training**

As always sitting in the sauna drinking my protein shake after my weights session is the highlight of my week.

**Diet**

Dry-on-man Still in full swing!

Alcohol and smoke free since week 1,.Still doing OK food wise during the day but turn into man possessed by night on the sugar hunt!!

**Ironman Training Week 5 of 28**

Monday : 1 mile Pool Swim

Tuesday : S&C @ gym

Wednesday : bike : 61 miles then 15 min brick

Thursday : Pool Swim 76 lenghts

Friday : S&C @ Gym

Saturday : 61 miles then 15 min brick

Sunday : 10k run

Can't believe it's February already!

The new month brings phase 2 of my training.

Its time to start increasing the bike mileage.

The IMUK bike circuit can be broadly broken down into 4 stages:

Stage 1 : 14 mile 'pre loop' From T1 to start of loop 1

Stage 2 : 47 Mile IMUK Bike loop – lap 1

Stage 3 : 47 Mile IMUK Bike loop – lap 2

Stage 4 : 4 Mile ride to finish

January saw me completing one full circuit of the 47 mile loop each week, which was fun, now I want to add  the 14 mile 'pre loop' element into my training.

I have 2 goals with this:.

1. To ensure the 14 mile pre-loop is completed within my 45 minute plan for IMUK
2. To Analyse the effect a 14 mile 'pre loop ride' has on my 47 mile IMUK circuit time

The rest of the plan for Feb is that my Sunday runs will stay at 10k but I will be increasing one of my swim sets to 1.2 miles, (the other one staying at a mile) with strength training twice a week.

I have managed to 'wangle' some free time on a Wednesday so if the weather is decent (and by decent I mean **not** 30 mph winds/driving rain/snow/ minus temp) I will do a 'big bike session' on the basis that you have to grab the good weather whilst you can.

The problem with doing the 'big bike' drill midweek is that I keep waking up on a Saturday to discover the sun literally  beaming through the curtains, so I go and do another! – this has to stop! From now on it's strictly one day or the other, not both!

Here is how I got on this week:

**Swim**

As it happened I had some extra time for both my swim sets, so managed to knock out 1.2 mile 76 lengths on both sessions. Time was 48 mins and 49 mins respectively against a planned allowance of 45 minutes, so not bad for a first attempt.

The key thing with the swim is I am still feeling very strong after the session which is exactly the feeling I am searching for!

## Bike

### 14 Mile 'Pre Loop' – Wednesday

By the time Wedneday came round I was absolutely itching to get out onto the bike and was really excited to see firstly how long the 14 mile pre loop would take me, and second, what effect it would have on my IMUK loop time.

I am going to change my pre loop circuit, the one I picked was absolutely full of potholes and was fankly a puncture waiting to happen.

I felt I was chasing the clock and pushing it harder than I ideally wanted at times, particularly in the second half, but I was delighted to end the 14 mile 'pre loop' in a time of 48 minutes, 3 minutes over my allowance – I was absolutely buzzing about this!

### 47 Mile IMUK Loop – Wednesday

I started the circuit on a high after my first successful 'pre loop' and soon settled into my stride, it felt great to be back in familiar surroundings, taking it really easy as I was unsure what effect the pre-loop was going to have.

The wind was starting to build and I felt sure I would be in for another brawl once I got round to the second half of the course.

As it happened, Once I got over sheep house, I was treated to the most beautiful afternoon.

I sailed round to the finish and was over the moon with my time of 3:27, bang on plan despite the 14 mile pre-loop.

The thing that un-nerved me was that for long periods I felt strong and full of energy, the longer I cycled, the stronger I felt, I ended the session with plenty left in the tank.

You would have thought that increasing the mileage would have the opposite effect, but it didn't, Wednesday was one of those amazing days when I felt like I could continue forever.

Maybe there was something in the water, maybe cycling 14 miles first acts as an excellent warm up, maybe it was the weather, maybe it was the corned beef hash that I had for tea the night before.

One thing is for certain, corned beef hash will become a pre-ride staple from now on.

## 14 Mile Pre-loop – Saturday

I went and did another 14 mile pre-loop on Saturday and recorded a time of 51 minutes against an allowance of 45 mins.

These 14 mile 'pre loops' are agitating me already.

The reward I am getting (time) does not equal the amount of energy (effort) I am putting into them, ie I feel like I am pushing myself way more than I want to be doing 'pre loop' without getting a particularly good time.

To use an analgy, Its a bit like having a 'warm up' fight with Les Dennis before getting into the ring with Mike Tyson.

You think Les is going to be a nice easy 'warm up' but he isn't, he gives you a good go, so you end up getting into the ring with Tyson sporting a broken nose, fat lip and a black eye from Les.

Not what you want to be doing.

These 14 mile pre-loops need more work, I am going to incorporate them into my training going forward.

## 47 Mile IMUK loop – Saturday

Once again I **wasn't** meant to be doing the 'big loop' today because I had already done it midweek but as always I awoke to discover the sun beaming through the curtains – how can I resist?

The 14 mle pre-loop didn't go particularly well, (see above) but once I got round to the start of the main circuit I felt, 'at one'.

Again I was treated to a pleasant enough day and I sailed round to Sheephouse where I met another first timer who had just joined the loop (bear in mind I had been at it for a good 2 hours by this point).

We rode the rest of the route together and he was pushing me to be fair.

I was pleased to end the loop recording a time of 3:22 which I should be over the moon with, but I wasn't, I felt tired and didn't really have much more left in the tank.

The feeling that I am stiving for is that of Wednesday's, finishing the loop full of energy, but this was not the case Saturday, despite my better time..

I'm certain the reason for this is because I am over-doing the mileage and going 'off plan' just because 'it's a nice day' – Saturdays lesson was that my  body is telling me to stick to the plan please,…….and body, ………..I hear Ya!…….. loud and clear!

Still managed a short brick run though and this felt surprisingly OK.

One big positive from this week : Early indications are that the 14 mile 'pre loops' do not seem to be making a massive difference to my 47 mile IMUK circuit time, this needs celebrating…..

Think i'll crack open a protein smoothie…..

## Run

I was hoping to enter a local 10k race on Sunday but it was sold out, which agitated me.

So I did my 10k as a lone wolf knocking out a time of 1:03 but strava didn't record it properly which also agitated me.

Nice steady pace, finished the run feeling strong and with plenty still left in the tank!

## Brick

Gentle 2.5km Brick after Wednesdays session, even this went well, my legs wanting to 'go', which I found bizzare! Wednesday was just one of those days!

Same again Saturday, whilst not as strong as Wednesday,my 15 min brick still felt OK

## Strength training

As always sitting in the sauna drinking my protein shake after my weights session is the highlight of my week.

## Diet

Dry-on-man Still in full swing, Alcohol and smoke free since week 1, plan is to continue for the duration.

Still doing OK food wise but caught myself gorging on bread a bit too much, putting a piece of bread into my stomach feels very much like putting a twig onto a roaring fire at times!

Need to focus on mastering the 'pre-loop' and stick to the plan – no more double 'big bike' sets  just because its a  nice day! oh and stop eating so much bread

Monday : Pool Swim 76 lengths

Tuesday : S&C @ gym

Wednesday : 61 mile ride then 15 min brick

Thursday : Mile Swim

Friday : S&C @ Gym

Saturday : 21 Mile Ride

Sunday : 10k Run

It's valentines Day on Tuesday, so I thought it would be apt to make a point about family/loved ones.

If you are single with no ties, you can pretty much do whatever you want, whenever you want  (how fantastic does that sound!)

But, When you have a family, in my case a wife and a little one, you simply cannot train for an IRONMAN  without first  getting their total buy-in and unconditional support.

Support doesn't just mean holding up a banner on the finish boulevard come race day.

It means supporting you in the middle of February when you say "Toodle pip, i'm off for a bike ride – see you in 5 hours"

"Oh and by the way, when I get back, i'll be going for a 20 minute run, then i'll need to re-fuel, take a hot bath, and then, after all that…….. I'll need a siesta"

Sounds horrendous doesn't it?

But that was my reality this week,

When I wrote this post I actually went and asked my wife why she puts up with it.

"Because I love you, I said I would support you, and I am"

Came the Awesome reply.....

"Besides, its only for 20 odd weeks, which in the grand scheme of things, is not a long time"

At this point I was about to call the florist and upgrade to the full dozen,  but then she finished with an absolute belter:

"But make no mistake, you are doing this Ironman thing ONCE"

Be sure to show your loved ones how much their support means to you this valentines day!

Here is how I got on this week:

### Swim

Managed to knock out x2 76 length 1.2 mile sets with times of 48 & 47 minutes (separate days), swim feeling good but lets face it, the test will come once the Open Water season starts.

### Bike

### 14 Mile 'Pre Loop' – Wednesday

Once again by the time Wednesday came around I was looking forward to the bike session.

I felt strong and was pleased to record a time of 48 mins, 3 mins over plan.

Whilst the pre loop continues to present a pacing challenge in that I still feel I am riding it a couple of notches harder than I ideally want to be doing, it did feel like it was getting ever so slightly easier.

I made a slight change to the route as my turning point last week was frankly dangerous, this meant that my pre loop ended up being 13 not 14 miles.

I am absolutely itching to ride the 'actual' pre loop to see what my 'real' time will be.

At this stage the logistics of doing so are a nightmare, so I am having to make do,  but it's firmly on the agenda later in the plan.

I have a funny feeling that this will be getting brought forward sooner rather than later!

## 47 Mile IMUK Loop – Wednesday

I started the circuit on quite a high given that the pre-loop went well.

The weather started brightly enough, but before long the skies turned a dull grey, whilst it wasn't training the roads were wet through, and there was a blustery, icy chill in the air.

I very much just got on with this one and grinded it out.

For a while I thought I was going to be on for a decent time, hitting one of my mid loop checkpoints with plenty of 'fat.'

For the first time ever I felt strong over the sheephouse climb, which was ace, but any hopes of a PB seemed to evaporate on the second half of the circuit.

A strange thing happened over on the country lane climb towards Brindle, a couple of ramblers were walking towards me – they stopped and started looking at me through binoculours which I found really weird as they were only about 100 yeards ahead!

They did give me a big smile as I passed, but seriously, WTF!

In terms of how I was feeling on this weeks long bike session, I would describe it as a bit up and down, strong/weaker/strong, which was a bit bizzare.

I felt I was riding the circuit hard at times, but this didn't really translate to a decent result as my time was 3:24, but hey, perfectly within plan.

That said, I ended the loop with plenty left in the energy tank, which is the goal.

**Bike -Saturday**

I managed to resist getting out onto the main circuit(whoop whoop) although this was a fairly easy decision as the weather was horrid.

Instead I did a 'trial run' of a new 14 mile 'pre loop' that starts from my gym/pool, in prep for Next weeks race simulation #2 of 6.

This went really well and I was literally buzzing to record my first sub 45 minute time of 44.50.

Just goes to show the difference the route makes....... either that, or I am getting stronger!(hope it's the latter!)

## Run

I knew before I even set off that I was going to have a decent run this week and was pleased to knock out my Sunday 10k with the watch displaying 58:18.

I 'mixed it up' a bit and it felt good to get under the hour mark but more on this in the coming weeks!

## Brick

Gentle 2.5km Brick after Wednesdays session, this went well, but afterwards I was not up to much, (this is becoming a theme after the long bike bricks)  once I had re-fueled and taken a hot bath, a siesta was very much required!

Same again Saturday, my 15 min brick still felt OK, not as tired after this one though!

## Strength training

As always sitting in the sauna drinking my protein shake after my weights session is the highlight of my week.

## Diet

Dry-on-man Still in full swing!

Still Alcohol and smoke free since week 1.

Not a great week diet wise, my standard meals are sound enough but sometimes I seem to turn into the incredible hulk and start losing the plot food wise.

Case in point – My little one absolutely loves jam butties (one slice of bread folded over) and whenever I make her one I end up treating myself to one too (when was the last time u had a 'folded over' jam butty on super soft, fresh white bread, with butter? trust me, it tastes AMAZING!).

If I eat one I appear to become possessed and end up munching half the loaf!

This needs to stop!

Monday : Swim 1 Mile

Tuesday : S&C @ Gym

Wednesday : Race Simulation #2 – 1.2 Mile swim 51 mile bike 10k run – see below

Thursday : OFF

Friday : S&C @ Gym

Saturday : 11 Mile Bike

Sunday : 11 Mile Bike 5k run duathlon

25% of the way there already! Eeeeekkk!!

The way I have structured my training means that once a month, I take part in a race simulation.

This involves completing a mock 'race' based on the training that I have been doing in that particular month.

In total there will be 6 'race simulations' throughout my plan.

I cannot over emphasise how powerful I find these 'mock races':

1. They keep me motivated throughout my training (lets face it – 28 weeks is a long time!)
2. They give me something to look forward to each month (i'm genuinely excited come 'mock race' day)

3. My time, but more importantly, the way I feel during them, gives me all the feedback I need as to what changes, if any, I need to make to my regime.

Furthermore, Each one acts as a 'stepping stone' to the next, and I feel sure that if I can successfully complete race simulaton #6 within the planned timescales, then the Ironman medal is almost certain to be mine.

This week it was time for Race Simulation #2.

I initially planned to do the simulation on Saturday, (to sync with IMUK) but after much internal deliberation, ended up brining it forward to Wednesday due to a mix of 'condusive' circumstances and fine (ish) weather.

Here is how it went:

### Race Sim #2 – 1.2 mile Swim : 14 mile pre-loop, 47 mile IMUK loop : 10k Run

### Swim : 76 Lengths / 1.2 mile – 46 minutes

With the bike firmly packed into the back of the car it was off round to david Lloyd to complete the swim element.

I have been knocking out 1.2 mile swim sets for a few weeks now in training and I find pool sessions the easiest of the three disciplines. (it wasn't always this way)

My swim started well enough, I had the luxury of a lane all to myself and quickly settled into my rhythm.

However, Within about 5 minutes, a guy gets into my lane and proceeded to swim 'at me' on several occasions, the speed of Michael Phelps.

'Great' I said to myself,   feeling certain I was to be in for a tough ride for the rest of my swim

Definitely not what you need on 'mock race' day..

There is something about wearing an Ironman swim cap (From my 70.3 in Dublin) that seems to 'agitate' a small percentage of people.

Don't get me wrong, 98% will see it, be respectful of your mission, and then very kindly get out of your way and leave you to your training in peace.

But, for the 2%, it seems to flick a switch inside them that says 'Ironman eh? – I'll show him'…………..

They then start to behave like neanderthal man, aiming 100% of their aggression, firmly at you.

As it happened, the guy swam at me Phelps style for about 6 lengths, spent the next 5 minutes wheezing by the wall, and then got out.

I was relieved to complete the rest of my swim in peace recording a time of 46 minutes, just 1 minute over plan.

## Transition 1 – 15 minutes

I spent a good 15 minutes in T1 (as plan) , although only 5 minutes of this was getting changed, the rest was walking to the car/sorting the bike out with security.

15 minutes felt very long, and by the time I started the bike, I felt rested.

## Race Sim #2 14 Mile pre loop – 44 Minutes

I was surprised to notice how strong I felt on the bike initially, but throughout my journey, the swim to bike transition I have always found easy.

I am certain that the reason for this is that I do very little kicking during my swim sets (the opposite of what most swim coaches will tell you to do).

This means that my swim sessions are more an upper body workout, so by the time I get on the bike I feel as though I am using completey different muscle groups.

Case in point, despite the  prior 1.2 mile swim, I was delighted to PB the 14 mile pre loop in 44 minutes, a good minute inside plan.

### Race Sim #2 47 Mile IMUK loop – 3:25

The weather was a good few degrees warmer than it had been recently, however the wind was starting to build and I felt sure this would prove menacing later on.

I hit a couple of my checkpoints within plan but I remember thinking that sheephouse felt a few notches more difficult this time round.

I was fearing the worst once I got over Rivington as this is where the course is most exposed to the elements, but as it happened it was pleasant enough.

I have to admit that my legs were feeling slightly tired round the second part of the course.

I am not sure if this is due to the swim,  a bit of fatigue creeping in, or the fact that I wasn't really mentally ready to be doing this race today as it was planned for weekend.

I need to keep an eye on this, I will be incorporating some swim/bike bricks into my training and from now on will be sticking to my plan like glue!

The Highlight of my ride was getting a big thumbs up from Barney, the landlord of the Cavendish Arms in Brindle as I cycled past.

When my freewheel started spinning both ways outside his pub once not only did he let me leave my bike in his boozer and call me a cab, but he also lent me £20 to pay for it!

Make sure you call to see him at least once on your many training rides as you pass, Barney is ace, so is his pub.

Despite feeling somewhat weaker earlier in the ride I felt strong for the last 30 minutes which puzzles me, you would think the further you cycled the weaker you become but with me it seems to be the opposite.

Maybe its the fact that the course finally lets up, maybe it was Barney, maybe I was on a high to be nearing the finish,………. maybe I am getting stronger…..

I finished the circuit recording a time of 3:25, which is  5 minuntes inside plan.

The massive plus from this session is that the prior swim (first time I have combined the swim/bike) made little difference to my loop time, which I am very pleased about.

### Race Sim #2 = T2 – 15 minutes

Once again I spent a good 15 minutes in T2 (as plan) , chilled, and took my time getting changed.

At this point my car was still at David Lloyd and my attention turned to mapometer to see how far away this was….

16km, came the reply....

## Race Sim #2 10k Brick Run

My brick run was meant to be a nice straightforward 10k, the exact distance that all my training runs have been so far.

However, As mentioned above, my car was still at David Lloyd, 16km away.

I am sure you can guess what happened next......

This was insanity really. (Seriously don't do it, stick to the plan!)

Ok, I ran a marathon as part of my training in October, but The furthest I have been running in training this year is 10k and it was now pitch black outside.

I justified it to myself by saying whilst I had already done a fair bit on both the swim and the bike, it's still only a fraction of what is required for Ironman, so I figured the 16k would be an excellent test of where I am at.

I would take it really easy, walk the hills, and stop for water on the hour.

When I first set off I couldn't understand how strong I felt given the prior swim and bike elements.

This strength continued throughout the run, on the bike my legs had felt drained at times, but now they felt strong, it was almost as if I was now using completely different muscle groups, this puzzled me.

I did have a slight wobble just after the hour mark (just beyond 10k funnily enough.)

I am sure this is purely due to lack of training the extra distance.

A stonking hill provided a welcome respite (it got walked) and then I finished the run on quite a high.

I was delighted to record a time of 1:45 for the 16k, at this pace it would be 2:10 for the 20k and if I can maintain this as my training increases for the other elements, I will be over the moon.

What unnerved me more than anything was that I was feeling much stronger than expected for large chunks of this run, not least towards the end – long may this continue!

## Race Sim #2 Summary

I was happy with the swim, a little concerned with how I was feeling on the bike at times and delighted with the run.

At the end of the day my times are still within plan so I have to be pleased, we will see what the coming weeks will bring!

## Post Race

Make no mistake, I was like a zombie on Thursday and took the day off from training.

Started feeling back to normal Friday but after my weights & sauna session was feeling a million dollars again!

By the time Saturday came around I was absolutely itching to get back onto the bike.

Thanks to the awesome @uktrichat on twitter I got wind of a fantastic free event held by the Endurance Store in Wigan, an 11 mile ride followed by a 5k run virtually on my doorstep and I figured this would make a welcome 'break' from my Ironman training.

I couldn't wait to get out onto their bike loop to 'rekki' the course for Sundays race.

11 miles when I have been used to 60 odd – easy right??

I went down there thinking I would 'smash it'

My goodness was I in for a shock!

Yes it was only 11 miles but 9 of those involved cycling up Parbold Hill which is a relentless very steep climb that goes on forever.

Cycling up Parbold Hill long and slow would make for excellent Ironman training.

'Racing' up it as fast as you can with a bunch of hardcore nutters from Wigan does not!

Is the penny dropping yet?

Monday : Pool Swim 1 mile

Tuesday : OFF

Wednesday : 28 mile bike 15 min brick

Thursday : 100 length swim

Friday : 75 Mile Bike

Satirday : Off

Sunday : 15k Run

The big news from this week is that the wife left me.

Before we all start doing the conga , it was unfortunately only for a few days whilst her and the little one visited family down south.

I jest, of course, but what this unexpected 'free time' gave me was a fantastic opportunity to do two things I have been wanting to do for ages –

1. Practice, practice and practice again the 'actual' 14 mile pre loop.
2. Ride the main IMUK loop in the correct order (ie starting at Babylon Lane)

Logistics had so far been a barrier to this as getting to Pennington Flash and back is frankly, a pain.

But now the stars had finally aligned, I booked some time off, and it was firmly 'on'.

Here is how it went:

**Swim**

Managed a mile on Monday in 40 mins, wanted to do longer but got trapped chatting to someone I hadnt seen for a while and couldn't bring myself to utter the socially fatal words:

'Sorry, must dash, no time for 'chit chat' – Ironman see'.

Thanks to storm 'Dorris' Knocked out the full 100 Thursday which was cool, 2 things causing me frustration:

1. I was messing about with my watch at length 50 trying to see my time – at length 100 it still said 30:02 (I had stopped it by mistake)
2. A lady was trying to tell me something at length 80, I tried to ignore her but she got to the point of literally manhandling me which resulted in me stopping.

All she wanted to say was – 'Can we swap sides please'

Really?

I am 80 lengths into my first ever 100 length set and you are making me stop to ask me that?

I am pleased to announce that I (somehow) managed to behave like a gentleman.

'Of course dear' I replied, before complying with her request.

**Bike**

**'Actual' 14 mile pre loop**

With the bike packed into the back of the car I was like a big kid as I made my way round to Penny flash to do something that I have wanted to do for ages and ages – the 'actual 14 mile pre loop'.

It was an absolutely awesome feeling to be cycling in the footsteps of the Ironmen from the outset and I got a surreal haunting feeling on more than one occasion.

Make no mistake, me cycling with the ironmen is like Yeovil Town playing in the premier league……

No…… make that the champions league.

This 'honeymoon period' was short lived however once the route began to bite…..

To give you an idea of what we are looking at here, once you get out of penny flash 'park' you cycle 'up' the A579 for 4 miles which is a busy main road and one of those surfaces that feels like you are cycling 'up' when you are not.

You then have a 2 mile climb up platt lane.

2 mile flat/descent down into Lostcock.

A mile up to Chorley new road.

Then 5 miles up and down (felt mainly 'up' on a somewhat challenging surface) through horwich and over to the bottom of Babylon Lane to pick up the main loop, 14 miles in total.

I don't know if you can relate to this but you know how on some rides you feel like you are constantly 'fighting' the route yet on others you are firmly at 'one' with it and glide along?

Well this is most defiantely the former!

I had been practicing 14 mile pre-loops in training and become quietly confident, but there are 14 mile rides and then there is an **Ironman** 14 mile ride!

All I can tell you is that I am glad I practiced this now, and didn't wait until race day!

One positive I did notice from being deep in Ironman territory – I got more supportive 'honks' of the horn than I have ever had (they saw my jacket) which was very much appreciated!

Despite the energy from the 'honks' I ended the route recording a time of 54 minutes for me 1st attempt and 53 for my second, two days later.

I either need to improve my time on this section by about 10 minutes, or I need to re-jig my plan.

I'll let you know which in the coming weeks!

### Bike – 47 IMUK Loop (Correct Order from Babylon Lane)

Up until now , I have been riding the IMUK loop, but I have been riding it in completely the wrong order.

What difference does it make?

47 miles is 47 miles right?

The loop is the loop – it doesn't matter which way you ride it – Right?

Wrong

I have been used to hitting the legendary sheep house lane climb after already being in the saddle for about 2 hours and first conquered Hunters Hill.

When you start Sheephouse with comparatively fresh legs, you feel like Superman.

For large parts of the route, I was hitting it full of energy where I would usually feel fatigued.

I went at it for the first 2 hours thinking I was Joe Skipper.

I was convinced I had discovered a magic new pill, that riding the route in the wrong order somehow makes Race day easy.

Not the case.

After about 2 hours I experienced the cycling equivalent of 'the wall'.

I was now hitting parts of the course fatigued where I am used to hitting them full of energy.

This is a surreal feeling and one that I didn't like one bit!

When I finally got to Hunters Hill it felt harder than ever, goodness only knows what it must be like after 90 odd miles!

I 'limped' round to the finish recording a time of 3:22, which is fine, but I wasn't, I was goosed!

The point here is that you can train all you like, but the power of getting out onto the actual route and riding it in the correct order must never be under estimated.

## Bike – Reverse 14 mile pre loop

With the main business of the day done and dusted it was time to make my way back to the car – the 14 mile 'reverse pre-loop' making an excellent stepping stone to the centuary rides to come.

I had more energy here than I thought I would have done, riding the route in reverse felt a darn site easier than it did on the way in, you can freewheel large sections of it for one, and it just goes to re-emphasise the point made throughout this post.

I recorded a time of 55 minutes, not that it mattered, I was just relived to get back!

## Run

Long slow runs increasing to 15k.

Having had some fun with the 10k's I'm back in that magical place where time is irrelevant and distance is everything.

Boy is than an amazing place to be! Took it really easy and felt strong for large parts. Gave any fellow jogger that came towards me a high 5 which gave me such an energy boost!

Delighted to return to base with the watch showing 1:39, not that time matters for these long slow runs (it really doesn't!)i

**Brick** : did a short brick after the Wednesday   session, didn't do one Friday more down to the fact that my car was parked in a very dodgy spot!

## Ironman Training Week 9 of 28

Monday : Pool Swim 1 mile

Tuesday : S&C Session @ Gym

Wednesday : 28 mile bike 15 min brick run

Thursday : Pool swim 100 lengths

Friday : S&C @ Gym

Saturday : 75 Mile Bike, 15 min Brick

Sunday : 15k Run

1/3 of the Way there already!

This weeks 'prelude' comes from the internet.

I am quite active on Twitter and am grateful to have discovered UKtrichat and Ukrunchat.

For the benefit of those that are not aware, these are fantastic free twitter communities filled with thousands of runners and triathletes from all different backgrounds, ages and abilities.

Those that come with the wrong attitude or with an ego soon loose interest, so what is left is an amazing community of like minded people who try to support, help and encourage eachother, everyday.

Uktrichat is amazing in itself, but what is even more fantastic is that every so often, a special guest will appear and you get the opportunity to interact with them online.

This week  Lucy Gossage. the Ironman UK female champion – Yes The female champion! appeared online.

How fantastic is that?

It was amazing to just sit back and watch Lucy answer all the quick fire questions that everybody threw at her.

What struck me was how grounded Lucy was, she was saying things like 'just enjoy it' 'don't take it too seriously' and 'loose the ego,' which I loved.

I asked Lucy for a good luck for Bolton and she gave me a 'whoop! see you there'

'See You there Lucy' – lol – no way!

Name me another sport in all the world where the average man (or woman) not only  gets to race with the champions, but interacts with them online first – how amazing is Triathlon?

Its the equivalent of your local sunday pub team having a match against Man Utd and they all get to have a good chat with Rooney beforehand…..

Never gonna happen.

What fascinates me more than anything though Is how tolerant the pros/elites are towards us humble first timers who just want to 'get round' and get our hands on the sacred Ironman medal. (It was the same at Ironman Dublin for the 70.3)

Whilst the pro's/elites  always set off before the amateurs, their paths will cross many times during the swim, and same again on the bike.

Imagine tomorrow morning you are late for work and whilst driving in you get stuck behind a leaner driver.

You finally manage to overtake, only to find 5 more 'learners' up ahead in a big long line, wobbling all over the road.

This is what it must be like for Lucy and  the rest of their 'ilk' on race day at times

Yet they remain unbelievably tolerant, welcoming and understanding of the first timer, almost to the point of actually embracing us.

I asked Lucy what her secret was to this, but she didn't reply.

In a way I love that I didn't get an answer to the question.

It serves only to deepen my fascination with it.

Maybe it's a case of "look, i'm happy to chat in a controlled environment – but don't think you can all start messaging me direct! I'll never get any time to train!" (Which I totally understand!)

Maybe the first timers secretly  'agitate' Lucy and all the pro's/elites, but they can't really come out and say that can they? wouldn't make for a very nice champion would it?

Maybe they don't want to' bite the hand that feeds' (I am well aware that part of my entrance fee will go into the prize purse and the more that enter, the higher the prize fund,  but make no mistake,  I hand this over to Ironman with a happy heart)

Maybe they  just love racing against thousands of other people and the 'more the merrier'

Maybe they adore the support that thousands
of spectators give them at events, well aware that a large chunk of these are likely to be friends and family of 'the first timers'

Maybe they want to be just as good at being an ambassador for triathlon as they are at racing it

Maybe they are not only truly amazing athletes, but truly amazing people

Maybe there is one final secret that I am missing

But Maybe, just maybe, they totally understand the incredible journey that someone like me goes on just to be lining up on the same start line as them, and they know exactly what hearing the immortal words 'You are an Ironman!' means to the 'average joe', so a little part of them quite likes the romance of it all…

Then again, maybe it's a case of….. 'all of the above'…..

And you can't exactly tweet that reply in 150 characters now, can you?

Thanks again to Lucy for taking time out to talk to us and to uktrichat on twitter for laying on such a treat!

On a high having got a 'Whoop! for Bolton' from the Queen, I was intrigued to see what would happen if I contacted the King, IMUK legend Joe Skipper, and ask him for one to match.

Guess what?

He Replied…

He gave me a 'Go on Iron, push your limits son!'

How ace is that??

How many times will I hear those words ringing in my ears 12 hours in?

Here is how I got on this week..

**Swim**

A mile knocked out on Monday in 40 minutes, and 100 lengths knocked out on Thursday sub 1 hour which felt good, despite being rudely interrupted at length 45.

My honeymoon period with the David Lloyd pool appears to be over, people are starting to do ridiculous things (like getting into my lane and walking when the rest of the pool is empty for example)

I reserve the right to have a good whinge about this in the weeks to come.

## Bike -Wednesday 14 mile pre & post loops

So after last weeks rude awakening, where I realised that there are 14 mile rides and then there is an Ironman 14 mile ride, it was back to Penny flash midweek to practice the 'real' 14 mile pre-loop, which I intend to be doing for the foreseeable.

I had treated myself to a new helmet and it felt like I was 'zipping' along better than before, although I am not sure how much of this was Purely psychological.

The pre-loop felt much easier than last week for some reason and I was feeling very strong.

None of this translated to a good time though, as I weighed in at 56 minutes, same as last week.

Much more to come on this tough little nut going forward..

The 14 miles back to the car its hardly worth a mention, it feels so much easier to me by comparison, re-emphasising the point that 14 miles isn't always 14 miles.

## Bike Saturday – 'Real' 14 mile pre loop – 47 mile IMUK loop – 14 Mile post loop

### 14 Mile 'real' pre-loop

I awoke Saturday raring to go.

Back round to Penny flash again to practice everything in the correct order.

Once again the pre-loop took me 56 minutes at a steady pace.

I am at a crossroads with the pre loop – I either start attacking it to improve my time by 10 minutes or I need to re-jig my plan.

I have not deceided which yet, more on this in the coming weeks.

### Bike – 47 mile IMUK Circuit

One thing I noticed before we get started – There are toilets at the bottom of Babylon lane – decent ones too – opposite the sweet shop – I must have ridden past them well over 50 times but only noticed them for the first time today!  just FYI, may come in handy, they certainly did for me!.....

See, you learn something everyday.....

As I made my way round the main circuit, I kept thinking to myself, the best way to to describe this loop, would be to say....

That It's like a lion.

If you attack the lion, it is likely to rip your head off, which is exactly what it did to me last week.

However, if you approach it with the total respect that it deserves, it may let you pass.

This time, I came with respect.

The effect was dramatic.

Here's what happened:

On the Sheephouse climb early doors, a couple of dudes came stomping past me.

Throughout the ride, people were overtaking me.

Instead of re-acting, like I did last week, I did something amazing.

I kept my ego in check, let them go, and continued to race my own race.

On hunters hill, 40 odd miles later, the dudes that came stomping past me earlier, were coming unstuck.

Yet, I was feeling stronger than ever.

What I love about the IMUK course is that it is technically brilliant, and whoever designed it is an absolute legend in my opinion.

I recorded a time of 3:22, perfectly in line with plan, but far more important, I was feeling strong throughout, not least towards the end.

What a difference a week makes!

I certainly felt like I could 'go again'

On that note, a couple of different dudes that I had been playing cat and mouse with caught me up on Babylon lane at the end of the circuit and asked me if I was 'going again'

"Not yet", I replied, my double loops not scheduled until phase 4, in a couple of weeks.

I was pleased to observe that they were though, as throughout my journey, I have created my own plans, and I am more than a little wary on this final one  of 'over doing it', but the fact that others on a similar quest are into double loops already gives me a welcome re-assurance in this regard.

## 14 Mile post loop

This post loop is so in-significant its hardly worth a mention but it makes an excellent stepping stone to the century rides that lie ahead.

The wind had certainly picked up on the way back which made it more challenging than usual and I recorded a time of an hour not that it matters as it really doesn't!

## Run

Awoke with everything feeling a little bit heavy and a little bit tight Sunday.

What happened is best summed up by a tweet I went on to post on twitter:

'When you awake on LSR day feelin 'heavy' but that warm fuzzy feeling 30 min later when endorphin oils kick in, that is why we run'

1:37 for the 15k with plenty left in the tank...

## Brick

2.5 km Bricks both Wednesday and Saturdy with Saturdays session feeling somewhat more difficult

## Ironman Training Week 10 of 28

Monday : Pool swim 1 mile

Tuesday : S&C @ Gym

Wednesday : Off

Thursday : Pool Swim 100 lengths

Friday : 75 Mile Bike plus 15 min Brick

Saturday : 15k Run

Sunday : Off

This weeks 'prelude' comes again from uktrichat on twitter.

If you do not know what I am talking about here, uktrichat is an excellent online twitter community filled with triathletes from all different backgrounds, ages and abilities, who support and encourage eachother, everyday.

There are always lots of ace questions on there, but someone recently posted a belter….

"What is the best piece of triathlon advice you have ever been given?"

Plenty of fantastic replies came in, but for me, one really stood out…

"Carry a spare set of goggles wrapped round your thigh on race day"

Allow me to set the scene………

You have paid well over £400 to enter your first ever Ironman event

You have dedicated every day of your life for at least the last 6 months training hard for it....

The big day finally arrives....

You make your way into the water, all excited, and ready to race....

The Claxton sounds, and off you go!....

However, 30 minutes into your swim, someone kicks you in the face & wipes your goggles clean off.

You frantically look around to find them, but they have vanished into the murky depths of pennington flash.....

Sorry, but unless you are Tarzan, there is no chance of finishing an Ironman swim front crawl without goggles at Pennington Flash within the cut off time......

That is your race potentially over, right there, in an instant.......

All those months of training....

*Wasted...*

All that hard work......

*For Nothing.....*

All those dreams....

*Gone.....*

400 Notes?

**Laters!…..**

Race Over, before it has even started….

A scenario that would never have crossed my mind, until this week.

I will certainly be carrying a spare as suggested come July 16th.

But it got me thinking about another scenario…

What would I do on race day if, 1 mile into the 2.4 mile swim, I saw another athlete get kicked in the face and loose their goggles when I am carrying a spare pair?

Do I hand them my spare and in doing so potentially sacrifice my own race should the same thing happen to me further down the line? Bear in mind there is still a good hour of swimming left to go?

Or do I pretend that I didn't see it and adopt the 'Sorry, every man for himself' type attitude?

I wasn't sure I knew the answer…

What would you do?

Intrigued, I posed the question to the uktrichat community in the form of an online poll.

Nearly 150 athletes 'voted'…..

The results surprised me…

Get this….

A **huge** 115 of them (80%) would hand you their spare

29 athletes (20%)  would adopt the 'Sorry, every man for himself' stance

I can't get over the fact that **80%** would give you their spare!

Either the people on uktrichat really are an ace bunch……

Or I caught the vast majority on a **very** good day!

Consider carrying a spare set of goggles at your next open water race.

If not,  lets just hope it's a 'uktrichat'er' that's swimming alongside you in your hour of need!

Here is how I got on this week..

### Swim

Mile done  sub 40 minutes Monday and then 100 lengths knocked out just over the hour mark later in the week.

I managed to get to length 98  without being interrupted (whoop!) at which point a guy decieded to walk straight into me!!

Didn't mind though as it was an old timer so I am pleased to report that I just smiled and apologised to **him** for getting in **his** way!!

Just on the swim,  Crooky, a multiple Ironman, said on twitter this week, "Pool is easy, the fun will begin once the open water season starts"…..

He makes an excellent point, thankfully not long to go now and the real swim work can begin!!

**Bike**

## 14 Mile 'Actual' Pre Loop – Friday

Yes you have guessed it, back round to Penny Flash to practice everything in the correct order.

As I said last week, there are 14 mile rides, and then there is an **Ironman** 14 mile ride!

I started this bit with the words 'This Pre loop aint getting any easier' and was planning to 're-jig' my plan for this section.

But then I looked at my time on Strava and it said 54 minutes, which is better than I was expecting, as I had it at 57.

I might not need to fly the white flag just yet!

One thing is for certain, these 14 miles deserve bucket loads of respect in my opinion!

## Bike 47 Mile IMUK Loop – Friday

When I started the loop I was treated to something pretty special on Babylon Lane.

An elderly couple, easily in their 70's were taking an afternoon stroll, hand in hand, and looked very much in love.

It was a most beautiful sight given the world we live in today and I told them so!

The lady gave me a huge smile but the bloke gave me a funny look....

Two other things of note, I spotted Barney, landlord of the Cavendish Arms in Brindle  and stopped to get me pic took with him:

This guy is ace, when I broke down on the bike outside his pub last year, not only did he let me leave my bike inside and call me a cab, but he gave me £20 to pay for it

Make sure you call in to see him at least once on your training rides, take your IMUK entry and he'll give you 10% off!

On a somewhat darker note,  2 separate occasions today drivers slammed on the brakes for no apparent reason when I was directly behind them at speed.

This is down right dangerous and something I have never come across before – take it easy out there the world appears to be going mad!

3:20 for this weeks loop in changeable and somewhat blustery weather – i'm getting there!

## 14 Mile Post Loop Friday

Hardly worth a mention but also did 14 miles back to the car to make it 75 miles for the day, bridging the gap to the century rides, took me about an hour.

## Run – 15k – Saturday

The first 2.5k of this everything was fairly stiff, however once my body realised it wasn't another brick session, magic happened.

I began to feel ridiculously strong.

I got more honks of the horn from cars today than I have ever had before (they saw my top) The thing is, as soon as one starts honking, they are all at it, and I love it.

I pushed it way harder than I should have really due to a potent cocktail of 1) being on a high from all the honks  2) feeling full of energy and 3) knowing that Sunday was a complete rest day

This was all fine until I got to the last 2.5k and it felt like a brick session again!

I returned to base with my watch showing 1:27 according to Strava I had recorded PB's for every possible distance between 1 & 15k!

These times are not particularly fast (although I noticed on one of the Strava segments I ranked #25 out of 90 – no way lol)

Fast really isn't the gig here, (when am I ever gonna learn)  but I aint gonna lie, it felt amazing!!

But, as I keep saying, when you are used to running having first cycled 75 miles, getting to run on fresh legs feels like heaven!

## Ironman Training Week 11 of 28

Monday : Pool Swim 1 Mile

Tuesday : S&C @ Gym

Wednesday : Race Swim #3 1.2 mile swim 75 mile bike 15k run

Thursday : Off

Friday : Off

Saturday : Off

Sunday : 10k

I discovered something magical this week.

My training is working.

Like really, really working.

On Wednesday I trained for 8 hours non stop in a 'mock race' situation.

I started swimming at 8am and finished running at 4pm with a huge bike ride sandwiched inbetween.

Whether you choose to believe me or not, that is up to you…..

But I can assure you, that is what I did.

Everybody said before hand that going for a swim first would have a negative effect on my bike time.

Everybody also said that 'your run time will always be slower after first swimming and cycling for 6 hours'

You would think so wouldn't you?

Makes sense, right?

What happened on this 'mock race' unnerved me……

The effect of an hour's  gruelling swim on a 5 hour bike ride?

I PB'd the bike……

The effect of 6 hours swim & bike on a 15k run?

My run time stayed the same as if I was running on fresh legs…..

More importantly, I was feeling stronger than ever……

Like ridiculously strong….

Sitting in the car at Leigh Sports village 8 hours after arriving, I couldn't help but think that this blog has reached a major fork in the road…

Not being funny, but the things I am now learning on a daily basis are way too powerful to be casually given away free of charge in a weekly blog post!

I am happy to continue with the observations, but if you want the plans, the training commentary, and the secrets, then you will find them in my book!

My observations from this week?

I bumped into an Ironman who's time last year began with an 11.

I managed to keep up with him for about half an hour.

I regretted doing that as I spanked a fair bit of energy in doing so.

What I didn't regret was the conversation I had with him.

It was nice to hear him echo the words of some of the other Ironmen I had met with his tips.

But there was one new one that I had not heard before.

It was all about cadence.

Can I be honest? – I had no clue what that word even means.

He went on to explain that Cadence is all about how you pedal.

I tried out what he told me for myself and it worked, (give your legs a break by dropping your gear and 'spinning' a lower gear)

Second, Leigh Sports village, or 'Leigh Baths' to you and I…..

It's FANTASTIC!

More on this hidden gem in the weeks to come….

Last but not least…..

The people who live / run businesses on the IMUK loop are ACE!

As I am sat sorting myself out at the bottom of Babylon lane, Phil from Grubber sweets comes out to say hello, ask me how I am getting on, chat about the Ironman etc,

How nice is that?

He even asked me if I wanted a brew?

How Ace is Phil?

I couldn't go without getting me pic took.

By the way, can I just say...... that isn't my belly under my jacket! it's a bum bag with all my puncture stuff turned the wrong way round!

Be sure to call in and see Phil and his lovely wife Liz as you train.

Grubber sweets are at the bottom of Babylon Lane right at the start of the IMUK loop and they will give u a 10% bonus if u mention this post!

## Ironman Training Week 12 of 28

Monday : Swim 60 lengths

Tuesday : Gym

Wednesday : Off

Thursday : Swim 90 mins

Friday : Gym

Saturday : Bike 47 mile IMUK loops x 2

Sunday : 15k

As my training ramps up to the next level, the true scale of the Ironman challenge finally dawned on me this week.

It was very much a tale of two big lessons...

Lesson #1 - The Swim.

Thursday saw me attempting 120 lengths in the pool non stop for the first time.

Bear in mind the pool equivalent of an Ironman swim is 150 lengths of a 25metre pool, and here I am having my first crack at 120.

The first 80 or so went by smoothly enough.

But as I got close to the 100 length marker, something weird started to happen.

I got this strange sensation, I find it hard to put it into words, but it wasn't a good one.

The closest thing I can describe it to is this:

Have you ever had a dream that you are swimming but not going anywhere?

Like you are swimming in one of those endless pools where you swim but stay still?

It felt a bit like that.

For lengths 1-89  I still had something in reserve, a sort of 'turbo' that I could call on if required at any point, but by length 90, this 'turbo' had well and truly disappeared.

Whereas for lengths 1-89 the sensation of my head being **out** of the water as I breathed felt different to  my head being **in** the water as I swam, by the time I got to length 90, it all felt 'as one' - and I didn't like it.

My eyes felt as though they were being sucked out of their sockets by my goggles, I felt weaker, disorientated, and nauseous..

I had tumble turned the whole 120 lengths and when I told Laura (a fellow IMUK first timer)  she replied 'I am not surprised you started feeling disorientated and nauseous!'

She has a point.

I guess even a champion gymnast would begin to feel just a little bit nauseous spinning 120 times on the bounce....

I have felt this sensation before, in Pennington flash, and it needs watching....

I managed to knock out the 120 in around 1:18

lesson #1 - This swim mileage needs more practice - and we ain't even in a lake yet!!

The above aside, I have discovered something excting about the swim....

Not decided yet if I should share it on here or add it to my book.....

2nd Lesson....

This week was also my first attempt at x2 IMUK bike circuits back to back (100 miles total)

My goodness....

It all started well enough...

I met up with Laura, a fellow IMUK first timer and it was by far the most beautiful day of the year weather wise...

We even had a laugh with some random people from Wigan who wished us all the best with the Ironman:

We took the first lap at a nice steady pace chatting about our lives and our journeys, the usual pleasantries...

A few people came stomping past us, but we didn't care, we were doing our own thing.

It was an absolute delight to be riding in the sunshine, although it was still fairly blustery at times, always a headwind of course...

2 hours in and we were traveling well, on for a fairly decent time....

All of a sudden....

Bang!

Laura got a puncture..

Got to be honest, I was initially pissed off about this.

Not with Laura, you must understand...

With the situation...

Up until this point I have very much been a 'lone wolf' in all my training.

Whilst Laura taught me that cycling an entire loop with a fellow 1st timer can be a pleasurable experience, sorry, but stopping to sort someone elses puncture out is not....

Especially when you are 'time trialing' a century ride for the first time....

As they say though, everything in life happens for a reason......

Once I had beaten my chest and let out a tarzan style roar, I set about Laura's tyre as if I was some sort of 'F1 pit lane' expert.....

It quickly became apparent just how crap I am at sorting punctures out.

It was clear that I have been naively floating along in my own puncture free bubble for way too long now....(The ironmen had told me about a special sort of tyre but these are no means bullet proof, as you will soon find out)

I don't know exactly how long we were stood by the side of the road, but it was easily a good 20 minutes.

Not only that, but when I finally got the darn wheel back on, I discovered that the valve was  sticking through the rim by just 1cm which rendered it neigh impossible to inflate the new innertube properly, so we had to settle for an approx. 70% 'inflation'.

When you plan to flirt dangerously close with the bike cut off times on race day, spending this amount of time on a tyre change is frankly unacceptable, and needs immediate attention.

In addition, trying to inflate an inner tube with a hand pump the size of a 'twix' is just ridiculous...

The lesson was clear, I need to get good at sorting punctures, pronto,  and I seriously need to ditch the 'twix' hand pump in favour  of the $CO_2$ cannisters....(thanks to the Welsh triathlete for pointing this one out)

If you are no good at sorting punctures, I seriously recommend that you get good - NOW! Especially if like me you intend to flirt with the cut-offs come race day.

We managed to complete the circuit in a time of 3:24 plus the stop, which we were both happy with, but poor Laura had to abandon mission thanks in no small part to my pathetic attempt at changing her tyre.

Great to meet you Laura - see you next time...

This left me to fly solo for loop 2.

My goodness did I feel this!

Once sheep house was out of the way for the second time my energy and fatigue levels were up and down like a yo-yo.

One minute I would feel strong, the next I would feel fatigued, it was a strange sensation.

That said, I sailed along fairly smoothly until I encountered an oncoming tractor carrying 20ft logs and one of them nearly took my head clean off as I made my way down a steep descent.

I defy even the most mild mannered of monks not to launch into a volley of expletives at said farmer for this ridiculous example of dangerous driving.....

When I got to the '2 hour checkpoint' 2nd time round I was a little unnerved to notice that I was now feeling fairly strong.

At 2:20 though, with just an hour left to do, it was my turn to get the dreaded 'BANG!'

Somehow, there was a huge tear in my tyre, I had one spare innertube and yes, you have guessed it, spare was knackered.

The thing with increasing your cycle mileage to nosebleed Ironman levels is that it also greatly increases the potential for things to go wrong, and unless you want to wave goodbye to your £440 Ironman fee without even seeing your running shoes on race day, you need to be fully prepared on the bike...

As you can see, well prepared I was not....

My first attempt at a century ride ended with me doing the cyclists walk of shame, carrying the bike on my shoulder, and marching, in cleats, to the nearest pub....

How I managed to resist ordering a pint of guinness or ten on arrival is beyond me...As I sit writing this blog from the warmth of my kitchen, covered in bike oil, protein shake in hand, one thing is for certain...These Ironman lessons just keep on coming....

**Ironman Training Week 13 of 28**

Monday : Swim 76 Lengths

Tuesday : Gym

Wednesday : Off

Thursday : Swim 45 lengths x 2

Friday : Gym

Saturday : Bike 2 x 47 mile IMUK Loops

Sunday : 20k run

Let me as you a question....

Are you superstitious?

I am...

I am very supersticious....

I play the same lottery numbers every week, I never walk under a ladder, and I hate it when I see a lone magpie....

So you can imagine my trepidation as I entered week 13 of my training...

I have been treading on eggshells all week expecting something  bad to happen....

Turns out, only fantastic things happened, but more on them another time...

I want this blog to be nothing but a celebration of my journey to Ironman, filled with positivity and happiness and sunshine (what's that?)

But I also want it to be an honest account, written from the heart.

You see week 13 brought an excellent opportunity for me to share with you a dark secret....

Something I have been wanting to share with you for a while now....

I want to be clear, what I am about to tell you needs to stay in the week 13 box....

And it will....

But I have discovered something powerful that has helped me in my training at times, so here goes....

In life, there are broadly 3 types of people.

Those that will be supportive of you

Those that want you to fail

And those that really don't give a toss either way

99% of the Ironmen (and women!) I have met have been 100% positive and supportive towards my journey and of what I am trying to achieve.

They are some of the most amazing people I have ever met in my life..

It's almost as if standing to applaud those on a similar quest is entrenched into their DNA.

How Ironman has been able to install this into virtually every single one of its superb athletes is one of the things that makes it so magical in my opinion.

Have you ever seen what happens for the final finisher at one of their fantastic events?

Just as you will ever only really understand what it is like to be a parent once you become a parent, you will only really understand what it's like to train for an Ironman once you have trained for an Ironman yourself.

The amount of supportive comments, help and encouragement I have reacieved both in person, and online, literally blows me away, everyday.

Make no mistake, these amazing people will be celebrated in a future post.

They mean more to me than they know.

But there will always be the 1%.

I am well aware that due to the way I am documenting my journey, I am potentially setting myself up for a rather spectacular fall, lol.

I am also pretty certain there are a couple of people out there who, for whatever reason, would love it if I failed at Ironman in July!

You don't get to almost 1,000 follwers on social media without meeting at least a couple of members from the 'number 13 squad'!

We have all met the person at the party  who  asks why you aren't drinking and then shouts 'Ironman eh? my mate Dave went and did an Ironman as his first triathlon without any training whatsoever'

Yeah, Top One.......... 'Dave'.....

Not want you want to hear when you have dedicated at least the last 6 months training hard for your day of glory...

The fact is,  very few people will ever complete an Ironman triathlon in their lifetime , such is the scale of the challenge (although I hope that my work might help to change that!)

Even fewer will just 'go out and do one straight off the bat' with no prior triathlon experience or fitness training.

Having cycled 100 miles 'straight' for the first time yesterday, trust me when I tell you.....

That really ain't the gig here....

Seriously, this isn't some 'jog round the park'....

This is the toughest one day endurance event in the world!

But someone within my 1% was exactly like the person at the party described above.

She "just went out and did an 'ironman' as her first triathlon with no prior experience or training"

You know, one of 'those'...

Except it wasn't an Ironman at all, despite the fact that she refers to it at such......

It was a long distance 'tri'.......

Anyhow, this person had a real bee in her bonnet every time I talked about Ironman being a journey.

You have to remember, when I first started, I was unable to swim more than a single length front crawl, hadn't ridden a bike for nearly 20 years and couldn't run more than 10 yards without wanting to stop.

Ironman, for me, has absolutely been a journey....

A beautiful, wonderful, fantastic, romantic, inspiring, uplifting journey....

The most amazing journey of my life.....

It's the whole reason for this website, my blog and my book, to help other first timers start or complete their own journey, provide a step by step guide of exactly how I did it, share the many secrets that I have learned along the way, and prove that 'anyone can do it'.

My point is, I am fairly certain that this individual would love nothing more than me to fail at IMUK in July....

Nothing would make her happier than to see the letters DNF next to Iron Rookie on the leaderboard

I'm not surprised she didn't actually do an Ironman as they would probably have rejected her entry application on the basis that she doesn't have the correct DNA....

But I have some news.....

And here is the dark secret.....

That person inspires me more than the people who want me to succeed.

Did you hear that?

That person inspires me more than the people who want me to succeed.

I am not joking when I tell you:

As I am swim length 120 of 150 and doubt that I can continue, I picture how smug she would be if I got a DNF on race day, and I instantly feel a strength, power and determination to succeed like nothing I have ever experienced in my life.

Same thing after 6 hours on the bike, and again on the run....

I cannot over exagurate how powerful the feeling is...

It's almost as if within all of us, there is a roaring lion, hidden away in a secret vault that we never even knew existed....

Whilst this person will no doubt appear again many times along my journey, not least on race day, her voice is sure to be drowned about by the many thousands of wonderful supporters that line every inch of the Ironman UK circuit and know exactly what this means to the 'average Joe'..

But for the strength and power she has given me, at exactly the points when I need it most, I will be forever grateful to her.

If you ever find yourself encountering similar people on your own journey, consider creating your own box 13, and tap into a secret power stronger than you ever imagined possible..

How was my training this week?

I have to tell you, I have had one of the best weeks ever....

I managed to nail 2 x 47 mile IMUK loops back to back for the first time by applying something that the Ironmen told me....

I found a couple more very powerful secrets that I added to my book.........

And I discovered something amazing that any potential first timer with any trepidation at all about the swim element absolutely needs to know!

**Ironman Training : Week 14 of 28**

Monday : Swim 76 lenghts

Tuesday : Gym

Wednesday : Off

Thursday : Swim 90 lengths

Friday : Gym

Saturday : 1 x 47 mile IMUK Loop

Sunday : 10k run

Week 14 has been the most amazing week of my journey so far for 3 main reasons...

First off, I am now officially famous....

The local paper picked up on my adventure and put a piece together for the world to see!

I was chuffed about this!

I first got that top made when I was training for the Marathon as something to keep me entertained as I ran for 2,3 and 4 hours at a time, often on my own (see back cover)

It started as a bit if fun, but I can't over exagurate how much it has helped me.

When you are out training for so many hours non stop, it all gets a bit lonely, and a bit boring, but the honks really keep me going - they give me such a boost, especially when the legs start to get heavy.

The thing is, when one starts honking, they are all at it, and I love it!

I always make sure I give every single one of my 'tooters' a wave of appreciation!

Sad but true, when this is all over, those 'honks' are one of the things that I am going to miss the most!

It was great to get some 'validation' of what I am doing off the press it really was but let me tell you, a single message from a stranger on twitter telling me that they found my work inspirational or motivating is all the validation I will ever need!!

Second bit of news, Open Water Swimming at Pennington Flash is now Open for business!

Pennington flash is where the Ironman Swim takes place.

This is squeaky bum time!

It's all starting to get real!

It's time to leave the comfort of the pool, don the wetsuit and wade into the murky depths!

Nailing the open water swim element is one of the final pieces of the jigsaw.

Nothing like hearing that the flash is open for business to get the stomach churning!

As many an Ironman will tell you, knocking out 100 plus lengths in a pool is one thing, but transferring this into open water is something completely different.

Much more to come on this in the following weeks!

**But by far the most amazing thing on my journey so far happened this week.....**

Yesterday I got to ride the entire IMUK loop with 7 x Ironman (4x Bolton) and local IMUK legend 'Crooky'

7 Times an Ironman!!!

He very kindly agreed to let me ride the loop with him and interview him at the same time!!!

How fantastic is that?

This experience was so amazing and so powerful that I have decided to separate it out from the 'Ironman diaries' and give it it's very own 'stand alone' blog post that it so rightly deserves!

**Ironman Training : Week 15 of 28**

Monday : Swim 64

Tuesday : Gym

Wednesday : Race Sim #4 – See report below

Thursday : Off

Friday : 20k run

Saturday : Off

Sunday : Off

An insane week this week for a number of reasons.

First off, more amazing Ironmen have very kindly come forward and agreed to let me run a feature on them for my blog!

Friday saw me out with 'Damo' who has 7 x Iron Distance finishes, 1 x 50km Ultra and 56 x marathons under his belt!

I can't begin to tell you how much getting to spend time with people like this means to me, I still can't quite believe it's all actually happening to be honest.

Again a separate blog post has been dedicated entirely to him and will be uploaded Sunday@ 7pm.

Trust me when I say, you really don't want to miss it!

In addition, a 3rd Ironman has come forward and you won't believe the amount of marathon/Ironman medals he has in his collection but more on him in the coming weeks.

Week 15 also saw me completing race simulation 4 on Wednesday, whereby I combine all of my training this month into one big 'race simulation'.

The distances this time were as follows:

90 minute non stop swim

100 Mile Bike (2 x 47 Mile IMUK loops back to back)

20km Run

It was by far my toughest challenge to date....

Here is how it went....

**Swim - 90 minutes front crawl**

My alarm went off at 5.30 am to get to Horwich leisure centre for a 7am public lane swim start.

I awoke not in the best of moods, one look out of the window to see the trees at right angles to their roots not helping matters in the slightest.

My mood was lifted however when, on arrival at the centre, I met Sue, one of the most helpful receptionists I ever met.

Annoyingly my phone was completely dead and as I really needed it for Strava, Sue very kindly agreed to charge it for me whilst I swam, she then lent me 50p for the locker because I didn't have one and said next time I come in I can have a free 7 day pass.

Love meeting people like this.

I ended up dedicating a blog post to her in the hope that someone sees it and gives her the 'employee of the month award'. http://iron-rookie.com/fantastic-customer-service/

My swim went well, there was plenty of room for all the swimmers and they kindly let me 'get on with it' with minimal interruption, which I very much appreciated.

I find swimming in the pool very easy these days and I found myself in that magical place where I felt like I could swim all day. (it wasn't always this way, when I first started I couldn't swim a single length front crawl).

**Transition 1**

I took my time in transition, I got changed into my tri suit and went to get the bike that was in the boot of my car, not before going back inside to get my picture took with Sue mind!

Some would say time is important in transition, that I should 'rush' like you see on the telly, but to me, some things are way more important than that, like letting Sue know how much I appreciated her help, for example.

**Bike 47 Mile IMUK Loop Lap 1 -Time : 3:24**

Leaving my car at the leisure centre, I started cycling the short distance to pick up the main route.

Within the first ten minutes I nearly abandoned mission to the point where I actually turned back.

Why?

The wind was completely ridiculous.

Not only that but it starts chucking it down, I only had my shorts on with no top base layers and it was freezing.

When I turned round though, something amazing happened.

The wind stopped and it was like It was a completely different day cycling in the other direction.

I figured that at some points on the course I would have a similar experience so opted to continue my mission, fuelled also by the possibility of a certain divorce should I deliver the news that Easter would not be spent with the family as originally planned.

So onwards I went.

As I am sat sorting strava out at the bottom of Babylon Lane a local, trying desperately to control his umbrella, sarcastically said 'Nice day day for it'

'When is it ever a nice day in Bolton?' I replied

I was reminded of the time I asked an Ironman if he ever looked at the weather forecast before going out to train..

"Why? I'm going anyway' came the legendary reply...

In fairness Once I got warmed up so did the course, I was forgetting it was a relatively early start and everything takes a while to thaw out round these parts.

Don't get me wrong, the conditions were still pretty hellish, gale force headwinds and cold driving rain being very much the order of the day.

I got round the first loop in 3:34 which I was pleased with given the prior swim, weather conditions and the fact that I took time out to have a photo-shoot with a Greggs flag half way round.

More importantly, I ended the first circuit feeling relatively strong.

### Bike 47 Mile IMUK Loop Lap 2 -Time : 3:45

After a quick chat with Liz @grubbers sweets it was off to start lap 2.

Half way up Babylon lane I saw a lady strapping a road bike to her car...

'Please tell me you don't live there' I said (meaning where the hell are you going with the bike strapped to the car when you live in cycling paradise)

"No!" She replied.

She went on to give me a supportive toot of the horn as she came past which I took to mean she is likely on a similar quest as myself.

Anyhow second time up sheep house went surprisingly better than expected.

However, once I got over Rivington and starts making my way to Abbey Village..

OMG!

The wind was horrendous!

This section of the course can either be the most rewarding or the most brutal!

It's just so open and exposed to the elements that even the slightest bit of wind is magnified tenfold.

On days like today, this section kills me, I spanked loads of energy negotiating it  and when I finally got to the other end I felt like I had been in an 'open air' boxing  ring with Mike Tyson somewhere freezing where it rains all the time (Bolton?)   .

That said, once the battle was over, the conditions began to settle down and my strength began to return a little.

2 Hours in and I was convinced I was going to be on for a positive split!

But somewhere between  the 2 and 3 hour mark I seemed to enter the twilight zone where the clock was running away with me and there was nothing I could do about it.

2nd time up Hunters was a killer as you can imagine but even before that I'd 'had enough of the bike'

Sorry but 100 mile grinds in conditions like this just aren't fun.

Towards the end it felt like my legs had lost all their power, my arse hurt, my shoulders hurt, and parts of my body that I didn't even know existed hurt.

I just wanted to get off the damn bike but I wasn't looking forward to the run that lay ahead one bit!

Once I realised it was soon to be 'all over' though  I felt a rush of energy and stomped round to Babylon lane where I recorded a time of 3:45.

Total time for the 2 loops 7 Hours 20 minutes, this is a good 20 mins over my allowance for race day (7 Hours)  and at 7 hours I am flirting dangerously with the bike cut offs as it is.

How much of this is down to the conditions, and how much is down to my ability, we will find out in the coming weeks!

**Transition 2**

T2 involved me packing the bike into the boot of the car and 'driving' round to a friends house that lives on the Reebok lol.

Sorry but I aint risking leaving the bike in the boot outside Horwich leisure centre whilst I go for a 20km run 9 hours after I first arrived  in a top that says 'trainee ironman'  all over it.

Besides it was only a short 5 min drive.

**Run - 20km Run along part of the IMUK run route : 2:20**

9 Hours after starting out, my phone died, which meant I couldn't record the run on Strava.

I'm annoyed with myself at this as we all know that if it isn't on Strava, it didn't happen.

Whether you choose to believe that I did this run or not is up to you, I couldn't give a monkeys either way to be honest, but I can assure you, this is what happened.....

It was great to follow in the footsteps of the Ironmen on parts of the actual IMUK run route but make no mistake, the legs certainly took a while to get going.

An hour In though and I was feeling surprisingly OK, on a high as I hit Bolton town centre.

However, once you hit the town you double back on yourself back up Chorley New road and this is when the fun really starts.

From the town centre up to Beaumont lane it is one long, slow, continuous 2 mile climb that feels like it goes in for ages, exactly the ones I hate.

Its not particularly steep, its just that the climb feels like it goes on forever.

This was hard enough first time round, goodness knows what it must feel like on laps 2 and 3! (on race day you do this 3 times!)

I then made the fatal error of turning left to Run to the end of Beaumont lane and back to make up the mileage. (don't worry u don't do this on race day!)

This is the equivalent of 'running' the big dipper in Blackpool.

It felt like it took me forever to get to the end of Beaumont lane where there was a petrol station (aka water station).

As I am stood in the queue waiting to pay for my evian, I watched open mouthed as the guy behind the counter picked something out of his ear before saying 'yes please'

I went and got another bottle  and left that on the counter with my quid coin as there was no way in hell I was letting him touch the one I was about to drink!

Back to the Beaumont lane 'run' and Large chunks of the return leg  got walked.

By this time it was starting to get dark and I must have looked like a right twonk bouncing around in me sunglasses.

I was very relieved to make it back onto to chorley new road however there was a further hill to greet me (great) and this  ran all the way back up to the golf club, but I didn't as  this again got walked!

Finally I hit the descent back towards the bee hive pub and felt a rush of energy as I completed the final stretch round to the Reebok.

That run was an absolute killer!

Those long Chorley New Road 'slopes' no doubt feel easy when you run them on fresh legs. (They definitely do as I found out on Friday!)

But running them 10 hours in let me tell you, they feel like running up Hunters Hill!!!

I was pleasantly surprised however to record time  of 2:20 for the 20k.

This is a good 20 minutes over my time for this distance in training but if the effect of a 90 minute swim, 100 mile bike and walking large chunks is that it increases my time by 20 minutes, I will take that all day long.

11 hours after starting, race simulation #4 of 6 was finally over!.

Hot Bath, Tea, Bed and Make no mistake, I wasn't up to much Thursday, spent most of the day spaced out!

But by the time Friday came round, I was full of beans again! (Excited to meet 'Damo'!!)

Many Ironmen will say that there is no need for me to do these race simulations and that I am over-training....

They are probably right!

But I have my plan, the way I want to do it, and I am sticking to it!

I have come this far by creating my own plans and I don't intend to change any of that now!

Failure is not an option for me at Bolton!

I want my body to get used to experiencing the sensation of running 20k up a hill after first swimming for 90 minutes and cycling 100 miles.....

So that when race day finally arrives.....

Well......

I'll tell you that one on race day!

So there we have it, a crazy end to what has been a crazy week.

But I have got to tell you.

I'm loving every second!

**Ironman Training : Week 16 of 28**

Monday : Off

Tuesday : Gym

Wednesday : 47 Mile IMUK Loop

Thursday : Swim 90 Minutes

Friday : Gym

Saturday : 5k Run

Sunday : Off

Once again lots going on!

Two more amazing Ironmen have agreed to a feature for the blog which Is absolutely mind blowing and fantastic news!.

Next week I feel very fortunate to say that I'll be spending time with a guy who has completed 10 x Iron distance triathlons and boasts multiple top 3 finishes in his age groups!!

If you have a question for him, please message me via twitter!

In terms of what I have been up to:

After lasts weeks insanities I treated myself to an 'easy' week this time.

I took some time out to go and give 'Big G' at Bolton Park run a 'High 5' - find out why here http://iron-rookie.com/bigg/

I supported the #rideformilla and I defy and parent to read that story and not immediately want to do their bit.....

And I let myself off the leash to have some fun with a single 47 mile IMUK loop on Wednesday and absolutely smashed it. https://www.strava.com/activities/948984877

I managed to record a time for the loop of 2:50 which is a personal world record for me by some distance and jumped a huge 500 places on Strava to now rank 816/1568 for the IMUK circuit!

My times for the loop had been peppering the 3:20 mark for a while now, so to drop half an hour is huge!

In all the times that I have ridden that loop my result has never began with a 2.

I can't begin to tell you how absolutely over the moon I am about this!

I set off thinking I was Joe Skipper but this time instead of feeling knackered 2 hours in I was able to push on still feeling strong all the way round.

I was way ahead of normal time at various checkpoints, not least the 2 hour marker and when I hit Coppul Moor Lane just over 2:30 I knew the magical loop time beginning with a 2 was finally mine!

What do I put this down to?

A number of factors....

You can't spend time with people like 'Damo' & Crooky and not have their influence rub off on you just a little bit

The weather was slightly more condusive (although there was still a strong headwind for large chunks)

Thinking about Milla helped, a lot.

However, those things aside, I would put it down to Two major factors...

Two huge things that I have learnt on my journey...

But sorry, they are way too powerful to be casually tossed away free of charge in a weekly blog post!

Guess you will have to have a look inside my book for that one.

(See secrets – dropping the distance back down & fuel)

Let us not get too carried away here though!

Going out and stomping round a single 47 mile IMUK bike loop with fresh legs and then going home for your tea is one thing.

Doing so after having first swam for 2.4 miles, then cycling the loop for a second time before  going on to complete a

marathon, is quite another....

**Ironman Training Week 17 of 28!**

Monday : Swim 64 lengths

Tuesday : Gym

Wednesday : 120 Mile Bike

Thursday : 10k Run

Friday : Gym

Another insane 7 Days!

Amazingly, I got to spend some time with a 10 x Ironman and multiple Kona qualifier!! I hope to be able to bring you the full interview on this next week - i'll keep you posted!!

I also rode the exact 112 mile IMUK bike circuit for the first time....

For the benefit of those who don't know the route, once you leave the swim exit at Pennington flash you cycle for 14 miles to pick up the main 47 mile 'loop' where you do 2 laps before heading over to the Wanderers stadium in Horwich to commence the Run.

Here is how it went....

**14 Mile Pre Loop - Pennington Flash (Swim exit) round to main circuit @ Babylon Lane - Time : 1 Hr**
**https://www.strava.com/activities/958696502**

This 14 mile pre-loop is my nemesis!

I had many a brawl with this section earlier in my training and it ain't getting any easier.

Compared to the 100 mile grind that lies ahead it should be a walk in the park, but it absolutely is not!!!

It's a real energy sapper!!

But what do you expect?

This is Ironman....

Large sections of this first bit are very exposed to the elements and despite my initial impression of it being a 'relatively nice day' -  20 minutes into the ride I felt like I was in the opening scene from the wizard of oz.

Not what you need as a pre-cursor to a 100 mile grind!

I was relieved to finally make it round to Babylon lane recording a time of one hour.

I was left battered, bruised and my feathers very firmly ruffled before I had really even started.

A gentle 'glide round' to pick up the main route this is not! - you have been warned!

**47 Mile IMUK Loop Lap 1 : 3:08**
**https://www.strava.com/activities/958887780**

Once I picked up the main circuit I felt very much 'at home'.

The first lap went well enough, a single 47 mile loop coming very easy to me now.

Again the wind was horrendous once I got over Belmont and headed towards Abbey Village.

What annoys me is that this section should be the most fun part of the course, it should be a long, fast, gradual descent all the way down to Wheelton, your reward for making it over sheep house lane, but with freezing headwinds like this, it's brutal.

Once that was out of the way I sailed round to Hunters without too much trouble, buzzing that the hurricane was finally over and the winds had returned to the standard 'gale force'

I am embarrassed to report though that a runner actually ran past me as I was cycling up Hunters Hill!!!

Of course he had the legendary marking on the back of the left calf!!

Turned out he was a 2 x Ironman and was going for the hat trick this year!

See you in July my friend!!

All in all I was pleased to end the first lap recording a time of 3:08, but I felt certain I had ridden lap 1 way harder than I should have and was more than a little apprehensive about lap 2.

## 47 Mile IMUK Loop Lap 2 : 3:40
**https://www.strava.com/activities/959185652**

After a quick stop at the water station aka 'Tesco express' it was time for lap 2.

Before I even started I knew this was going to be a tough grind.

Second time up sheep House and my legs lost all their power.

Not only that but  I knew what was waiting for me once I got over Belmont and boy did this give me one hell of a kicking.

I swear I nearly turned back at one point near Bolton sailing club, the wind was just a joke,  my legs were already energy depleted so the prospect of another 40 odd miles in these conditions and i'm in the equivalent of cycling hell.

Somehow I managed to make it through the cyclone that is Abbey Village.

Once that was out of the way for a second time the weather finally settled down, as did I,  just 'getting on with it.'

What un-nerved me more than anything though was this :  about 90 minutes into the second loop, my energy began to return.

Don't get me wrong, my strength was up and down for long periods, and I certainly felt like I was 'limping round' at points.

But I have to say, 2nd Time up Hunters Hill felt easier than 2nd time up Sheep House!

How can it be that you feel stronger after 90 miles than you did after 45?

How is that even possible in science?

But it happened, and i'll take it!

Once you complete Hunters for a second time it feels like all the hard work is done and this gives you such a lift.

Finally I made it back round to Babylon Lane recording a time for lap 2 of 3:40.

Secretly I was hoping for 3:30, but i'll take 3:40, especially given the conditions which were hellish in parts.

So there you have it, my time for the first 108 miles being 7:50.

Add 1:30 for the swim, 10 minutes for T1 and 15min for the final 4 miles and that will see me entering the run on race day with the clock showing 9:45.

This gives me over 7 hours to run the marathon and get my hands on the sacred medal!

I'll take that all day long!!!

**14 Mile ride back to Penny Flash : Time : Who Cares!**
**https://www.strava.com/activities/959295574**

I now had the nightmare situation where my car was still at Pennington flash and here I am sat on my bike 14 miles away at the Bottom of Babylon lane having just cycled 108 miles straight.

I was fully expecting this ride back to be torture.

But do you know something?

It was surprisingly OK!

It's almost as if your body says 'You know what, I aint even going to bother saying anything to you anymore'

In fact, today's whole experience could be best described as follows:

Body : 'Stop!'

You : No!

Body : 'Stop!'

You : NO!

Body : 'STOP!'

You : NO!!!

Body : 'OK then, you win.....  I suppose I best get on with it!'....

9 Hours after first arriving, I finally made it back to Penny Flash.....

As I'm driving home, sipping on a protein shake, I couldn't help thinking.....

Today, I cycled a grand total of 122 Miles...

One Hundred and Twenty Two....

Do you know where you can get to if you drive 122 miles north of Bolton?

Scotland.....Yes.....Fookin Scotland.....

This is insane.....Ironman is insane.....

But I've got to tell you.....I'm loving every single second of it!!!

## Ironman Training Week 18 of 28

Saturday : 1 Hour speed session on bike

Sunday : 25k Run

Monday : Swim 64 lengths

Tuesday : Gym

Wednesday : off

Thursday : Off

Friday : Gym

So the highlight of this week was that I finally got to meet 'Dave' landlord of the Rigbye Arms on High Moor Lane just after the Hunters Hill climb.

This is the guy that is responsible for the sign that you can see in the picture, it reads 'Free water refills for Ironman cyclists' and takes pride of place outside his pub from March onwards.

The first time I saw that sign I honestly cried. (see pic week 14)

The position of it, 40 odd miles into the Ironman route (or 90 if you find yourself on lap 2!) and coming just after the toughest climb on the course, I found it haunting, it really moved me.

By this point many of us have been cycling alone for at least 3 hours, often battered by gale force winds, soaking wet from driving rain, freezing from the sub Siberian temperatures and cream crackered from our battle with the IMUK loop thus far...

Each time I see that sign it speaks to me....

Here is what it says....

"Hey lone warrior on the Ironman Quest"

"I just wanted to tell you something"......

**'I'm rootin for Ya!'**

It's one of those beautiful, magical, iconic things that only those that have trodden a similar path will ever understand....

Here is what else happened this week....(4 Points)

## Point 1

Tomorrow I will be with a guy that has done 14 'Iron' Distance Triathlons, 1 Double 'Iron' Distance and well over 100 Marathons.

This blows my mind.

The 'interview' will be uploaded to this blog Sunday 14th May.

Keep an eye out for it.....

(There is still time if you want me to include a question, but be quick!)

## Point 2

Last Sunday I went out for a 25k run.

I dis-respected it.

My attitude was all wrong....

'It's only a run on fresh legs - piece of cake' I said to myself...

I went charging off for the first 5k thinking I was Mohammed Farrah, even getting into a 'race to the traffic lights' with another jogger at one point.

The run kicked my arse.

Once I got past 10k I found large chunks of it tough going.

By the end of the 25k I could hardly walk.

https://www.strava.com/activities/964643906

Do not under-estimate these long runs, they deserve total respect and need more focus.

## Point 3

On Wednesday I wanted to go and 'smash out' a single 47 mile bike loop but when I looked out of the window I saw a bird flying backwards, the trees at right angles to their roots and rthe wind doing things to the grass that was just plan wrong...

I also felt like crap as I had 24 hour man flu.

For possibly the first time in 18 weeks I managed to resist the urge to 'go out anyway' and forced myself to take a day of rest instead.

It's now Saturday and I feel like I could go and fight a lion.

I'm absolutely itching to get out and 'have it' with the bike loop.

Never under-estimate the power of rest!

I'm also finally learning to play the weather at it's own game (thanks Damo!)

## Point 4

The interview with 10 x Ironman and multiple Kona qualifier 'Marc Laithwaite' will be uploaded to blog tomorrow morning (Sunday 7th) at 10am.

I found his story fascinating and he gave loads of great tips for first timers like me!....

Trust me when I say, you really don't want to miss that interview!

To Your amazing journey!

## Ironman Training Week 19 of 28

Saturday : 10k Run

Sunday : 47 Mile IMUK Loop

Monday : 64 length swim

Tuesday : Gym

Wednesday : 47 Mile IMUK Loop & OW swim training

Thursday : Off

Friday : Gym

This week saw me focusing on the final piece of the jigsaw....

Nailing the Open water swim.

It was finally time to dust down the wetsuit (£40 ex-hire special) and make my way round to 3 sisters in Wigan for my first open water swim of the season.

I think for many of us first timers, the swim is the one that strikes the biggest fear into our hearts.

'How did it go?' asked Paul, a fellow IMUK 1st timer....

The answer to the question is that I loved it.

In order to explain why I loved it, I need to give you a bit of background.

When I first started out, I was unable to swim more than a single length front crawl.

My first tritathlon required me to swim 16 lentgths of a 25 metre pool without stopping.

That was a big deal to me at the time.

I taught myself how to swim the entire 16 lengths front crawl by following a simple training plan.

That plan is in my book.

I then took it all the way up to a mile (64 lengths) without stopping, tumble turning each lap for good measure.

That plan is in my book too.

By the time I entered my first Olympic distance triathlon I was very comfortable knocking out a mile in the pool without even thinking about it.

But being able to Swim a mile In a pool is one thing....

Doing so in open water is a very different proposition, as many an Ironman will tell you.

It's why I have dedicated an entire chapter of my book to it, 'Making the transition from pool to open water'.

Last year I went on to complete the Ironman 70.3 in Dublin, which featured a 1.2 mile swim in the North Sea.

Not being funny, but if you can do it in the North Sea, you can do it anywhere. (That comment better not come  back to bite me on the arse!)

Without typing out the whole chapter of the book on here, There are 4 or 5 huge things that I learnt which helped me massively when making the transition from pool to open water.

One of those was getting used to swimming in a big crowd of people, as this is exactly what happens on race day.

I spent large chunks of last year swimming in Pennington Flash as part of their weekly 'group' open water sessions.

Those sessions are great but the thing is  you are mostly swimming on your own due to the course being so vast in size.

That is all well and good, but it's the open water equivalent of having a 'private lane'  every time you go down to your local pool...

That aint what happens on race day at Olympic distance and above...

There are no 'private lanes'.

You are thrown into the water with everybody else in one big mass or rolling start.

There can be anything from 100 - 2000 swimmers in the water at the same time, all going for the same 'line'

Lets have it right....

It can be a brawl at times!!

You will swim into the back of people...(especially when they just 'stop' for no apparent reason!)

People will swim into the back of you....

You will swim into the side of people...

People will swim into the side of you...

You might get kicked....

You might get elbowed...

You might get a 'crack'

But let me tell you something.....

It really isn't a big deal....

It doesn't 'hurt' in the slightest

99% of the time they will just 'bounce' off you

No one is doing any of it on purpose..

They don't want to swim into you any more than you want to swim into them!

But it happens....

**And It only becomes a 'big deal' if you are not used to it!**

Which is exactly why I loved the session at 3 sisters as instead of swimming on your own you are swimming in a big group.

There must easily have been 70-80 in my cluster!

It's the closest thing to a 'race simulation' that I have ever experienced as 'all of the above' happened to me this week!!

In fact on several occasions I purposely positioned myself so that I would be in 'the thick of it' once the drill got going...

Mad Eh?

Maybe...

But What am I going to do on Race day if this starts happening?

Get out and say 'I'm not playing?'

I don't think so....

It's like everything else in life, the more you do something, the more tolerant you become if it.

I have been wallowing in the tranquil luxury of the pool for way too long now...

I need to get used to the 'rough and tumble' - getting the odd whack now and again...

I will certainly be making my way back down there every week for the next 9 weeks!

If you are considering it too don't worry, there are several sessions available from complete novice to podium contender and you can have it as 'gentle' or as 'rough' as you want by positioning yourself accordingly within each group!

If you live elsewhere in the country, I seriously recommend you try and find something similar to this as it's one of the best race specific Open Water training drills I've ever done.

PS, I could 'stand up' virtually the whole way round which is very re-assuring but felt a bit like cheating so i'm going to combine my swims here with Penny flash to get experience of the two!

Next week at 3 sisters its a time trial race simulation for various distances, i'm excited about this as it will be a great indicator of 'where I am at' against my goal time of 1:30 - Pretty sure i'm going to have a crack at 'the big one' - 3.8km.

As far as what else has been going on this last 7 days.....

I banged out a 10k Run on Saturday and had lots of fun with that trying to move up a Strava segment.
https://www.strava.com/activities/973032698

On Sunday I did a 47 mile bike loop with the guy who has completed 14 Iron distance triathlons, 1 double iron and well over 100 maras - you don't want to miss that 'interview' - it will be uploaded to the blog this Sunday @ 10am.
https://www.strava.com/activities/975128987

Monday and Tuesday were pool and gym sessions.

Wednesday I had a day off work, it was superb weather  so I went and smashed out another 47 mile IMUK bike loop and PB'd it which I was chuffed with.
https://www.strava.com/activities/979639096

I then stupidly went and did my 1st open water session later that day which I don't recommend doing at all -  although to be fair it turned out alright in the end as above.

Thursday I took a day off as I was like a space cadet having speanked loads of energy Wednesday.

Friday I went down the gym for a strength session and the all important Sauna with protein shake!!

I've got some exciting plans for this weekend and am looking forward to the open water TT in the week ahead!

I'll let you know how it goes next week!!

## Ironman Training Week 20 of 28

Saturday : 1700 metre OW Swim then 28 Mile Bike

Sunday : 25k run

Monday : 64 lengths Swim

Tuesday : Gym

Wednesday : 47 Mile IMUK Loop (am) 2.4 Mile OW swim (eve)

Thursday : 10k Run

Friday : Gym

So the big news from this week is that I was absolutely buzzing to knock out the full Iron distance swim in 1:24 down at three sisters on Wednesday!

This was my first attempt at the 3.8km in an open water race simulation and I loved every single second of it.

Whereas last year I went charging down to Pennington flash as soon as it opened it's doors for business in April and, as complete novice, paid the price for my naivety.....

This year, I bode my time, trusted in my pool training, and waited for the water to warm up a little.

I only went for my first open water swim of the season last week!

What I loved even more was this:

When I asked the organiser what the relationship was between peoples times for the 3.8km at 3 sisters and their time down at pennington flash come race day, he said that you need to add no more than 5 minutes, usually 2-3.

I can't begin to tell you the confidence boost this knowledge has given me.

All I need to do now is replicate that swim time down at Pennington Flash.

I'm not going to lie though, I still find swimming in the flash 'challenging'

I say this even after returning victorious from my battle with the North Sea in Dublin for the 70.3.

But what do you expect?

A swim in a beautiful, warm, tranquil lagoon?

I don't think so.

This is Ironman.

And part of the process of becoming an Ironman is learning how to conquer the flash.

So that is what I will do.

But this time, I will take a 'two pronged' approach, combining 'the flash' with 'the sisters'.

One thing is for certain.

Penny Flash.....

**You will not win!**

Here is how I got on this week.

**Saturday : Swim in the flash then Babylon Lane and back on the bike** https://www.strava.com/activities/983868583

First swim of the season down at penny flash, somewhat challenging. managed 1700 metres in about 50 minutes.

Straight onto the bike to Babylon Lane and back (28 miles)

You would have thought a prior swim would be detrimental to the bike, but I found the opposite!

It felt really good and I was feeling very strong.

I couldn't believe it when I PB'd the 14 mile 'pre loop' from the flash to Babylon!

I wasn't even really trying that hard as I was purposely trying to get my pace right for race day!!

**Sunday : 25k run** https://www.strava.com/activities/985836431

I'm fine with the runs up to 20k and feel that I can knock these out all day long but as soon as I start taking it over 20k I find it tough going in parts.

My second attempt at 25km and I found that the point at which I start finding it tough is increasing further into the distance which is a positive.

I think I need to introduce more running so have added some midweek 10k's into the mix and we will see what effect that has on the LSR's!

## Monday

Pool swim 64 lengths - was expecting it to be much easier than it actually was!

## Tuesday

Gym & Sauna!

## Wednesday 47 Mile bike loop am then 2.4 mile open water TT pm https://www.strava.com/activities/992123219

am - 47 Mile bike loop - I thought I was going to be on for a decent time 2/3 the way round but it didn't pan out that way - still just over the 3 hours though which is fine - managed a cheeky 10 min brick too - I need to analyse my PB of 2:48 on Strava and work out where I need to be by when!

pm - Group open water TT at 3 sisters buzzing as above!

## Thursday 10k Run
https://www.strava.com/activities/994552291

Tried running 'fast' - not liking that much

## Friday

Off

I have a huge weekend planned and this will be my toughest test yet! - more on this next week!

## Ironman Training Week 21 of 28

Saturday : Race Sim #5 – See Report (in hindsight, no need to do this)

Sunday : Off

Monday : Off

Tuesday : Gym

Wednesday : OW swim training 1 hr

Thursday : Pool Swim 100 lengths

Friday : Gym

Like everybody else, I find myself sickened, outraged, deeply traumatised and extremely angry at what happened in Manchester this week.

The youngest victim, a beautiful little girl called Saffie Rose, went to the school round the corner from my house.

She was just 8 years of age.

I run past that school at least twice a week.

My training runs will never be the same again,

Ever.

One of the other victims attended Runshaw college.

We cycle past that college on the Ironman bike route.

Twice.

My training rides will never be the same again,

Ever.

Got to be honest, as the father of a beautiful little girl myself...

I'm struggling right now.

I think we all are.

For many of us, the appalling events of this week feel incredibly personal.

I cannot begin to imagine what it must be like for the families of the victims and their friends.

If I hadn't have already written my training update then there wouldn't be one this week.

However it was already written by the time the atrocity occurred so I have taken the decision to share it in it's original, un-edited form.

Here it is...

Those of you who have been following this blog for a while will know that once a month, I take place in a race simulation.

Last weekend saw me completing race simulation #5 of 6.

The purpose of these race simulations is to see what happens when I combine the three elements of my training for that particular month, with each one acting as a stepping stone to the next.

Race simulation #5 involved:

2700 metre swim in Penninton Flash

The Full 112 mile IMUK bike route following the exact IMUK circuit

25km run

It was by far my toughest challenge to date.

I have purposely not read any other training plans but I doubt you will find one that tells you to do anything like this.

Most coaches would also probably question the need to do these race simulations, dismissing them as 'empty miles'

But for me, doing the individual elements or even shorter distance tri's and then hoping that iron distance will somehow all magically come together on race day is too much of a gamble.

Failure is not an option for me at Bolton.

Not an option.

You can smash out hour long turbo sessions all you like, but the only way you can prepare yourself for what it feels like to cycle up Hunters Hill 2nd time round on race day  is to swim in the flash for an hour, cycle 90 odd miles of the IMUK bike route and then try and cycle up  Hunters Hill for a second time.

Further….

The only way you will know what it's going to feel like 25km into a run having first swam in the flash for over an hour and knocked out 112 miles of the IMUK bike route is to go for a 25km run having first swam in the flash for over an hour and knocked out the 112 mile IMUK bike route.

So that is what I did...

And here is how it went.

### Swim : 2700 metre swim in Pennington Flash - 1:15

This was only my second swim of the season in Pennington and it certainly felt much easier than first time out.

I had to laugh to myself as I heard the usual shreaks of horror from fellow athletes as they 'waded in' and one lad shouted 'It's always this cold - deal with it'

Penningotn Flash is vast and there are a hundreded different courses available so everyone does their own thing and as opposed to a 'mass start' like you get at 3 sisters its much more relaxed down at Pennington with a steady trickle of people coming to join the party from 7am onwards.

I opted for the 'short course' which involves three buoys in a massive triangle and according to the official website measures 425metres but according to the lad in the kayak it's 450, so we will run with that.

I very much just got my head down and got on with it.

I paused at 4 laps (1800 metres) to check the time and I was at 45min so as this is pretty much half way in the ironman swim i'll take it.

By laps 5 and 6 I was really getting into it even 'showboating' a little.

Whenever I encountered another swimmer I would try and swim next to them, this I absolutely adore, I even tried 'getting onto one lads feet' (hark at me knowing what that means!)

I can't over exagurate what a massive difference having clear googles makes in open water - I bought some special 'de-mist' spray in the week and it worked a treat.

I was pleased to exit the swim having knocked out the 2700 metres in 1:15 and was feeling good.

## T1 - 15 min

T1 was interesting!

Whenever I exit an open water swim I always feel a bit dis-orientated, as if I am going to fall over, and something weird happens to my speech, it's almost like I am having a mini stroke.

This is due to a combination of 3 things:

- being absolutely freezing
- being tossed around in the washing machine that is Pennington Flash for over an hour
- being absolutely buzzing to have reached the shore victorious.

I went and got my bike from the lads in the office and cycled over to my car in the wetsuit - you can imagine the looks I got from those who were just on 'swim day' - they were ace!

I spent a good 15 minutes In T1  which is in line with plan for race day

## 14 Mile ride Pennington Flash to Babylon lane to pick up the main circuit - 57 minutes
## https://www.strava.com/activities/996528896s

I was still feeling a little bit dis-orientated for large chunks of this and was very much waiting for myself to 'come round'

I was careful not to push this 'pre ride' as I was well aware of what lay ahead, cycling very much 'within myself' the whole time.

I was pleased to arrive at the bottom of Babylon lane in 57 minutes which is well within plan for race day of an hour.

## 47 Mile IMUK loop lap 1 - 3:30
## https://www.strava.com/activities/996871045

The omens were not looking good when I came out of the toilet at the bottom of Babylon lane to see the lads from Tri-Rivington putting their waterproof 'capes' on outside Grubbers Sweets.

It all started well enough, I was even treated to the beautiful sight of a long line of cyclists making their way up the last bit of sheep house lane towards 'the tree'.

This is something that I have been lucky enough to witness on several occasions now and it's certainly one of the many treasures of my journey thus far.

Once I got over Belmont however, the rain arrived.

Well I say rain, it was more like a Monsoon.

I swear to god I am emigrating after the Ironman.

The weather in this country is an absolute joke.

It is meant to be summer.

It felt more like the middle of winter.

It didn't stop raining for the next 3 hours solid.

I got absolutely soaked, constantly battered by a freezing wind for good measure.

The highlight of the first lap was seeing a bloke running down Chorley road bare Chested, it looked like he had a wetsuit on with the top bit folded down!

I gave him a multiple fist pump as I cycled by and he gave me a big thumbs up with a massive smile on his face as if to say 'We are off our heads aren't we out in this?- but ain't it just ace?!'

Also near the end there was a wedding being set up with an outside marquee that looked like it costs thousands.

This I found quite sobering.

Here is me moaning about the weather ruining my training day and those poor sods are getting married in it!

I was pleased to end the loop on 3:30 given the conditions and the prior swim.

This is bang on plan for my time for race day.

### 47 Mile IMUK Loop Lap 2 : 3:43
https://www.strava.com/activities/997279289

I took ten minutes between loops to stop at the water station aka Tesco express and sort strava out for the second lap.

Thank goodness the weather improved but the damage was already done.

I was soaked, cold and energy depleted from my first lap.

Off I went and the 10 minute power break had worked wonders.

If time allows I may seriously consider having one of these on race day.

Sheep House felt fine second time around and for long periods I even thought I was going to have a 'positive split'

It was a weird sensation, on the one hand I wanted to push for the positive split, on the other I wanted to hold back as I knew what was waiting for me once I had finished the bike.

I opted to hold back.

This worked a treat as on 2 hours I was feeling stronger than ever.

I have noticed on these long rides that there comes a point many hours in that you feel stronger than when your first started!

How can that be!

I wanted it to last forever but sadly it did not!

Second time up Hunters was tough as you can imagine in fact I found the whole of the last hour 'challenging'.

I had lost my drinks bottle fairly early into the second loop and this was far from ideal, but I managed to complete the second circuit in 3:43.

OK this is 13 minutes over plan, but I know from my training that the weather makes a massive difference to my performance on the circuit, massive, like 20-30 minutes a loop.

We would all be very unfortunate to experience conditions like these come race day in July so all things considered, i'll take the 3:43.

**T2 - 13 mins**

T2 Involved the wife bringing the car and my run round to the bottom of Babylon Lane!

This went well, I took 13 of the 15 allowed and it felt like a long time!

We now have the situation where my own car is 25km away over at Pennington Flash sailing club in Leigh.

How are we going to get it?

Run of course!!

**Run : 25km Bottom of Babylon lane to Leigh Sailing club @ Pennington Flash : 3 hours https://www.strava.com/activities/997583817 - (strava error - bat died!)**

My goodness gracious.

You do not know what a brick run is until you try running after you have done 'all of the above' let me tell you.

Usually I find my brick runs a 'piece of cake'

Not this time...

The first ten minutes were hell.

Minutes 10-40 were still hell but a slightly more watered down version.

Of course the sun began to beam down on me for good measure..

Thanks a bunch - Where the hell was you 7 hours ago you ****?

At around 40 minutes I stopped at the co-op to put the lottery on.

This was like some sort of magic trick.

After the short stop I felt very refreshed and sailed through to about 1:20.

At 1:20 I had a bit of a wobble but 1:30 - 2 hours was plenty of down hill which helped.

2hours - 2:30 I somehoe got through.

2:30 - 2:45 were very difficult!

@ 2:46 I have never been so pleased to see Pennington Flash in my whole life!

The last 15 were torture!

Once I finally made it to the road that the sailing club is on I walked / hobbled down to the car.

It's now 10pm.

I think I arrived at 7:40 am.

This is insanity.

But as I sit here, typing out this blog post having spent the entire day in bed Sunday, I have to tell you something....

I can't wait to 'go again!'

*Although after what happened in Manchester this week.*

*I'm not sure about anything anymore.....*

## Ironman Training Week 22 of 28!

Saturday : 1 Hour OW swim then 28 mile bike

Sunday : Rossendale Sprint Triathlon

 Monday – Day Off

Tuesday – Gym – Weights & sauna

Wednesday 2 x 47 Mile IMUK Bike loops

Thursday : Pool Swim 120 lengths

Friday : Weights & Sauna Session

The big news this week was that I managed to nail 2 x 47 mile IMUK circuits back to back well within my planned time for race day, but more on that in a minute!

First, I just wanted to share something that I have been meaning to for ages….

And that is about food.

My goodness what is happening to me?

I have never known hunger like it…..

I buy a loaf of warburtons fruit bread that would usually last a week and it now lasts about 24 hours.

The entire loaf gone, before you can even think about putting it under the toaster..

Worse still, it's the combination that frightens me.

Peanut butter on the warburtons fruit bread anyone?

What the hell is going on?

Am I pregnant?

I feel like a man possessed as I ransack the cupboards night after night in some crazy, sugar enduced rage.

Entire packets of Fig Rolls are obliterated in one sitting.

When I put things like a kit kat into my stomach it feels like putting a twig onto a roaring fire, nothing happens, it just instantly evaporates….. so I gorge on the whole sleeve.

The other night my wife came into the kitchen at midnight to ask me what I was doing….

'Making some rice' I replied?

Also, See the picture to the left?

That is not me joking around.

That actually happened.

Cocco Pops are meant to be what my little girl has for breakfast, but now there aren't any left….

It has got to the point where my wife actually hides food from me in a secret stash…

The final straw came when I was making my porridge the other morning.

As I reached into the fridge to get the milk, half a twix was somehow left over from the night before….

I used the twix to stir the milk into the oats before putting it into the microwave then happily chomped on the chocolate whilst I waited for my porridge to cook.

Seriously, wtf?

If you too are experiencing similar pangs then don't worry, you are not alone!

Apparently it is quite common amongst trainee Ironmen!

The other thing I found is this….

You know those people that say 'I'm training for an Ironman, I can eat whatever I want and I never put on any weight'

Well I found this to be bollocks.

My personal experience is as follows…

It doesn't matter how much training you are doing….

If you eat a sufficient number of Kit Kats, you will still pile on the pounds!

At the start of the year, I weighed 13 stone 11.

I have been hovering around the 13 stone mark for weeks now.

Ok, I have lost 11 llbs…..whoopy doo…..

But the reason I have not made my way down into the magical 12 stone?

Diet….

Simple  as that!

Whilst we are on this subject, one final thing I discovered deep into Ironman Training....

There is a direct correlation between the food I eat and the way I feel the next day!

It's almost as if when you are training for an Ironman, eating bad food gives you a hangover!

I must try and remember that next time the 'red hunger mist' descends! (tonight)

Here is how I got on with training this week:

**Saturday:**

**Swim in Penny Flash then Babylon Lane & Back on the bike (28 miles)** www.strava.com/activities/1007617487

So I am in a nice little routine now where I practice swimming in the flash every Saturday then immediately get onto my bike to ride the actual 14 mile 'pre loop'.

For those that don't know the IMUK bike route, once you leave the flash you cycle for 14 miles over to Babylon Lane where you pick up the main 47 Mile bike 'Circuit'.

I was late down to the flash this week so only managed to squeeze in 1300 metres.

I wanted to do more but its my own fault for being late.

Went and collected the bike from security and have to say am loving practicing the actual 14 mile 'pre loop' directly after a swim.

I was within the allowance of an hour for this section and upon arriving at Babylon lane was absolutely itching to go and 'bang out a loop'.

Thankfully I managed to resist and made my way back to the flash instead!

### Sunday : Rossendale Triathlon – 400 metre swim, 21km bike, 5km run

I retuned to Rossendale Tri last weekend, the place where it all began.

I will probably never be fitter than what I am in my life right now so I was really interested to see what effect my new found fitness would have on my time.

I thought I would smash it.

I did not.

In fact I was 3 minutes slower than last year.

Two key differences:

1. I found the hill climbs much easier this time round
2. At the end of the race, Instead of feeling like I needed a lie down like I did first time I had a crack, this time I felt like I could easily 'go again'

At the end of the day, point 2) above is what my journey is all about right now, So I'll leave chasing rainbows for another day.....

**Monday – Day Off**

**Tuesday – Gym – Weights & sauna**

**Wednesday 2 x 47 Mile IMUK Bike loops**

**Lap 1 3:08 (strava error)**
www.strava.com/activities/1014299874

It was a beautiful day on Wednesday, red hot with little wind, so I was well up for the bike as you can imagine.

I was really excited to see what effect going out in beautiful conditions would have on my time.

Out on the loop, I found myself caught in a very strange situation.

Part of me wanted to 'go for it' and try to PB.

The other part of me wanted to 'hold back' as I knew I had another circuit waiting for me once this one was out of the way.

I ended the loop on 3:08.

I should be pleased with this as my plan for race day is 3:30 but I wasn't….

I had 'the needle' for 4 main reasons

1. It felt like there was a strong wind for the last 40 minutes which agitated me.
2. I was disappointed that I didn't go sub 3.
3. I was expecting the fine weather to make the circuit feel easier but it didn't, I still had to 'work it'
4. I ended the first loop feeling considerably more fatigued than I would have liked given my performance from a time perspective.

## 47 Mile IMUK Loop Lap 2  – 3:22 (strava error!!)

After a 5 minute 'power break' I started lap 2 with a completely different attitude.

Forget the PB, give me 3:30 and i'm over the moon for this second lap.

I was more than a little weary as I made my way up Babylon Lane for the second time.

My energy was lifted however when I passed a girl pushing her bike up sheep House as the sun beamed down on us….

'Alrite Babe?' I asked her

'No I am Not' came the stern reply.

Got to be honest, this gave me a boost.

It was the way that she said it and the look on her face, it made me laugh.

But make no mistake, we have all been there, myself included.

I got a further boost when I hit the other side of sheep house with the clock showing 30mins, on a par with lap 1.

This time though I was going to play the course at it's own game.

I know that loop like the back of my hand and I know exactly where all the 'free gifts' are.

I can't over emphasise the advantage course knowledge gives you from a first timer perspective.

Knowing when you need to pedal and knowing when you can 'freewheel' – it's gold dust.

If you are a first timer yourself, get your arse up to Bolton, I don't care where you live. there are still 6 weeks left. Stop making excuses and get up here, get out onto the loop!

Before you start saying 'it's alright for you' bear in mind that Penny Flash is still a near 2 hour round trip for me.

But if you want something, you will find a way.

Back to lap 2 and whilst I spent plenty of time in 'cruise control' I still had checkpoints that I wanted to hit and pushed myself to do so.

By the time I got round to Hunters Hill for the second time though, I'd had enough.

Ok, I made it up Hunters fine, but I found the last 50 minutes 'tough going',

I get to the point on these long rides where I am sick of pedalling and just want to get off the damn bike!!

I made it round to Babylon in 3:22 which I should be over the moon with as it was within budget of 3:30 however got to be honest....

I was spanked.

But let's have it right, Cycling nearly 100 miles on the bike is a big ask, nice day or not.

On reflection, two things need celebrating.

First, my plan for race day is 7 hours for the two loops.

Today I did it in 6:35.

The other thing was this….

Whilst I felt considerably fatigued at the end of the bike, after about 10 minutes of 'chilling' by the car, my energy started to return and I felt ready to 'kick on'.

One thing is certain – The double loops need more practice!!

**Thursday : Pool Swim : 120 lengths**

It comes to something when you don't feel like you are getting going until length 90!

That was very much the case here.

I was only going to do 100 but kicked on to 120 and by the end felt like I could go forever which I was pleased with,

**Friday – Gym – Weights & Sauna Session!**

Next Update : 10/6/17.

Can't believe that there are just six short weeks to go!

Saturday: 1 hour open water swim then 28 mile bike

Sunday : 30k run – 3:35

Monday: Mile pool swim

Tuesday:Weights & Sauna session

Wednesday: 10km Run am then Iron distance (2.4mile) swim TT pm

Thursday: 47 Mile IMUK loop from Babylon Lane 3:17

Friday: Day Off

Couple of things I wanted to mention this week before going into the training that I have been doing:

**First : Sleep!**

Last week, I talked about how I have never been as hungry in my life.

Well you can add another thing to that:

I have also never enjoyed sleep so much in my life!!

If you want to know the secret to a fantastic nights sleep – train for an Ironman!

Out like a light and sleep like a log, every time without fail!

This isn't a recent 'happening', I have been noticing it for weeks now.

Worringly, the only time I do not feel tired is when I am actually training!

When I wake up, I am excited and itching to get stuck in to whatever session the day brings….

And during the actual training itself, I feel great.

Its when I return to base that the problems start!

Often, the only thing I want to do upon my return is eat some food, have a hot bath, and go for a nap!!

But my 3 year old usually has a different agenda!

If, like me, you find yourself 'craving' your bed at 3pm each day during this process then worry not, you are not alone – it's perfectly normal!!

## Second : Open Water Swimming

I am about to tell you something that I never thought I would hear myself say….

I am starting to really enjoy swimming in open water.

In fact I would go further….

I now actually prefer OW to swimming in a pool.

I find it much easier, there are far less distractions (like a wall every 25 metres for example!) and I find that you can totally absorb yourself in your rhythm, breathing and technique, especially when you are swimming with other people….

Yes! **especially** when you are swimming with others!

Learning how to swim with other people in OW and 'play' them to your advantage is one of the biggest things I have learnt on my journey and something I talk about in great detail in my book.

I went and knocked out the full iron swim in 1:17 down at 3 sisters and I have to tell you, I didn't even feel like I was trying particularly hard – I just relaxed, focused on my technique and it all just seemed to 'click'.

What I love most though about Open water TT's is this:

Once the initial 'scrum' is over and you settle into your rhythm, you will inevitably be joined by someone who is of a similar pace to yourself.

Swimming side by side with a total stranger as you make your way around the course together like a couple of dolphins is a wonderful sensation and one which I absolutely adore.

But I must re-emphasise the point that it wasn't always like this for me.

Far from it in fact……

The first time I got into Open water I think I lasted about 2 minutes and hated every second, despite being a competent mile pool swimmer at the time.…

Anyone stuggling with the transition from pool to open water right now believe me – I truly feel your pain, I was there myself not that long ago……

But let this post be your lighthouse in the dark as to what is possible if you stick at it!!

Here is how my training went this week:

## Saturday: 1 Hour Swim in the flash then Babylon lane & back on the bike (28 mile)

I have established a nice little routine now where I swim in the flash on a Saturday  morning then immediately get onto the bike to follow the exact 14 mile IMUK bike route round to Babylon lane which is precisely what we will do on race day.

The flash was a complete dream today, warm and calm.

I even managed to swim all the way out to the furthest buoy!

I did 3 laps of the short course (1350 total) then 1 lap of the bigger course which I thinK is 900metres so roughly 2250 for the session which I was pleased with.

One thing I noticed when getting onto the bike was that I was freezing for quite a while so this needs to be monitored.

I sailed round to Babylon lane within an hour but two things happned.

First, I dropped my water bottle about 5 mins from Babylon lane.

'No problem, I will get it on the way back' I thought to myself.

When I returned 10 minutes later – it had gone!

Who would take a used drinks bottle, £2 from Sports Direct?

Seriously, why would you do that?

Second, I dropped my mobile phone on the way back to the flash!!

I could not believe it when an elderly gentleman called the wife to say he had found the phone on Chorley New Road!

With everything going on in the world right now people like that simply warm the heart!

## Sunday : 30km Run – 3:35

So I have taken the long slow runs up to 30k.

I made sure I took the pace really slow and concentrated on completing the distance rather than speed, taking regular breaks.

The first 20k was fine, I feel like I could knock 20k's out all day long now.

To 25k was just about ok.

25-27.5 was a challenge.

The last 2.5k I found tough.

By the end I could hardly walk.

It's always like this first time for a new distance.

3:35 would give me nearly an hour and a half to complete the last 10k on race day to fall in line with my plan of 5 hours for the run, so i'll take that.

Slow, I know, but I don't give a shit – running over 20k I find tough – always have and probably always will!

It's weird, for LSR's my 5k time is always 30 mins, 10k = 1hour and 20k = 2 hours dead….

But as soon as I take it over 20k that nice little matrix goes completely out the window!

I am going to try a new strategy for next weeks 30k, i'll let you know how it goes.

**Monday: Mile swim in the pool**

Easy, felt nothing more than a warm up, not being arrogant, that's just how it felt.

**Tuesday : Weights and sauna session**

**Wednesday – 10km run am then 'Iron swim pm'**

10km run, nice and easy sub 1 hour, I then got some issues with my bike sorted by Ian @ wigan bike tec fantastic service as usual

Open water TT went really well as above – Highlight of the swim was seeing Nick doing his David Hasselhoff impression keeping all the swimmers safe whilst stood on his paddle board!- I shouted 'alrite Nick' as I passed him on lap 3 'mid stroke' and I could tell by his reaction that I was probably the only one to do this!!

**Thursday – 47 Mile IMUK bike loop from Babylon Lane 3:17**

I shouldn't have gone really as the weather was poor but I had booked a day off and was itching to get out, convincing myself that 'it wasn't that bad'

As soon as I pulled up in Babylon Lane to unload the bike, the heavens opened. I got drenched and battered by a constant headwind for large periods. It is now June and there is still no sign of the gale force winds receeding out on the loop.

I swear I am buying a 'twat hat' for the rest of my training, I don't care what I look like – every time I go out on that circuit I feel like I am in the opening scene from the wizard of Oz and I've had enough!

## IMUK Training through the eyes of a first timer! Week 24 of 28

Saturday : 1 Hour open water swim then 28 mile bike brick

Sunday : 30k run – 3:10

Monday : Mile Swim in the pool

Tuesday : Gym strength & sauna session

Wednesday : Double IMUK loops back to back : 2:53 & 3:24

Thursday : Pool Swim 100 lengths

Friday : Gym Strength & Sauna Session

Many people have said many different things to me throughout my journey.

But one of the most profound is this…..

"*Compete* or C*omplete*? – There is one 'L' of a difference?"

I love that statement.

I really love it.

It goes straight to the bullseye of what my journey has been about from day 1.

I am not striving to achieve a certain 'time' in order to 'be happy'.

Never have been….

My journey has been based on the amazing sense of achievement one gets from taking something that you believe to be impossible, be that a 10k run, a 70.3 or a full Ironman triathlon and slowly bringing it into your reality, step by step.

The joy of the 'doing'

The joy of simply getting the medal and proving to yourself that 'anything really is possible', despite your limiting beliefs.....

So why this week why do I find myself attacking the Ironman bike circuit thinking I am Joe Skipper trying to PB it simply because it is a 'nice day' when I am meant to be doing long slow double loops?

"If you can't PB on a day like this then you never will" I said to myself as I went stomping up Sheep House first time round.....

Ok, I went Sub 3 on the first lap, even knocking out a half average time of 2:53.

But boy did that come back to bite me on the arse later.

As soon as I started lap 2 I thought to myself 'why the hell did I just do that?'

The first 2 hours of the second lap were ok, but hours 2-3 were absolute torture and that's before I even got to Hunters Hill 2nd time round....

Bear in mind the small matter of a marathon will be waiting for me after the 112 mile bike which is a bit like a tiger waiting for you having first been mauled by a lion!

The trouble is, when you surround yourself with people that have completed the iron distance many times over, it is very easy to become complacent about it.

Make no mistake, I have total respect to all those who go into every Iron distance race and push themselves to the absolute limit, striving to be the very best that they can be – total respect.

But let's have it right.

'Just' completing an Ironman triathlon  is a truly wonderful achievement for a first timer.

Truly Wonderful.

And the way I see it, you can make it as easy or has hard as you want….

Remember always that I only ever had one objective….

And that was simply to get the sacred IMUK medal….

So…..

I have allowed 3:30 for both my 47 mile IMUK loops.

Let me tell you something.

Weather permitting, I now find that easy.

Very easy.

So why make this thing more difficult than what it needs to be Iron rookie?

If I had the race of my life and went sub 3 on both loops then half killed myself on the mara I might, if I am really really lucky, be able to scrape 12:30.

Kona in my age group requires a time of 10 hours.

Never gonna happen!

So what would a time of 12:30 really achieve in the grand scheme of things?

looking at last years results a time of 12:30 would rank you around 500 out of 1800 finishers, such is the quality of the athletes that we are racing with here.

OK you will be In the 'top third'....

Whoopy Doo!

So I push myself to the absolute limit and stress about 'my time' all the way round to finish #500?

No thanks....

I would much rather relax and enjoy it, take everything in, really savour the experience.,....

It reminds me of my first ever 10k race.

First time I did a 10k I was just absolutely buzzing to be lining up on the start line.

I was totally relaxed, soaked up all the atmosphere, and enjoyed every single second of simply completing the distance for the first time and collecting the medal – it was a very pleasant experience.

Now when I go to a 10k run what happens?

I almost give myself a heart attack trying to beat my previous time and come away from the race pissed off because I was 30 seconds behind my PB...

It is no longer a pleasant experience!

Far from it!

Do you see the difference?

Well in my mind, it's the same here....

Iron Rookie, would you like your first IMUK to be easy or hard?

Erm.....

Easy please....

Would you like to enjoy it or suffer?

Erm....

Enjoy it please!

*Compete* or *complete*?

I'll take *complete* all day long thank you very much!

OK Then you are the boss!

Cruise Control it is!

Here is how I got on this week...

**Saturday Dip in the flash then Babylon lane and back on the bike (28 miles) – Sub 1 Hour each way**

www.strava.com/activities/1029389138

Once again I was late arriving – I really need to sort this out!

The flash was in a bad mood this week, harsh, cold, dark and very unwelcoming.

I made the mistake of not wearing my neoprene 'helmet' and very firmly paid the price.

Was glad to get out to be honest – hate the flash when it's in a bad mood!

I think I have cracked the ride round to Babylon lane, I am able to glide round within the hour without even really trying – exactly what I am looking to achieve.

I then found out this week that they had made a change to the 14 mile pre loop – typical – i'll check it out and report back!

### Sunday 30k Run. – 3:10

Last week my 30k run was 3:35.

This week I got it down to 3:10.

For my mind that is a very big difference.

What I did differently was this.

Instead of trying to run 30k 'straight' I did 10k x 3 with a 5 minute break inbetween each one and I found that each 10k I managed to get under 1 hour exactly like my 10k's are in training!

I stretched, took a gel and drank some electolytes inbetween each set.

Try it! – it may just change your life like it did mine!

## Monday – Mile swim in the Pool

Very easy, not even a warm up now.

## Tuesday – Gym strength work and sauna session

## Wednesday – Double IMUK loops back to back 2:53 & 3:24

www.strava.com/activities/1036045480

www.strava.com/activities/1036304805

See report above

## Thursday – 100 lengths in the pool

Not difficult, boring to be honest. didn't warm up until length 60 odd! much prefer OW but no way I am going down to three sisters after a 100 mile bike!

## Friday – Gym strength and sauna session

Saturday: 1 hour OW swim, 14 mile pre loop, 47 mile IMUK loop (3:13), 14 mile 'post loop'

Sunday: 10k run 58 minutes

Monday: Mile Pool Swim

Tuesday: Gym strength & sauna session

Wednesday: 47 mile IMUK bike loop & 15 min brick

Thursday:10k run – 57 mins

Friday: Gym strength & sauna session

'Aren't you meant to be tapering?' Someone said to me in the pool last week.

Good question.

There are 4 things I wanted to cover off before talking about my training over the last 7 days, so let's start with 'tapering'.

1) The Taper

It seems to me that everywhere you look right now people are getting their knickers in a twist about how to Taper for an Ironman triathlon.

It also seems to me that just like every other aspect of Ironman training,  some insist on making it way more complicated that it needs to be.

Make no mistake, there are people out there way more qualified than I, (my only qualifications are my race medals) and always remember I am not chasing some phantom 'time' at IMUK in order to be 'happy' –  my goal is simply to get my hands on the sacred medal….

But here is how I see it….

A week is a very long time in triathlon training.

Very long.

Further.

3 days is a long time.

Let me give you an example of what I mean.

Lets say I go out for a 'long' bike ride on a Saturday (50 miles +)

By the time Wednesday comes round (my next cycle day 3 days later) I am absolutely itching to get back out onto the bike again.

If I take the Wednesday off and wait until the following Saturday (7 days later) I feel like a crack addict who has been locked in the house for a week going mental for his next fix.

What about swimming and gym work?

Got to be honest –  they feel like 'days off'.

Running 20k?

Not even out of breath.

Not trying hard enough?

Come and tell me that when I am holding the sacred medal.

So there we have it.

My plan is to continue with my training 'as normal' all the way up to race week and ok I might take the Wednesday bike off, but that's about it!

**2) Watches**

A good lad that I know who is also training for IMUK very kindly offered to lend me his posh watch this week – it was a really nice gesture and one that I very much appreciated, but it reminded me of something I have been wanting to talk about for ages.

You can go out and buy a watch today that will do pretty much everything apart from complete the actual Ironman for you.

Over and over again people on social media will say things like 'thinking of doing an Ironman and cant decide between this watch at £300 or this one at £350'

Let me tell you something....

See this watch?

Guess how much that watch cost me?

£9.99 from Argos.

Yes, less than a tenner.

That watch has been with me since day 1 and has served me extremely well through super sprint, sprint, Olympic and 70.3 triathlons as well as 2.5km, 5km, 10km, HM and mara runs inbetween.

I use mapometer.com to plan my routes and distances free of charge and record my activity free on Strava via my mobile phone.

I have become very attached to that little watch and it will take pride of place on my wrist for IMUK!

But what about heart rate I hear you all cry!

Let me tell you something else…

I have never owned a heart rate monitor.

Could the quality of my training have been improved if I had one and used it properly?

Probably, but remember always the saying *'compete or complete – there is one 'L' of a difference'* – and my goal – which is simply to collect the sacred Ironman medal.

That said.......

At the start of the year my time for the 47 mile IMUK loop was 3:24.

Recently I got that down to 2:48 for the exact same loop.

36 minutes quicker over the same 47 miles is a big difference.

Huge.

My average speed for the loop has increased from 13.8 to 16.8 mph.

I feel certain most coaches would be shouting from the rooftops about such a dramatic improvement in performance.

Yet there was never a heart rate monitor in sight.

No different training 'zones'…..

No 'VO2 Max'…..

No complicated training plans…..

Just simple, straightforward training.

My point?

You can spend an absolute fortune on a watch as a first timer……but you really don't need to!

**3) I must not race…**

On Wednesday I went out and tried to smash a single 47 mile IMUK loop.

My plan for race day is 3:30 loops.

This week I recorded 2:57.

Instead of being happy that I did a loop 30 minutes inside my plan I was pissed off because I didn't PB.

letting myself off the leash and 'going for it' on these 'shorter' rides makes excellent training for two major reasons which I talk about in my book, but I must remember not to do this on race day!!

It's like when you was at school and the teacher made you write the same sentence over and over again 100 times so that it would sink in…

Well I think I seriously need to do that with the following:

'I must not race the IMUK loop on race day'

## 4) Insider Tips

I met a lad on Babylon lane who was going for his third IMUK.

He gave me 3 cracking first timer tips, these I already knew, but they are powerful so I wanted to share them:

1. Ride the first loop totally within yourself, at 70% of your potential
2. When you first leave the flash there will be stray drinks bottles everywhere because of the speed bumps and adrenaline fuelled animals will come stomping past you, be aware of both
3. Race your own race

The guy was Ace but then again he was a 'Babylon Babe' so that makes him ace by default.

Here is how my training went this week:

**Saturday** : 1 Hour Swim in The Flash then bike : 14 Mile 'Pre Loop' (58 min) : 47 Mile IMUK loop (3:13) : 14 Mile 'Post Loop' (59 Mins)

I did 3 loops of the 'small' swim circuit then got cocky and tried a big loop and got to admit me arse went but managed to get back to shore after a good hour 'at sea'.

One thing I have been aware of for a while is that I completely adore swimming alongside others – I find it is a completely different experience versus swimming on your own.

I didn't really feel like I got going on bike during the 14 mile 'pre loop' but still managed sub 1 hour so the feedback here was not to panic, you are often doing better than what you think!

The main loop was ok, I managed a time of 3:13 in lovely conditions but felt a little more fatigued than was expecting, I put this down to the 100 miler that I had done just 2 days previous – I shouldn't really have structured it this way but glorious weather, days off and penny flash swim restrictions forced my hand!

When I returned to the flash my car was locked in the car park!

If this every happens to you simply drive at the locked gate and it will open automatically!

**Sunday :** 10k Run – 58 mins

Standard sub 1 hour 10k

**Monday** – Mile pool swim

Instead of counting lengths I focussed on my technique and in particular my breathing, trying to breathe every 8 lengths instead of every 4 – this I very much enjoyed and I know will help me no end once I get back in OW!

**Tuesday** – Gym strength and sauna session

**Wednesday** – 47 Mile IMUK bike loop – 2:57 & 15 min brick- see above!

www.strava.com/activities/1047329094

**Thursday** – 10k run – 57 minutes

www.strava.com/activities/1049386725

Tried to beat the one Strava segment that is on my run – missed it by 10 seconds – this is a slipperly slope as time and time again people tell me that trying to run fast over shorter distances  is when the injuries are most likely to happen – serioulsly Iron Rookie stop it, stop it now….

**Friday** – Gym strength and sauna session

Saturday: 1 hour OW swim, 14 mile pre loop, 47 mile IMUK loop (3:24) 14 mile 'post' loop

Sunday: 30k run

Monday: 40 minute pool swim

Tuesday: Gym Strength Session

Wednesday: 2.4 mile open water Time trial swim 1:19

Thursday: 10k run

Friday: Gym Strength & Sauna session

I am absolutely buzzing this week.

I feel like everything has just all of a sudden fallen into place for me.

I say this for 3 reasons.

**First, the run.**

I went and ran the actual IMUK run circuit on Sunday – I did 3 x 9k laps up and down Chorley New Road exactly like we will do on race day and I came away on such a high I can't begin to tell you how buzzing I was about it!

My Times for the 3 were 54:17, 51:58? (buzzing after lap 1!) and 53:29 against an allowance of one hour per lap.

Ok, on race day we have the additional 9k ish from the Macron to the Beehive and then the 'victory' parade down into to the town centre at the end but still, 2:40 for nearly 30k of the actual route Is  good for me...

Very good.

Or so I thought....

Laithwaite collared me before the TT swim on Wednesday and said "Rookie.... a word"

What he said to me was this.

'I have been watching your blog and I have got to tell you something – When you first started this project, it was all about 'could you complete an ironman' but from your training you now know that it's not going to be a problem. Unless you have a complete disaster, you're going to get round without any issues. It's moved on now and become something else, it's not about completing, it's about doing yourself justice and seeing how far the training has brought you, its about going out there on race day and being absolutely the very best you can be'

How amazing is this guy?

I'm not even one of his clients!!

On the back of that I returned to chorley new road the next day in a spanking new pair of Mizunos and do you know what?

I ran a 41:17 lap.

www.strava.com/activities/1059438255

Mental aint it?

How can words have such a dramatic effect on performance?

Yet we must never forget that all I ever wanted at the start of this journey was to get my hands on the sacred medal.

I didn't believe it would ever be possible for me.

It shouldn't be possible really.

But Ironman has been trying to tell me that 'Anything is possible' all along...

I wonder what would happen if we applied that attitude to race day?

I wonder indeed....

Whilst on the subject of running I promised some other first timers from distant lands  an overview of the run route the way I see it.

Remember always I haven't actually joined the ranks of the legendary Ironmen yet, but I have been out on the course every week for pretty much the last 6 months  and  know it like the back of my hand!

So here is my take on the run route written from a wonderfully naïve, first timer place as requested!

Many of those that already have the sacred medal will no doubt read this with a wry smile (You just wait till race day Rookie)  but here goes...

For me, the IMUK run route can be broken down into 3 parts.

Well 3 and a half parts and a couple of cheeky hills to be precise!

## First Bit – T2 at the Macron Stadium round to the main lap circuit on Chorley New Road) 10km (ish)

I have ran this section before with Damo and I have to tell you it is nothing to be worried about. (yes we started at the beehive so add 5 minutes!)

www.strava.com/activities/941354666

OK, when you leave T2 at the Macron there is a big hill virtually straight away up through the new estate, but it took me no more than 90 seconds to 'power walk' up it – feel free to go and spank all your energy charging up it like Tarzan but this is not what Iron Rookie will be doing, let me tell you.

Once you get onto the main road it's all downhill to the beehive pub then a very gentle climb up chorley new road for a kilometre or so  and then downhill again to the canal where it is all completely flat.

When you get off the canal there is another steepish hill that leads you up to the main 'lap' circuit on Chorley new Road but once again this got walked in about 60 seconds.

I would say 8km of the first 10km are downhill and flat with the rest a very gentle climb.

My time with Damo  was just over 50 minutes which is much faster than my usual 10k time in training.

I have also ran this bit after a 100 mile bike and of course it is somewhat more challenging than running it on fresh legs but I honestly didn't find it a big deal.

People more experienced than I tell me that this section is very exposed to the sun (what's that?) so make sure you have plenty of suncream in your T2 bag not that we have seen the sun in Bolton for well over 12 months like.

Also, support on this leg of the route is a little bit thin on the ground as you are out of the way but fear not – fantastic crowds are waiting for you once you get onto the main lap circuit – so let this be your motivation!!

Just on that note I got wind that  a little boy will be standing on the white bridge near the end of the canal route cheering for his mum who is another 1st timer- the little boy is called Harry – keep an eye out for him – stuff like this gives me goosebumps!

## 2nd Bit – Main Lap circuit – 9k ish a lap – 3 and a half laps

So this is the bit that I did at the weekend.

If you look at the picture to the left, that's me on  Chorley New Road in Bolton which is where the actual run will take place on race day and I love it.

You can break each lap down into three parts.

### First part

Run from Beumont Road junction all the way down Chorley New Road into Bolton Town centre (4.5km)

You run **down** a gently sloping hill the whole time – piece of piss!

Once you get into the town centre you run onto a cobbled street (not shitty cobbles, ace cobbles) then round a hairpin bend called Le Mans crescent (how fab is that) – here the atmosphere is electric and is something I cannot wait to experience!

## Second Part

Run from the town centre back up Chorley New Road to the Beaumont Road junction. (4.5km)

You Run **up** a gently sloping hill the whole time – not a piece of piss!

(But the crowds will carry you through)

## Sandwiched inbetween

Just before you get into Bolton Town centre you run down a really steep hill.

It's Famous amongst the legendary Ironmen.

It's called Chorley Street Hill

Guess what?

You have to run back up it on the way back.

Nautie!

Very nautie!

But don't worry about it – I discovered something.

I can walk up that hill and it takes me 2 minutes.

I could run up it in what? a minute?

But i'll sacrifice a minute per lap all day long for the difference in the way I felt once I got to the top of that bastad hill!

I also found out this week that some ace people are planning loads of support on there for us with a disco and fancy dress etc etc so this will no doubt ease the pain!

**Final Bit**

Once you have completed 3 laps you then start your 'victory run' which is half a lap but you will be delighted to hear that this is on the downhill section of chorley new Road!

So there you have it, I hope that helps!

My advice to you would be to get your arse up to chorley New Road and get your trainers out!

Failing that find a 5km stretch of road near you with a continuous gentle slope then run up and down this section of road three times!

Don't say I never give you anything

**Second Point – The Swim**

Penny flash has long had a hold over me ever since the first time I went down there and lasted about 30 seconds before instantly dismissing open water swimming as 'impossible.'

The flash still intimidates me to this day, but I finaly feel like I have got the upper hand.

On Saturday I did 5 x small loops of 450 metres and by the 5th loop it felt like I was just getting started.

In an audacious display of arrogance and defiance I tumble turned against the safety boat on my final lap before making my way back to shore.

I felt a bit like the kid at school who was being bullied but has secretly been having kick boxing lessons late at night.

I told you I would get you in the end Penny Flash….

### Third : Weight

At the start of the year I weighed 13st 11.

I weighed myself this morning and I am now 12st 11.

My goal was to get to the same weight I was before the 70.3 in Dublin and that was 12st 9 so I am almost there!

I am so happy about this as I find it makes a big difference to the way I feel.

I would have arrived here miles quicker had I not eaten so much crap food throughout this process but got there in the end!

Here is the training that I did this week:

**Saturday** : 1 Hour Swim in Pennington, Bike :  14 Mile 'Pre Loop' 56 minutes : 47 Mile IMUK loop 3:24 : 14 Mile post loop – 1  Hr

Was buzzing about the swim (see above) and then also pleased that the diversion on the pre loop to avoid the roadworks at lostock train station had little impact on my time despite a cheeky new hill (junction road west) recording 56 minutes however I did 'tag on' to a couple of the team Deane lads – interestingly these boys were also allowing 1 hour for this section on race day and they are way faster than me for the main loops!

I tried to aim for a 3:30 loop in line with race day and this was quite easily achieved as the wind was once again horrendous slowing me down and stealing my energy as standard.

**Sunday :** 30k run – Ace! See above!

**Monday :** 40 minute pool swim – Not really even worth a mention!

**Tuesday :** Gym strength session!

**Wednesday :** Open water TT down at 3 sisters. 1:19 for the full iron distance. got a tow all the way round by my new best mate Paul – Cheers P!

**Thursday :** 10k run – Buzzing – see above

**Friday :** Gym

In addition, the most beautiful thing happened today….

As I am running up Chorley new Road a guy is running towards me in the opposite direction and we recognised eachother as trainee ironmen a mile off (you know when you just know)

 Anyhow The guy was easily in his late 40's / early 50's and as he gets closer he is screaming at me 'WE'RE GONNA DO THIS! WE'RE GONNA DO THIS!' at the top of his voice, eyes bulging with excitement and an expression on his face that I will never forget as long as I live.

If you could 'bottle' what Ironman 'is' then that for me was it right there, in that very moment….

Saturday: 2 x 47 mile IMUK loops (negative split)

Sunday: 27k chorley new Road Run (IMUK lap circuit x3)

Monday: 40 minute pool swim

Tuesday: Weights Session

Wednesday: 47 Mile IMUK loop (2:38 PB!) & 10K brick run

Thursday: 10k Chorley New Road Run

Friday: 24 mile escorted ride for an IMUK legend

4 things I wanted to cover off  in the penultimate update before the big day!

**First – Don't be shit**

I will never forget the first time I cycled the Ironman bike route.

It wasn't long after the race and hundreds of messages of support that had been chalked onto Hunters Hill were still clearly visible in the tarmac.

Those messages gave me goosebumps.

All the hopes, dreams and individual journeys that they represented, I found them haunting and truly beautiful.

But amongst all the words of support and encouragement, one particular piece of grafiti stood out.

It read 'Don't be shit'

Now I long had an issue with this particular message as it never made any sense to me.

How can someone be shit if they are attempting an Ironman I thought to myself – these people are amazing!

What the hell are they going on about?

But this last week or so it clicked….

I now know exactly what those words mean, and they are very significant.

Let me tell you something.

When you are the one stood in the crowd swilling beer on race day you are in awe of the amazing ironmen and your mindset is that what they are doing would be impossible for you.

Even many people who are already into triathlon look at the iron distance and doubt that they would ever be able to conquer it.

But once you understand the secrets and follow a simple plan, something amazing happens.

You begin to realise that not only is it possible, but being able to complete it is almost a given.

When the penny finally drops you scream 'Eureka!' from the top of Hunters only to find the existing ironmen looking back at you with an expression on their face that says…..

And?

Not such a big deal afterall is it?

Come join the party…..

Just don't be shit.

Now what they mean is, there is being able to *complete* an ironman, and then there is being able to *compete* at Ironman – so don't be shit – compete.

It's almost as if there is an unwritten rule:

Once you know the magic, 'just' completing it is not enough anymore, you have to race.

But wait a second.....

Do you know how many people will actually complete an Ironman Triathlon in their lifetime?

Less than 1%

Way less....

Why?

Because most people believe that it would be 'impossible'.

So on that basis what is wrong with simply celebrating the wonderful achievement of taking something that you thought was impossible and getting your hands on the sacred medal?....

Let me tell you what is wrong with that....

Absolutely Nothing!

Nothing at all!

Completing an Ironman triathlon is a phenomenal achievement and one that should be celebrated for many months, years or even a lifetime.

Never forget that.

Ever.

You see the trouble is, many of the existing Ironmen who have been at it for years and years have long since forgotten what it is like for the average guy or gal stood in the crowd on race day.

But I haven't.

I know exactly how you are feeling!

I was there myself not that long ago!

And that is exactly why I made this website and wrote my book!

My whole journey has only ever been about one thing.

How you take something that you  believe to be impossible (complete an ironman) and slowly bring it into your reality.

Now many people have said to me that my journey has evolved, that it isn't about just completing an ironman anymore, it's about trying to get a really 'good' time – about not being 'shit'.

And I agree.

I believe my journey has evolved.

It has evolved into something else way beyond just 'completing it'

But exactly what it has evolved into I will share with you once I am (hopefully) holding the sacred medal next week!

## 2) Self Discipline

As anybody who knows me will tell you, it wasn't that long ago that I was the first one to arrive at the bar and the last one to leave it.

Yet do you know when Alcohol last touched my lips?

New Years eve.

Yes, well over 6 months ago.

I have turned down pretty much every single social invitation that involves alcohol which means I have turned down pretty much every single social invitation.

Besides, got to be honest, idle chit chat bores me these days....

Do I miss it?

Not really.

As we all know, alcohol is a slipperly slope, you can never just 'have the one' so a quick pint easily turns into a skinfull.

Smokes often make their appearance and you end up eating all the wrong foods, like a kebab and then a full English the next morning for example.

Hungover and feeling like shit you inevitably miss training the next day which turns into a week and then all of a sudden its spiralled out of control.

But hey, at least you had a 'great night'.

No, one must resist.

I definitely find I can dig a lot deeper on the centruary rides/nosebleed runs  alcohol free.

That said, As I passed the Top Lock this week there must have been at least 50 cycles outside, (see pic) some lads from Wigan on a charity ride having stopped off for a pint or two in the sun mid route.

As I munched on a protein bar and sipped on some electrolytes, I couldn't help but wonder what the hell I am doing with my life....

Bide your time Rookie, bide your time son.

**3) Negative Split** www.strava.com/activities/1066404636

For those Unfamiliar with the term 'negative split' it involves completing the second half of a ride faster than the first.

Now being able to do this at iron distance is for me, very significant.

Going for a 100 mile ride is a big enough challenge in itself.

But riding two 50 mile loops of the IMUK bike circuit back to back with the 2nd circuit at a faster pace than the first I found a very difficult skill to master.

After 3 months of trying, I finally managed to nail this at weekend.

Once you can do this, you own the Ironman bike circuit as far as I am concerned.

## Point 4 – PB the loop
www.strava.com/activities/1068760452

Having negative split the circuit at the weekend I returned to the loop Wednesday for one last, somewhat emotional final attempt at a single loop.

I knew from the outset that I was going to 'go for it' (and not 'be shit' lol).

I was over the moon to smash out a loop time of 2:38 – this moved me about 400 places up the strava leaderboard and puts me just under top 25% of all time Ironman loop rides.

Can't begin to tell you how buzing I was about this.

Exactly how was I able to do it?

It's in my book.

## Ironman training through the eyes of a first timer! Week 28/28

Saturday : OFF

Sunday : OFF

Monday : 40 min pool swim

Tuesday : Gym

Wednesday : 10km Chorley New Road Run

Thursday ; 40 min pool Swim

Friday : Off

Race Week! - No Way lol

What a crazy six months!

Looking back, I have had the most amazing journey.

'Self discovery' bit aside, the greatest part has without doubt been the wonderful people I have met during this process, they have made it magical, they really have.

Everyone from  Liz at Grubbers sweets who gave me the biggest smile every time I sat outside her shop on Babylon lane, Sam, Steve Cook, Damo, Ironman S, Laithwaite, Nick Thomas, Katerina Tanti of the excellent @uktrichat on twitter who has supported me since day 1 and Deca Dave who did 20 Iron distance triathlons back to back breaking the world record in the process......

When I really think about all the amazing people I have been lucky enough to meet, it brings tears to my eyes, it really does, hundreds of people, from all walks of life......

I wont half miss the banter I have had on social media too, the guys on twitter @uktrichat in particular, honestly, those guys are just the best.

It was fitting to  end my journey at the Ironman Welcome party last night with Crooky, the guy who's interview kickstarted a chain of interviews that will motivate the like minded for generations to come.

We had an ace night, it was great to catch up with him (and Sam!)

Ironman not only do the best triathlons in the world, they do the best welcome parties in the world too.

There is a school of thought that says you don't become an Ironman on Race day, you become an Ironman during your training.

Look at the pictures to the left. (see website)

I barely recognise the person I have become....

Who is he!!

Iron Rookie is the guy stood at the bar, not the one running around in the Tri Suit!

I have to say though, it is madness how 6 months of training all boils down to one single day.

Its a bit like studying for something for 3 years and it all comes down to one exam.

As many a teacher will tell you, anything can happen on exam day.

That is why they changed it to coursework, so you are judged on your performance throughout the process and not just the result of a single 'test'.

If Ironman was 'coursework' I am certain I would have been awarded the medal months ago!

But Ironman aint 'courseowork'......

Ironman is all about Race Day....

I feel like I have been sailing the 7 seas for the last six months en route to the greatest roller coaster in the world.

Well it is time to board that coaster.

I am strapped in and I am ready to go.

Hold tight kids as this is going to be one hell of a ride!

My fate now lies in the hands of the iron gods....

If you are joining me then may the gods be with you, I look forward to seeing you out on the course, give us a whoop whoop as you overtake, you'll spot me a mile off.....

If not you can track me #1424 - I believe my name will come up as the iron rookie (love that it will do that)

There are many other things that I want to tell you, but I need to wait until I am holding the sacred medal first!!!!

In other news Social media went into meltdown on Wednesday after one of the volunteers noticed the name 'Alistair Brownlee' on the Pro Athletes board at the IMUK volunteers briefing .

Will he race, Won't he race, everyone getting their knickers in a twist about it until the guy from tri247 popped all the balloons by saying he had spoken to his manager and was told Ali will not be racing on Sunday.

Yet there was total silence from the man himself.

I got a right bee in my bonnet about this.

I think it is completely unfair on all the fantastic supporters - People see that name on the board in the registration tents so they talk and they come out to support him all excited yet he cant even be arsed to send a simple tweet to let everybody know that he ain't coming.......

If you plan to DNS your first ever Ironman then say so, in order that we can all start taking the piss......(and boy will the piss be royally taken on this side of the pennines if he doesn't show)

I chanced my arm and sent him a couple of nice messages via Twitter....

Of course he did not respond to little ol me....

Can I tell you something Ali?

Lucy Gossage responded....

Joe Skipper responded.....

**Ironmen respond**....

Maybe he will understand one day if he ever actually becomes one himself...

Oh and by the way, he is an Englishman so it has to be Bolton, England, no fukin off to Europe for a nice easy course now-don't even think about doing that - come and show us how it's done up Hunters Hill 100 miles into the bike please.......

We are waiting......

If he fully intends to race and can't/won't say anything for reasons unbeknown to me then Sorry Yorkie, I take it all back, blame the tri247 guy that said he spoke to your manager and I really look forward to seeing you on Sheephouse cocker, as do we all...

Next update : ASAP - Well Rookie??

# IRONMAN UK, BOLTON, ENGLAND.... RACE DAY!!

May I begin by sharing with you the biggest thing that I have learnt on my journey?

Ok, come closer so I can whisper it to you.....

Are you ready?

Here goes......

Race day should only ever be one thing.....

A celebration of all your training.....

And That is exactly what Ironman UK felt like to me.....

A celebration.

From the moment that I arrived in the registration tents until the minute I crossed the finish line, IMUK was quite possibly the most amazing experience of my life.

Before we get started, I want you to promise me something.

If you are not already an Ironman, please make the decision to become one now....

Right now.

If you would like some inspiration on how this will be possible for you then please consider signing up for my book and read how I was able to go from being..

- 'One of the lads' always in the pub
- Very overweight and unfit
- Unable to swim a single length front crawl
- Hadn't ridden a bike for almost 20 years

- Couldn't run any more than ten yards without wanting to stop........

To Becoming an Ironman myself.

Its not just 'another inspirational story' it's a step by step training manual detailing exactly how I did it., race by race, together with the many secrets that I learned along the way.

You might also want to join the @uktrichat community on twitter and get involved.

Why?

Before the race I got literally hundreds of supportive messages via social media that reduced me to tears and you will too if you interact with these amazing people online.

Now in my case, this was obviously a double edged sword as I would have looked a right clown if I had failed on Sunday and I am sure you can imagine the added pressure that this brings......

However during the race the reaction I got from not only the crowd, but many of the other athletes, blew my mind, as you will soon find out...

Here is how it went...

(You might want to get cosy and make yourself a brew.)

### Race Eve

They said at the race brief that you will not be able to get to sleep on race eve.

Trust me when I tell you - you will not be able to get to sleep on race eve.

I think I managed the grand total of 2 hours.

Not exactly the dream start to the biggest day of your life is it?

Just keep this is mind as you read.

## Race Day

What I love about Ironman events is that they force you to be organised, come race morning simply put your wetsuit on and you are ready to race, everything else has already been taken care of the day before.

I arrived at the flash in good time - the entrance to the athletes area was packed out with members of the public and it was difficult to get through - make way for the athlete now, make way....

First job - check my bike.

I was absolutely convinced something would have happened to it overnight (you rack your bike the day before so it is all ready for you on race day)

Obviously I have been shouting my mouth off on social media about this crazy adventure for months and have generated a fair bit of attention.

Whilst 99.9% of people have been nothing but wonderful with me, I half expected someone to say 'there is that dick Rookies bike - slash his tyres' to the point where I seriously considered standing guard over it for the entire time transition was open...

Thankfully I was delighted to observe that everything was still in order in this regard so OK to proceed.

**The Swim 2.4 Mile Swim : Pennington Flash :**

**Cut Off : 2:20  Race Plan : 1:30 Actual Time : 1:30**

At Ironman, instead of 2,000 people all getting into the water at once, you self seed in a big long line based on your estimated swim time like you would if you was lining up with the pacers at a marathon.

I still had my wetsuit down showing my tri-suit underneath with Iron Rookie all over it and already people were coming up to me saying that they had seen me online and wishing me all the best which was a lovely touch.

for some reason I moved up to the 1:20 pen, laithwaite had told me that the trick is to swim with people slightly faster and it was interesting to observe how the aggression/seriousness/growling seemed to increase the further I moved up the line.

I broke the ice with a couple of lads around me and we ended up having a right laugh.

The adrenaline rush you experience when you are stood on that start line of your first full Ironman event is like nothing I have ever experienced in my life.

The announcer said that Lucy Gossage (female winner) was dancing on the pontoon to the music - this I loved. I would later see her handing out medals to the final finishers some 6 hours after she had finished her own race - This I loved even more.

Once the national anthem finished I let out a roar with mixed reactions from my fellow athletes, some joined in, some laughed at me, some jumped out of there skin and some looked at me as if I was a psyco.

In Dublin for the 70.3 in the North Sea the roar that went up once the Claxton sounded will stay with me for the rest of my days.

I wanted the roar to be even better at IMUK but it was more a nervous silence, almost as if many were thinking 'Oh Shit' rather than 'let's have it'.

That certainly appeared to be the case around me although we must remember nearly 50% of the field were fellow first timers and me letting out a roar like that, eyes bulging wild with excitement probably didn't help their nerves one bit.

I do think though that Ironman should make it a condition of entry that after the national anthem you have to make a roar.

Anyhow race gets underway and we are all stood in a big long line waiting to 'get in'

My race plan was based around the bike cut offs so I had to be in the water by 6:15am, simple as that.

6:14 and i'm still stood with the 1:20 guys prob a good 5 minutes away from the pontoon.

Fuk it i'm getting in.

I then walked round the outside of the queue towards the water, which the stewards appeared to be very impressed about and I ended up getting in with the 1:15 boys.

Now normally when I get into the flash I prance about in the water for a good few minutes to allow my body to acclimatise.

There is no 'prancing about' at IMUK - you are straight in son, sink or swim.

Those first few seconds were horrible, the shock to the system whilst your body acclimatises, it makes getting your head into the water very difficult.

That said, after a short while I began to settle into my rhythm.

Like everybody else, I have heard all sorts of horror stories from people saying they got punched, kicked, bitten, winded, swam on, ribs broke etc at the Ironman swim start but get this.....

About 3 or 4 times early on people crashed into me.

Guess what happened?

They said Sorry!

Pardon?

Did you just say sorry?

You have got to remember that I have been used to swimming down at 3 sisters these last few weeks in a big pack of ex rugby lads from Wigan..... i'm used to having a brawl!

I thought IMUK was going to be twice as bad, but here I am surrounded by athletes saying excuse me and sorry?

Wtf?

I remember thinking this is a bit like expecting Millwall at the football but Burton Albion turn up instead....

Once the initial 'scrum' was over there was plenty of room and we all just 'got on with it' - felt like it took forever to get to that first turn though!

Settling down nicely and I noticed a fluorescent green swim cap cutting through the field swimming in a perfect line with the buoys (one of the pros on lap 2) for a split second I thought about getting on their feet  - don't you dare Rookie....don't even think about it sunshine.....the thought made me laugh though.

Watching the pro effortlessly cut through the field like that whilst everyone else was hard at it was one of the most beautiful things I have ever seen

I was really interested to see what would happen when our group got to the first turn buoy.....

No drama, everybody around me played nicely, slowed down and navigated the bend perfectly.

I tend to find this often happens if you are a middle of the pack swimmer, you will find yourself surrounded by people who 'play the game' so to speak.

'Boy what a long way I have come since the first time I went for a swim in Penny Flash last year' I thought to myself - i'm holding my own here!

Back to the race and I had been looking for a suitable 'partner' for a while and I finally found him.

We settled into a nice rhythm together for a good 20 minutes or so.

There is something that you need to learn  that will make your life much much easier on the swim.

I can't go into detail about what that is without giving it away but lets just say the guy eventually stopped swimming.

I said to him 'why did you stop I was enjoying that'

He laughed and replied 'I know, that is exactly why I stopped'

I continued looking for my next victim and noticed a guy swimming front crawl with his goggles over his head instead of over his eyes.

'What are you doing I asked'

'What do you mean' he replied.

'Your goggles are on your head?' I said

'Oh I prefer it like this' he replied?????

I thought I was hallucinating but no, this definitely happened.

As you make your way down the home straight you can hear the music pumping and the dj talking, this is the best feeling in the world ever!

I gets out to see the watch displaying 45 minutes so bang on plan.

You take a short walk round to start lap 2 and this section is packed with supporters looking out for their loved ones.

I started screaming 'Coooomeee Onnnnn' 'Easy' and 'Again' at them and they responded with a mix of cheers, whoops, laughter and looking at me as if I needed locking up.

Roar kids, I want you to roar! Roar back at me!!

Lap 2 with my confidence sky high - 'Piece of piss this' I thought to myself.

This time I was going to make a bee line for the buoys and swim as straight as possible.

Still plenty of room with everyone nicely spread out but then all of a sudden 'whack' someone smashed me full in the face and nearly took my googles clean off.

Fuk! Millwall are here I thought to myself but thankfuly it wasn't a marauding mob just a random loose cannon.

It doesn't hurt you must understand, it would have hurt his hand a darn site more than it hurt me, its more the fear of losing the goggles that I was worried about, but they were sandwiched inbetween 2 hats so they were going no-where - thanks to Sam for that one!.

Further round and I got a bit frustrated with a couple of swimmers swimming a bit erratically in front, I tried to overtake but it was difficult to get past them,  either relax or get out the fookin way please!

I spent the rest of the lap a bit bored to be honest, just kinda doing my own thing.

I amused myself by saying 'areeet cocker?' to the guys in the kayaks as I passed them, I often do this at events, I love seeing the expression on their face, I can tell that hardly anyone does it!

Just before the turn for home one shouted back at me "1:25" which I took to mean I was on for a 1:25 swim - cheers dude I'll take that all day long.

Beng able to see the finish arch is just the best feeling ever but it felt like it took ages to 'wind it in'

Crossed the timing mat with 1:30 on the watch, nearly an hour inside the cut-off.

Now I stressed to the max about that swim before the race.

Stressed to the max.

Pennington Flash is about a 40 minute drive from my house and you can go down there to practice open water swimming a couple of times a week at the organised swim sessions at leigh sailing club.

Now when I say 'organised swim session' - pay a fiver and get in on your own with a couple of safety kayaks  would be the more accurate description.

I will never forget the first time I went down there last year - I lasted about 60 seconds in the water and hated every single second, despite being a competent mile pool swimmer at the time.

I hated the flash from day 1 and it has had a hold over me ever since.

The size of it, the depth of it, the colour of it (everything is grey) I always found it intimidating, there is something eerie about the place that I simply don't like.

However I kept going down there week in week out to battle my demons with it.

But let me tell you something.

The Ironman swim is a million times easier on race day than it is swimming in the flash on your own in training....

Yes - one million times easier!

Why?

It's in my book.......

**T1 : Race Plan 15 Mins : Actual time : 12 Mins**

I wont bore you with a report about T1 - after celebrating with the crowd I got changed into bike gear...simples.

I spent 12 minutes in there but I don't give a shit, it was my reward for my hard work in the flash plus I had allowed 15 so well within plan.

**Bike - 14 Mile pre loop penny flash round to Babylon Lane**

**Race Plan : 1 Hour**

**Actual Time : 53 Minutes**

First off pleased to report there were no issues with stray drinks bottles on the escape road from Penny flash, the odd one or two but nothing like I was expecting.

Either Ironman were all over this or athletes took heed of the great iron rookie (lol)

The bike was feeling good, I'd had a good week and a bit 'cycle free' and the legs were feeling strong.

The first 14 miles were fairly un-interesting really except for the fact that nearly ever other person that came past me shouted my name (it was printed on my top) or said they followed my blog, some even calling me a legend!

The thing was it wasn't just fellow first timers that were saying it, many of the legendary Ironmen were saying it too!

I cant begin to tell you how this made me feel.

The other thing I noticed was that already quite a few fellow athletes had suffered punctures or tec issues and I saw many a bike upside down by the side of the road.

I didn't half feel sorry for these poor people - tec issues so early on into the bike would be my worst nightmare.

I always said if I was going to fail I wanted it to be because of a physical failure on my part not a mechanical one and prayed that the iron gods would be smiling down on me throughout the circuit.

This section was taking me an hour in training and if I remember right I came in around 53 minutes despite taking it relatively easy so I was very pleased about this.

**Lap 1 47 Mile IMUK loop from Babylon Lane :**

**Race Plan 3:30**

**Actual Time : 2:50**

It was ace to get onto the main loop and get my first taste of the fantastic crowds on Babylon Lane, we have all seen the wonderful photographs, but now it was time to experience them in real life.

As always, the guys from COLT (Lancaster Tri) were amazing, cheering every single one of the athletes, not just their own.

I got a huge cheer and loads of  high 5's which I absolutely adored.

When you have ridden Babylon lane on your own over a hundred times like I have with your only supporter being Liz of Grubbers sweets, to have crowds like this roaring you on is just the most exhillarating experience in the world and worth the Ironman entry fee tenfold.

On to sheephouse and more athletes were catching me up and saying hello including Laura (Lara) who was making me laugh keep shouting my name at the top of her voice. The lads from

Rochdale Tri doing there bit to warm us up nicely before the sheephouse climb which was very much appreciated.

I took it slow over Sheephouse, once you got over the other side there were excellent crowds waiting for you outside the Black Dog pub so I gave them what they wanted by charging up the hill shouting 'EASY!' at them and once again they erupted.

Wonka, one of the local lads had come stomping past me on Sheephouse earlier and took the mick - he was shouting 'come on cocker' at me (I called him cocker once on FB and he didn't like it) but I got him on the other side as we made our descent down towards Abbey Village - 'Come on then Cocker' I shouted back at him as I freewheeled past and I could tell he was pissed off lol. - Banter like this keeps you going, it really does.

More fantastic crowds once you got over to Wheelton at the Houghton Arms (Team Foggaty , Blackburn Road Runners, Tri Preston, Team MGPT ) and again give them what they want and they will treat you like a legend.

These crowds, honestly.

The only thing I can describe it to is like being a footballer and scoring a goal so the crowd start gong mad just for you, well imagine that but every 20 minutes!!

This magnificent support powered me round and by the time I got to Buckshaw village I was well ahead of time.

I really appreciated the closed roads and riding with so many other kindered spirits.

I dropped down onto my aero bars and started to put my foot down, my bike was making that amazing noise, like a whirling, - u know the one I mean.

At Buckshaw one girl nearly took me clean out when she pulled out without looking but thankfully I managed to swerve just in time and no harm was done.

Fellow athletes continued to fall foul of the tec issues and I continued to pray to the iron gods.

I pushed the first loop way to hard, 'If Ironman are going to close the roads for me the least I can do is go for it in return' I thought to myself.

When the adrenaline is pumping, the roads are closed and everyone is shouting for you it is very difficult to resist, very difficult and you start to dream.

Over to Hunters Hill and I was really looking forward to this as I knew there would be loads of brilliant support on there for the 'Hubsters Hill Party'.

Not only that but I was sure tri Preston would be waiting outside the Rigbye Arms once you got to the top.

They didn't disappoint.

Please enter IMUK to experience these sensations.

I got high 5'd all the way up Hunters Hill by Scouse tim, Team Pie, St Helens Tri, Warrington Tri and the Endurance store race team!.

Once I got to Rigbye arms at the top I roared 'COME ONNNN!!!' as loud as I could at the tri preston lot and this was like chucking a grenade as the place exploded.

A couple of the lads that were behind me on the bike at the time caught me up shortly after and said it was the most amazing noise they had ever experienced.

Turns out Tri Preston had been joined by the red and black of invictus tri Wigan which was a bit like having the toon army and the tartan army in the same place at the same time.

I rode the adrenaline wave for the rest of the loop  high as a kite and was delighted to end the first lap with the clock showing 2:50 - 40 minutes ahead of plan.

This put me 1:30 ahead of the bike cut off when I planned to be only 45 minutes ahead.

I was over the moon.

The other highlight of this first loop was seeing a couple of the pro's in action.

One of them showed us all how it is done up Hunters Hill, zig zaging inbetween the stragglers without muttering a single curse.

The other further on, a huge guy dressed all in black I could hear coming a mile off, the noise, it was like a pack of ten were coming behind me but it was just him, I made sure I shifted out of his way pronto!

Also I swear one of the female pros turned back and waved at me near the end of lap 1 then again maybe I really was hallucinating this time.

## 47 Mile IMUK Loop Lap 2

**Race Plan : 3:30**

**Actual Time : 3:10**

Whilst I had pushed the bike way too hard on lap 1, I now had well over 4  hours to complete lap 2 to stay inside the cut off.

Got to be honest, the feeling I got by being 'ahead' of time helped me a lot.

I knew I could now coast round and still be well within plan.

I made the decision to take it easy this second lap and just enjoy it.

I had ace banter with a bunch of blokes behind me on Babylon who pointed out that my water bottle was leaking and one of the lads said 'Thank fuk for that, I thought he was having a piss'.....

I nearly fell of my bike I was laughing that much.

Many many athletes were still callin my name and wishing me well as they passed.

The crowds were once again absolutely superb in all the places that I mentioned above but I was reminded this week on FB of other people.

Like the little old Indian lady that was stood outide her house on lap 1 clapping all the athletes and was still there in the exact same spot on lap 2.

Or the lovely old man with the huge beard at the top of Babylon with the biggest smile on his face as he waved at you - people like this, they make you cry.

Despite the fact that I was meant to be taking it easy I was travelling well on lap 2 although I thought my thighs were going to cramp up at times towards the end - this is something I haven't experienced before but I put it down to all the adrenaline and 2 only hours sleep!

Just before I got to hunters I had a bit of a wobble when my chain stopped turning - please god no - but thankfully all that had happened was my drinks bottle had slipped down - watch this with the course issued bottles, I found they didn't fit in my drinks cage - not complaining, not at all - just saying (By the way the drinks and food stations were excellent as you would expect)

Team Pie and their mates got me up Hunters second time round but when I got to the Rigbye arms at the top the most wonderful thing was waiting.....

Tri Preston had joined with invictus to make a big Mexican wave arch for you to ride under as the crowd roared their approval which was just the best sensation in the world ever.

This experience was so magical I almost turned round so I could ride through it again.

I ended lap 2 buzzing on 3:10 ish.

I make that a total double loop time of 6 hours versus a plan of 7 and more importantly I absolutely smashed the bike cut offs.

Can I just say thank you to all the wonderful supporters on that bike circuit, all the tri clubs in particular, the way you were with me today when I am not even a member of your club was absolutely brilliant and you made my race, you really did.

I was relieved to have ended the 2 loops without any tec issues whatsoever save a split drinks bottle.

I started to make my way over to the Reebok to start the run - this final bit of the bike took longer than expected, 20 odd minutes if I remember right, not that it mattered, I was celebrating the whole way.

## T2 Plan 15 Minutes : Actual : 16 Minutes

I knew if I made T2 the sacred medal was going to be mine.

I had done loads of partying on the bike as I cruised round to T2 but upon arrival I felt horrible, I had been high as a kite from all the supporters but now I was coming down, coming down fast!

It felt a bit like I was just getting in from an all nite rave, the best all night rave of my life, but instead of curling up and going to sleep, I now had to run a mara.

I chilled for a bit in T2 and sorted myself out, thinking about the amazing crowds that were waiting for us in Bolton town centre kept me going.

## Run : 26.2 Miles!

OMG...

You don't know what a marathon is until you try and do one up and down chorley new road after all that let me tell you.

I had written about how easy I had found my chorley new road runs in training.

How the legendary Ironmen that had actually done this as part of their Ironman didn't rip me to pieces I will never know.

Trying to run up Chorley new Road from Bolton Town centre feels like trying to run up a 20ft brick wall on lap 1, never mind lap 3.

But put that to one side for a second.

I learnt things about this run on race day....

Many things.....

Yes it is a marathon, but it is nothing like what you imagine.

It's not what you think it is....

Let me tell you something.

IMUK is going to stay in Bolton town centre for the next 5 years.

They are very unlikely to change the run route.

Once you learn, understand and apply what I tell you in my book, you will realise that the Ironman medal can easily be yours too if you want it.

Wonderful thing hindsight isn't it?

Congratulations, you get to benefit from it....

Aside from that, Many other things get you through the run....

The amazing volunteers on the aid stations - one lady outside Bolton school handing out drinks was literally dancing every time I saw her - stuff like this is magical....

Seeing my brother, seeing my family, seeing Crooky, Sam, Mel, Paul Fisher and countless others and giving them hugs as we crossed on the run.

Hearing numerous other athletes shouting my name as they passed.

Seeing the turtle doing the funky disco on chorley street hill.

I seemed to have acquired little pockets of supporters dotted all around the town centre that would go mad when I ran past them shouting my name - Carol Spoor and her crew in particular who were just ace for me - I don't even know these people yet their support for me was unbelievable!

Steve cook and his gang who sadly did not make the cut offs himself but still came into the town centre to  cheer me and his other favourites on.

Then there was big G, every time I turned the corner to make my way onto Le-mans crescent he would introduce me at the top of his voice every single lap - he was stood there with all his family  with a huge smile on his face,  he was paying me back for the time I went down to Bolton Park run to give him a high 5 after he posted on twitter that a runner left him high and dry when he was stewarding there once.

Boy did Big G and his family pay me back big time!!

But my greatest memory of all has to be this,

I had been having amazing banter with all the lads stood drinking outside both the lion of Vienna pubs and retreat on Chorley New Road.

It all started when one of them spotted my Bolton Wanderers badge on my Tri-Suit and he shouted 'White Army' at me so I shouted it back.

That was it.

From then on every time I passed those pubs they were looking out for me and they would all start singing 'White Army!' at me with me singing it back to them as I ran past.

On my last run out of the town centre some of the supporters from retreat invaded the course, put their arms around me and began to dance, sing and run with me up Chorley New Road.

But that wasn't all…For my final lap I had a surprise for them.

When my dad died he left me a Bolton Wanderers flag,

I had a vision of running onto the finish boulevard waving that flag in order to feel that somehow my dad was with me as I completed my amazing journey.

The flag was waiting for me at the Top of Chorley New Road on my final lap.

You can imagine what happened when I ran past those pubs for the final time waving the flag with the 3 bands on my wrist.

The places went mental.

Eurphoria!…….

Right There….

Total euphoria!

I had done it…

I had done what I set out to do all along.

I had proved that anything is possible with hours to spare (14:49)

But way more important than that….

I had the time of my life as I did it cocker….

**The Interviews**

Whilst I was training for IMUK I began to write a weekly blog about my adventures in training.

During this time I began to meet even more inspirational Ironmen, separate to the ones I had already met and upon which this book was originally written.

I found their stories fascinating, so included them in my blog.

These 'interviews' proved extremely popular.

Their appearance in these pages is not an endorsement of my work, rather an agreement to feature in the hope that their story will further inspire, motivate and help you in your quest, sharing their many tips along the way.

**The Ironing Mum that turned into an Ironman!**

I figured it was about time I ran a feature on an inspirational female!

Throughout my journey, many people have often said things to me like 'I would love to be able to train for an Ironman, but I have got kids so there is just no way'

Or 'I would love to be able to train for an Ironman, but I just don't have the time'

Or 'I would love to be able to train for an Ironman but......(Insert random excuse here)..

So how about we run an interview with amazing lady that will be lining up at IMUK for the 4th time this year whilst single handidly bringing up 3 kids?

Not only that but one of those children has special needs.

Please allow me to introduce Sam, aka @ironingmumtakesonironman on facebook!!

She might only be 4'10 but what she lacks in height she more than makes up for in personality as you will soon find out!

**So Sam 4th Time for you at Bolton this year - where did it all start?**

I only recently got into fitness, these last few years or so - it was the Ironman that got me into it.

I used to take the kids to go and watch it as it comes near to my house - I was in awe of all the Ironmen, I found them really motivational - they inspired me to start running!

**So you went down the running route first?**

Yes I started running round our estate at first, then did a little bit more and more like you do and ended up entering a half marathon! - I loved it!

**Then what?**

I did a couple more half's then set my sights on the big one, the mara

**How did that go?**

Yes I managed to do it and I was well chuffed.

**So What got you into triathlon then?**

After Ironman inspired me to take up running, I returned to watch IMUK the next year with the marathon under my belt, I had done a little bit on the turbo and I thought to myself, I can run, I can do a bit on the bike, the only thing I cant do is swim.....

But I can learn!

As soon as the race was over I thought fuk it i'm signing up and registered for IMUK as soon as it opened the next day!

**So Ironman was your first triathlon?**

No I entered a local sprint distance as part of my training for it

**How did you find learning to swim?**

I joined the local leisure centre and taught myself how to swim, the more I practiced, the more confident I got.

**How did you find the transition from pool to open water?**

I hated it!

I will never forget the first time I went to pennington flash - I was in the water for an hour and a half and I swam for about 12 seconds! (see pic)

I sat by the side and had a little cry and thought to myself 'what am I doing?'

**How did you get over that?**

I kept at it! (Sam is such a trooper)

They did some lessons down at 3 sisters so I signed up to those and slowly but surely I got better!

**Did you follow a training plan for IMUK?**

Yes I followed a very well known plan but adapted it to suit my needs

**How the hell did you manage to fit in all the training as a single mum with three kids and one with special needs?**

The turbo and the treadmill became my best friends.

Once I had seen to the kids and put them to bed that is when I would start my training, on the turbo downstairs late at night. (how amazing is this lady?)

Either that or I would set an early alarm and get on the treadmill before they got up.

I would try to get out onto the course when I could but the vast majority was done indoors, If you want something badly enough, you will find a way.

**What was your first Ironman like?**

Amazing, just the best feeling ever, you cant bottle that buzz, when I did my first one there was only about 10% women, you can imagine what the women in the crowd were like with me!

**What did you like most about IMUK?**

The spectators, the atmosphere, everyone shouting your name, its just electric

**Why do you keep coming back every year?**

Once you run down Chorley new road on race day you will understand why I keep coming back

As soon as I finish one I sign up for the following year straight away, its the atmosphere, once you experience it you want it again and again.

I know a lot more people now (fellow competitors)  so that is great too - we all shout for eachother - its amazing

I also like being fit and healthy and the general way of life the Ironman demands. (Sam showed me a picture of her before she started doing Ironman and she now looks like a completely different person!)

But got to be honest I have never really 'gone for it' I am far too busy chatting and having the time of my life!

I'll never forget my first one, many people around me were struggling, being wrapped in silver blankets and all that, but I felt totally fine!

Part of me feels like I have cheated, like I should really go for it and see what pain feels like, I keep saying i'm going to see what I am capable of -  maybe I will this time!

## Which race was you most proud of?

Probably my first, but last year I had a lot of stuff going on so that too.

## How have you got on with Injuries?

I used to get injured but now not as much, I have learnt to listen to my body and I know when I am pushing it too hard

## What is the Biggest thing u have learnt on your journey?

In your head you have a perception of what an Ironman would look like, but It doesn't matter what shape or size you are, Ironman is possible

You put your own barriers up and make your own excuses - only you can take them down.

## Funniest thing you have seen on your journey?

I was so paranoid about the cut off times first time round that I wrote them on my arms but after the swim they had rubbed off!! arrrgghhh!!!

## What do you know now that you wish you knew before your first Ironman?

I was stressed to the max about everything and its easy to say it but try not to be, If you have put the training in everything will be OK, try to relax, try to enjoy it!

Ironman is what you make of it

Its addictive!

## What are your Top Tips for first timers?

If you have invested a year of your life training for it you have got to enjoy race day

Don't put any pressure on yourself

Have Fun!

If the crowd can see you enjoying yourself they will give you everything

Don't get down because there aren't many supporters on the first 10km of the run - don't worry they are all waiting for you once you get onto the main lap circuit!

Bolton school is where they give the bands out on the way back up chorley new road - dont panic! you haven't missed them! (first one about 15km into the run)

Get the fuel down

Two hats for swim with your goggles sandwiched inbetween and they are going nowhere

Its about managing your time to get your training in

If its something that you want you will find a way

If you miss some training days its not the end of the world

It doesn't matter what shape or size you are its possible

Compete is pressure

The special needs bag is a god send - use it but prepared to lose it - you don't get any of that stuff back at the end of the race get out onto the loop

Fate plays a part on race day

don't worry about people overtaking

But most of all ENJOY YOURSELF!

As you can see from the above, Sam is a truly amazing, inspirational person and I found her story fascinating.

You wont find anyone that goes to IMUK intent on having a bloody good time and enjoying every single second of it more than Sam. (well apart from Iron Rookie □)

But there is a fascinating twist to her tale.

Sam told me that part of her feels like she didn't deserve the medal.

What do you mean? I asked.

"When you see people all around you struggling, looking like they are going to collapse having given it their absolute all yet you feel totally fine, you feel cheated."

"Part of me wants to feel like they did, but the truth is, I haven't."

There it is again!

Compete or Complete!

We then spent ages talking about this  subject as I too find myself torn in this regard!

We eventually came to the conclusion that people should never get confused between 'not trying hard enough' and 'having a fantastic race strategy' as there is a huge difference between the two and learning how to feel strong throughout the toughest one day endurance event in the world is something that should be celebrated.

I am sure many people will draw inspiration from this amazing lady.

Having found myself at a bit of a crossroads recently Sam has certainly helped me hit the nail square on the head with defining who I am, what I am about and what I have been trying to do all along!.....

But more on that very soon!

You can follow sams excellent blog on facebook @ironingmumtakesonironman

## The Day I Cycled the IMUK loop With 7 Times an Ironman 'Crooky'!

So, 14 weeks into my amazing journey, a most magical thing happened.

7 times Ironman (4 x Bolton) and local IMUK legend 'Crooky' very kindly agreed to cycle the 47 Mile IMUK loop with me.

This sent me into dreamland!

Getting to ride the entire loop with someone like this and interview them at the same time was definitely one of the highlights of my amazing journey so far!

I should point out that me and 'Crooky' didn't really know eachother before today, but I hope that I will be seeing him again many times on my journey, you will soon discover why!

I should also point out that Crooky has an issue with me calling him a 'legend' and I quote "I am just a normal bloke with a little too much time on his hands that likes to exercise a bit"

Likes to Exercise a bit?

The man has already completed 7 full Ironman triathlons and has his eye on doing 12 for goodness sake!!!

The fact that he plays it down in such a humble way makes him even more of a legend as far as this first timer is concerned!!

At the end of the day, for me, when someone like Crooky speaks.....

I listen!!!!

Here is how it went!

Given recent 100 mile 'grinds' I had been planning to take full advantage of the sunny weather this weekend  by treating myself to  a single loop on Saturday afternoon and was really looking forward to it.

But then I got a message from Crooky late on Friday night.

'Doing the loop tomorrow 7:30am start if you are about'

I had been pestering him to do this with me for a while and finally, here was my chance.

It took me about 10 seconds to abandon my plans and snatch his hand off!

With the 'meet' arranged my attention was drawn to sorting the bike out.

My front tyre had been 'going down' inbetween rides and I decieded that it would be a good idea to change the innertube.

I wont bore you with all the details but 1 hour and 3 'dud' innertubes later the front wheel was finally good to go.

This is seriously unacceptable to the point where tyre changing training sessions are now actually inked onto my Ironman training calendar going forward.

With that out of the way I finally gets in bed for a relatively early night setting my alarm for 6am to be at the bottom of Babylon lane for a 7.30 meet.

At 2:30am I wakes up 'ping' wide awake.

I was simply unable to get back to sleep – I was more excited than what I am on a race day! – my mind was whirling with the excitement of riding the loop with a 7x finisher and all the questions I planned to ask him.

I pretty much lay awake until 5:30 in that awful state where your body is technically 'resting' as it is just lying there but your brain is working at a million miles an hour.

I arrived at our meeting point in good time and was surprised to see Crooky already there complete with his distinctive yellow and black 'pirate top'.

For those who do not know who the pirates are, they are a group of Ironmen, large in number, that go by the name 'Pirate ship of Fools', often abbreviated to PSOF and I doubt it is any coincidence that this triggers the words 'Piss Off' in the mind.

Legend has it that it all started with one guy who, whilst training for Ironman on a budget, developed his own aero bars using empty Pringles dispensers and a Smarties tube.

Then, in his small daughter's school bag, he found the pirate sticker, which sat happily on front of the now legendary 'AeroPringles'.

If, after reading that, you don't immediately want to become one, then don't worry about it…

You likely never will……..

But the pirate's website continues…

"People who take themselves too seriously or demand respect because they reckon they are 'great triathletes' soon lose interest. So we are left with a great bunch of people, with a huge can-do attitude who aren't afraid to laugh at themselves and each other in the process. That's what the Pirates are all about"

Make no mistake though, some of these Pirates have gone on to record many fantastic times at Ironman, times many a 'expert' would be more than a little envious of….

Anyhow once I got myself sorted we cracked on up Babylon lane and I started to fire the questions at Crooky:

**So How many times Have you Done the Ironman Crooky?**

7

**Wow! which ones have you done?**

IMUK Bolton four times, Wales, South Africa and Lanzarotte

**Which of those was your favourite?**

Bolton, for the atmosphere, but South Africa for the beautiful scenary

**And The Most Difficult?**

Lanzarotte- Heat, Hills everywhere  and you haven't seen wind until you have cycled in Lanzarotte!

**If you don't mind my asking, How old are you, what do you do for a living,  and are your family supportive of your Ironman adventure?**

I am 46, I work full time in solar energy, my girlfriend is very supportive of my adventures – she is even starting to get into it herself lately!

## How Did You Get Into Triathlon?

I went to watch the Ironman in Bolton town centre and I loved the amazing crowds and the fantastic atmosphere, when I saw what happened to the final finisher I thought to myself 'I want a bit of this' and signed up for the next race pretty much straight away

## Had you any prior triathlon Experience?

No

## Wow You went and did an Ironman as your first triathlon?

Yes! But don't get me wrong, I trained really hard for it!

However prior to the Ironman, I had not done a triathlon before

## I'm surprised you came out with me today given what I worte last week!

I totally understand your journey and what you are trying to do, Iron

## What training did you do for your first Ironman?

I trained for pretty much 12 months solid, my training started the day I entered the event

## Specifically what training did you do?

At that time the course was different, you had to do Sheep House Lane 3 times instead of twice and there was no Hunters, so I went out and practiced sheep House Lane almost every morning before work for three months together with regular runs and brick sessions.

## What about the swim?

When I first started I could only swim breast stroke, but this got me round the swim element fine

## That's an amzing 'tip' in itself! Any more about the swim?

Due to the rolling start it can take you up to 25/30 minutes to enter the water after the race has begun! – The pros have often already completed their first lap before I even get in!

Many people don't realise this!

## Do You Still Swim Breaststroke at events?

No, I can do front crawl now

## What would your top tip be for people that want to learn front crawl?

Learn how to use the pull buoy, it really helped me

## How did you find balancing all the training with working full Time?

I got up earlier and trained every day before I went to work and again at weekends.

If you want something badly enough you will find a way.

## Which of your Ironman races was you most proud of?

Obviosuly my first, you will never forget your first one, ever!

But I had a bad injury before another race yet still went on to complete it, so that one is right up there too.

**Talking of Injuries, Have you had many issues on that score?**

Touch wood, I have been very lucky.

But as I mentioned above, There was one time that I pushed it a bit too far on steep decent, hit a pot hole at about 35mph and came off the bike, I was so badly injured that I had to phone for an ambulance and my knee was in a right mess.

It wasn't long before the Ironman race  but I didn't let it stop me from completing it!!

In typical Ironman fashion Crooky made sure that I understood his bike was OK after the accident!

More importantly he went on to make a good recovery, but pointed to a big scar on his knee!

**Is that why they call you Crooky then!**

Yes! partly because of my Crooky Knee!

**Speaking of the Bike, You have a very nice looking one there Crooky! looks like it would be more expensive than some of the cars on this street! How much did that cost?**

You are right!

**What was your first Bike?**

I did my first Ironman on a £400 aluminium Trek and got round fine!

## Having Ridden Ironman on Both, What difference Does the expensive bike make?

Is it the bike or is it the rider? that's the million dollar question, I think its a mix of the two, heavily weighted towards the rider, as a crap athlete on a fantastic bike is still a crap athlete.

An expensive bike is the cherry on the cake, but first you have got to bake the cake.

Just on that note whenever I got a bit 'lively' and went charging off I loved the way Crooky would effortlessly come gliding past me in a way that said 'nice try but don't even think about it sunshine'

## How Are you at Sorting Punctures?

Front i'm OK but back does my head in!

Whenever I am out though I always carry at least 2 spare innertubes and a couple of bottles of Co2 Gas

## Have you ever had puncture/tec issues on race day?

Again I have been very lucky, but once my tyre went down the day before a race for no apparent reason  (how spooky  is that)

I racked my bike at transition and pumped it up fine, but when I came back the next day it had gone down again, I should have changed it, but I didn't and just pumped it back up.

Anyhow second time round sheephouse on race day and what happens? Tyre goes down.

## How Long was you by the side of the road?

I don't know exactly but probably a good 20 minutes, you try not to panic and stay calm but that is easier said than done when the clock is ticking and all the other athletes are whizzing past! even for me!!

I think you are right when you say you need to practice punctures as part of your training!

**Are you a member of any Tri or Running Club?**

Other than the Pirates, No, I have thought about it but I would prefer to do my own routes on a day/time to suit me

**Tell me more about the Pirates**

The Pirates are a group of Ironmen that subscribe to the mindset you talk about above (aeropringles, attitude, etc) some do train together but mostly we train alone (due largely to the fact that we live all over the place) we interact online and then 'come together' to race certain events throughout the year, there are often large numbers of pirate supporters in the crowd that go mad when they see the kit.

When I first went along they were very welcoming to me and we had such a laugh, it was ace!

**Going back to Bolton, what do you love most about this event?**

Without doubt the atmosphere from the thousands of spectators.

They are all superb but you will see certain ones that really stand out from the rest – case in point There is one lady who completes the Ironman herself and then goes and stands in the middle of the run course and shouts encouragement at every single athlete that runs past, she has done that every year since goodness knows when, look out for her. (OMG!)

## Lovin That! Any other tips specific for Bolton?

When you hit the amazing crowds on Hunters Hill you will feel a rush of energy but resist the urge to get out of the saddle and go stomping up it, many a time I have done likewise then got to the top and thought 'why the fuk did I just do that?'

## Do the Pros Ever Talk to you as they come past?

You will hear the other athletes shouting for Lucy (gossage) as she passes them and if you do likewise she will always smile at you and say thank you, every time.  (Can I just say I had tears in my eyes writing that!)

## What Is the funniest thing you have ever seen on your journey?

In South Africa a couple of guys came stomping past me on the bike dressed as a cow (and yes they were racing in the event!)

## Looking Back on your journey is there anything you would change?

I would have liked to have trained more for some of the my more recent events

## I have heard talk about 'post ironman blues', have you had any experience of this?

Not really because as soon as I finish an event I sign up for another!

## So are there Any 'Secrets' that you would be prepared to share with me?!

Crooky went on to confirm quite a few things that I had already been told by the Ironmen, which was very re-assuring! but he added a couple more, one of which I had partly heard of, the other I definitely had not, and he kindly gave me permission to add these to my book.

**What do you know now that you wish you would have known Before your first Ironman?**

That everything is going to be alright

**What Top Tips Would you Give to Other 1st timers Crooky?**

1. Carry a mobile phone with you at all times during your training, you never know when you might need it
2. It can take ages to enter the water after the race has started due to the rolling start, (sometimes 20 min plus) bear this in mind with your plans
3. Keep your transition simple, the amount of people I see with huge transition bags the size of a suitcase and 80% of the stuff in there they really do not need
4. Trust Your Training – if you have trained hard for it you will be fine, do not worry about anything on race day, you will worry though  (even I still do) but if you have trained properly, everything will be alright, trust in your training
5. Enjoy every second and don't forget to smile the whole way round (Whenever I ask an Ironman this question this is the one that comes up every single time)
6. **The guy who finishes in 10 hours is called an Ironman, so is the guy who finishes in 16:59**
7. Time passes fast, 6 months is nothing, maximise every second

**Thanks! They Are SUPERB! What's Next for you then?**

I am doing Bolton, Italy and Lanzarotte again this year

## 3 More in 2017! What is your motivation to keep entering Ironman events?

I am never going to win, but after I experienced the amazing atmosphere at my first ever one I instantly wanted to do it again!  after that my girlfriend  is from South Africa so I thought we could kill two birds with one stone, combine another Ironman with a holiday like….

But then I got wind of the Kona legacy…

### The Kona Legacy? What's that?

If you complete 12 Ironman events you can apply to enter the Kona Legacy, it is like a lottery where our name goes into a hat and if you are successful you get to race at Kona, that is my dream.

### That's amazing Crooky! Good Luck With That! My goodness we are nearly at the end of the loop already! One last tip?

"The biggest tip of the lot, On your final lap of the run, say thank you to all those people out on the course, all the volunteers, the marshalls, the event crew, the people on the feed stations,  all the supporters….

They have been on their feet all day……

### For you…..

Make sure you say thank you to every single one of them as you pass".

With that 'lump in the throater' one of the most amazing IMUK loops of my life drew to a close.

I can't finish without telling you one other thing…

See This Picture?

Some other cyclists from Preston kindly took that for us outside the legendary Rigbye Arms at the top of Hunters Hill, not before I had re-arranged the 'Ironman' sign mind!

It was hidden from view by a big wagon and the lads watched open mouthed as I went and fetched it!

We had a laugh with them, exchanged the usual pleasantries and they asked me about my jacket before quickly boasting 'I did IMUK for the first time last year' and I did the 'Lakesman' and 'I did this, I did that'....

I looked at Crooky and was amazed at how he just sat there listening to them go on without uttering a single word...

When they finally got it all out of their system I looked again at Crooky with a 'Go on then!  TELL EM!!!' Expression but he just continued to sit there in silence with a big smile on his face.

I am not having a go lads, I enjoyed the conversation,.

But I thought this summed up beautifully the quality of guy we are dealing with here! (as if that wasn't evident already!)

I was very aware as we went round of constantly being 'in the moment' and  that I was creating memories today that will last a lifetime.

A million thanks to Crooky for taking the time out to do this, it means the world to me and I feel certain many a first timer will benefit form his words in the months and years to come!

But what was our time for the loop I hear you all cry?

Really?

Have you not learnt anything at all here, lol?

Seen as you ask the question…..

Thanks to Crooky, I recorded my best time of 2017!…..

You can follow crooky's amazing Kona adventrure on his twitter feed @crookybwfc

## My IMUK Run With 56 x Marathon 1 x Ultra & 7 x 'Iron' Triathlete 'Damo'

My Goodness! What is happening to me?!

Remember always that I am just an Ironman first timer who is absolutely buzzing to be a part of the whole thing and trying to do my bit to help smooth the way for other first timers in the future by sharing my experiences as I train....

Remember also where my journey started, very over-weight, very unfit, couldn't swim more than a single length front crawl, not ridden a bike for over 15 years, unable to run any more than 10 yards without wanting to stop...

Yet on the back of my ride with the legend that doesn't like to be called a legend 'Crooky' I unbelievably came into contact with 56 x Marathon Runner, 1x 50km Ultra Runner and 7 x Iron Triathlete 'Damo'.

'Damo' told me that he knew the IMUK run course very well and I have been wanting to practice this for a while now as I was unsure of the route.

When 'Damo' altruistically (great word that isn't it?) offered to take me round, I immediately snatached his hand off!

We had arranged to meet at 8am Good Friday morning at the Bee Hive Pub on the IMUK run course.

It was freezing cold and absolutely chucking it down (as it always is in Bolton).

I arrived at 2 minutes to 8 fully expecting to find 'Damo' sat in his car with the heater on waiting for me to arrive.

As I looked around the car park all of the cars appeared to be empty.

I sat waiting in the comfort of my own car and after about 5 minutes became convinced that he had 'stood me up'.

I went on a mission to check there wasn't another car park somewhere else and was absolutely astonished to find shorts and T-shirt clad 'Damo' warming up  in front of the Bee Hive Pub in the torrential rain!

Don't know about you but I sense another 'legend' coming on here!!!

We set off for a 10k run that ended up turning into almost 20k!

It was probably one of the best runs of my life....

Here is how the 'runterview' went!

### So Damo, 56 Marathons, 1 Ultra and 7 x Iron Distance triathlons! Where did it all Start?

Believe it or not at school I was hopeless at running, I would always come last at everything as I was very overweight and very unfit.

### What Prompted you to change?

When I got older I made the decision to 'get fit' and used running to do it

### That's amazing! tell me more

I signed up for a 10k race and used that as my motivation to train, conquering that first 10k felt amazing even though it fet like a marathon to me at the time!

**And where did your journey go from there?**

I stayed at the 10k level for a bit, had some fun with it but then like everyone else began to look towards the half and then eventually the full marathon

**Which was your first full marathon?**

Fleetwood in 2010

**And how many marathons have you completed so far?**

56, number 57 will be in a few weeks!

**Wow!**

**Which one was your favourite?**

It's a top 3 rather than a top one!

Liver Bird Double which takes place on NYE/NYD it's a small but really friendly race

Bolton Hill is incredible and i'm glad it's back this year

And Windermere because you are running round the most beautiful part of the UK

**And the Toughest?**

Hell of a Hill. It's organised locally and takes you up Rivington Pike an outrageous number of times!

Despite it being the toughest of races, it's also one of my favourites and I make sure I'm signed up for it every year!

You can do it five days in a row but I can't get the time off school for that unfortunately!

**What was your first mara time?**

4:30 at Fleetwood in 2010

**And which One did you PB?**

Gin Pit in 2015 where my time was 3:14

**How did you get your time down so much?**

I found that the more I ran the better I got at it, due largey to the fact that you learn something each time and therefore become more intelligent with your training.

Bear in mind the PB came 5 years and countless more marathons after my first ever one!

**What Tips would you give to Marathon First Timers?**

Enjoy yourself, relax, don't worry about time for your first one, train properly, trust in your training and sign up for another asap!

**What is your motivation to keep entering so many marathons?**

I love running, (it was abundantly obvious to me that Damo absolutely loves running no matter what the weather)

I want to get into the 100 marathon club (there is a special club for people that can prove they have entered 100+ maras!!)

I also do a bit for my favourite charity, the RNLI https://rnli.org/what-we-do

Plus I like visiting new places and combining a marathon at the same time

## How Did You Hear about the 100 Marathon Club?

I saw someone wearing one of the T-shirts at an event and that was it! I had found my next challenge!

## That's Ace that Damo, so what got you into triathlon?

After I had done a fair few marathons I went to watch the Ironman in Bolton Town centre, after experiencing the amazing atmosphere as a spectator, I wanted to experience it as a competitor so I signed up for the next race pretty much straight away

## How Many 'Iron' Distance Triathlons Have You Completed Damo'?

7

## Wow! Which Ones Where they?

Ironman® Bolton 3 Times, Ironman® Copenhagen, Challenge Roth, Challenge Almere & Outlaw

(The last 3 are not Ironman® branded events but they are the same 'iron' distance, 2.4 mile swim, 112 mile bike, 26.2 mile run)

## Which One Was your Favourite?

Without Doubt Challenge Roth, for me it's the best triathlon in the World

## What makes you say that? (Sulking because he didn't say Bolton)

Just everything about it, the scenary is amazing, the bike course is smooth like a billiard table (!?! Count me in!!)
The crowds are 7 or 8 deep on the hills like they are in the tour

de france! One of the hills alone has about 20,000 people on it cheering you on!

The run course is great and very well supported,  its a tiny little village in the middle of no-where set in the most beautiful countryside yet hundreds of thousands of spectators come from all over the world to see the athletes on Race Day!!!

Bolton is great though too! - do Both!

## And The Most difficult?

Again challenge Roth for no other reason than the heat! yes it was absolutely my favourite but it was 30 degrees out there and I ain't used to training/racing in that sort of heat - we don't get many days like that round here!

## Was Ironman Bolton your first triathlon?

It was my first Ironman but it wasn't my first triathlon, I completed a local sprint and Olympic distance first as part of my 12 month Ironman plan

## What training did you do?

After I had entered Bolton I sat down and worked out a 12 month plan on how I would get there, I would have killed for something like what you are doing at the time but I had to work it all out myself!

## What did you find the most difficult?

I knew I had the running under my belt but putting all 3 together was a totally different proposition!

## How did you find the swim?

I could swim front crawl, albeit badly, but I invested in a swimming coach early on and it was one of the best things I ever did

## What would your top tips be to people who are anxious about the swim element

Hire a Swim coach!

## Was your first triathlon Pool based?

Yes

## How did you find the transition from Pool to open water

I'll never forget my first open water swim in Salford Quays, I got cramp quite early on and finished the rest of the swim using only my arms!

Like anything though it gets easier the more you practice

## What would your top tips be to anyone nervous about the Open Water Swim element

Practice, hire a coach

## What bike did you do your first triathlon on?

a £900 boardman from Halfords and that got me round fine

## What bike have you got now?

A £3k Giant

**Having ridden the Ironman on both, what difference does the more expensive bike make?**

*I saw this question on your interview with Crooky and think its an excellent one*

*All I would say to you is this*

*Have you ever heard of Chrissie Wellington?*

In answer to Damo's question I only recently came across this amazing lady so for the benefit of those that haven't she started out in triathlon with a £300  third hand Peugeot road bike and went on to become Ironman world champion 4 times and is now involved with grass roots fitness at ParkRun.

Pretty amazing lady right?

You ain't heard the half if it....

This is what she said about becoming Ironman world champion for the first time...

'To win the race was something that hadn't crossed my mind, so to find myself in the lead at about 120km on the bike, to cross the line in first place and be crowned World Ironman Champion was amazing, surprising and incredibly overwhelming. **And more importantly to stand there until midnight watching people achieve their dreams is a memory that will never fade and one which I will treasure forever.**'

I purposely highlighted the last bit because If that doesn't bring a tear to your eye then sorry, nothing ever will!

When I pushed Damo to tell me what his own experience of the more expensive bike was he very much echoed Crooky's comments when he said that *'the bike is the 'icing on the cake' but first you have got to 'bake the cake.'*

When I asked him if he would swap back to the cheaper bike he said *'I would like to think that I am a better athlete now than what I was then'*

It was clear that the focus should be on becoming a better athlete and not on getting a 'better bike'

## How Are you at Punctures?

Pretty Good

## How Long Does it take you to change a tyre/innertube

About 5 Minutes!

## Have You ever had any puncture tec/issues on Race Day

Touch wood no, but there was this one time that I didn't prepare properly for the race and 20km into the bike something didn't feel right.

I said to myself 'if there isn't something wrong with the bike I am withdrawing from the race'

Turns out I had not put my back wheel on propely so rode the first 20km with the  brake rubbing against the rim of the wheel!!

You can not be too prepared for your first  Ironman race, give yourself plenty of time, check, check again then double check everything before you even get to transition.

**If, on Race day, you saw another competitor broken down with a puncture at the side of the road, would you stop to help?**

That is something you should be able to do on your own and need to practice if you can't!

But I'll slow down and ask a person if they are alright/need help. If they said they needed it, I'd like to think I'd help!

**How have you got on With Injuries?**

Again touch wood, I have been very lucky in this regard.

I have my fair share of niggles and went over on my ankle at a run not long ago which still isn't 100% but other than that I have been very fortunate

**Are your family supportive of your Iron/Marathon Adventures?**

Yes, my girlfriend is very supportive of my adventures, she is very independent and has her own hobbies friends and interests that keep her entertained whilst I train

I try to combine as many holidays and events as possible so we can kill two birds with one stone so to speak

But I am not going to lie, it can be tough, especially at this time of year when the trainining starts to ramp up.

**How do you manage to balance working full time with training for an Iron Distance Triathlon?**

Again, its tough

I am lucky because I work relatively close to where I live so I can be out  within 10 minutes of finishing work but there are all the usual early morning starts and weekend training sessions but you have got to love training for it otherwise what's the point?

## Are you a member of any Triathlon/running club

'For many years I was not, one of the biggest things I have learnt about my training is not to become too fixated with a certain 'plan' or tying myself to doing certain things on certain days.

If Saturday is meant to be my long bike day for example and I take one look out of the window and it's freezing cold with driving rain then guess what?

I ain't getting on the bike! - i'll go for a run instead.'

What I loved about Damo was his enthusiasm for running, he had this magical way of turning bad weather into a positive, "*if the weather is poor on bike day then great! i'll go for a run*!"

Damo continued....

'I do what I fancy when I feel like it, If I feel like speed work i'll do that, if i'm in the mood for a long grind, i'll do that, i'm very flexible with my training.

Also, when I am out running I never take my mobile phone with me so I get to escape from whatever has happened that day and completey switch off, running helps me totally relax.

Having said all of that I recently joined my local tri club, there are many Ironmen there and you can always learn from people better than you and besides we have a good laugh, which is important too.

Being in a club isn't always the best if you're as 'flexible' as I am but I've found that's not the case with Team Deane. It's something I wish I had done earlier to be honest as they're helping me improve as an athlete.'

## Going back to IMUK Bolton, what things do you love most about this event?

The supporters are amazing, I love that it is right on my doorstep so it is very convenient for me, I find the bike course very technical yet very enjoyable and being a local lad its great when you recognise so many faces in the crowd  (and they recognise you!)

## Do You have any specific Tips For IMUK Bolton

Do not find yourself sat at the pasta party the night before the race bricking it about Sheep House Lane or Hunters Hill

Get out there and practice them!!!

If you can't because of logistics then go and find a similar hill of a similar size and length and go practice that one instead

## What is The funniest Thing you saw on your journey?

Last year at Bolton when I was stood at the swim start I saw a guy with his wetsuit on the wrong way round,  his zip was at the front.

I went and talked to him and he said he had never done an open water swim before and had slept in his car the night before wearing the wetsuit ☐

I told him that he needed to go and 'sort it out'

**If a Marathon sits above a 20k and an 'Iron' triathlon sits above a Marathon, where does an Ultra sit in relation to an Iron distance Triathlon?**

Good question, these things are always very course specific and the weather also plays a huge factor on race day, my ultra was 'only' a 50km one and I have to tell you, the first marathon was fine, but the second time round, I hated it, by the end I was goosed!

So my answer would be that they have the potential to be on a par.

**Some Questions from twitter now..(Damo loved all of these by the way)**

**Have you got your eye on the Kona Legacy (12 x Ironman) Like Crooky?**

No, Kona would be way too hot for me - I don't like racing in the heat!

**56 x Marathons and 7 x Iron Distance Tri! How Do you follow that, what challenge is next?** *Jodie, @jandkpike*

I am doing 2 further Ironman branded triathlons this year, Bolton because it is convenient and Copenhagen is the one I am going to have a 'good go at' but also getting into the 100 marathon club is my big focus

**What Drove you to do 7 x 'Iron' Tri's? Improving time, regime of training, something else?** *Eileen, @eilewoo*

It's a mix of the three

But I very much like the person I become when I am training at 'iron' distance, its a cliché but doing an Iron distance triathlon isn't so much a race, but more a way of living your life on a daily basis.

I enjoy all aspects of the training, trying to eat right, the general state of well being you experience when getting to a certain level of fitness that the 'Iron' races demand.

**Did your Marathon & 'Iron' races get progressively easier as you found new training techniques etc?** *Harriet, @hjrbrandwood*

*Yes! Absolutely!*

This was probably the best question of the day (miles better than any of mine!) as it held the key to one of the biggest things I got from Damo, as he raced more he learnt more and therefore become more intelligent about what worked for him and what didn't so absolutely they got easier for him the more races that he did.

But he also became a better athlete during the process, as you will soon find out.

**Which Iron Distance Race was You so Proud of?**

At the end of the day you never forget your first race so I will always be more than a little attached to Bolton.

But the race I was most proud of has to be Outlaw. (Not an Ironman branded event but it is the same 'iron' distance 2.4 mile swim, 112 mile bike, 26.2 mile run)

**Outlaw, Why?**

At my first ever Ironman, my time began with the number 15.

At Outlaw my time began with the number 11.

**What? You managed to knock 4 hours off your 'Iron distance time?**

Yes

**OMG how did you manage to do that?**

What Damo told me next was beautifully simple yet clearly very powerful.

'The greatest gains for me where to be made on the bike'

So He hammered the bike in training.

Practiced it over and over, joined a cycling group and learnt to get quicker.

**Any other Secrets?**

The course can make a big difference to your time

**What Would Your Top Tips be for 'Iron' 1st Timers Damo?**

- Do not be precious about time for your first Ironman, save that for the next one
- Smile, all the way round, you have spent probably six months of your life training for your big day, you have annoyed your other half, you have annoyed your mates, you have trained really hard, made many sacrifices, been out in all weathers, ENJOY RACE DAY!! the amount of 1st timers I see with a face like thunder because they are 5 minutes off their PB on race day is ridiculous! Enjoy yourself and SMILE!
- Things like Hunters Hill and Sheep House lane should not be a shock to you, practice them, if you can't get up to Bolton find similar hills near you and practice them instead
- Foam rollers are very underestimated

- Consider hiring a swim coach and practice Open water in a group
- Soreen malt loaf is very underestimated
- I put a big bag of Haribos into my bike pouch and give myself a treat when the bike gets tough - who desn't like Haribos and we all deserve a treat now and then! (Crooky does this with sports mix!)
- Try not to panic about anything, you will, we all do, but try not to
- Get organised and give yourself plenty of time to get organised, do not leave anything to the last minute
- Do not stress about things outside your control like the weather or punctures or getting kicked in the face on the swim, at my first Ironman I was checking the weather forecast every 5 minutes but why? if it's raining am I not going to race? of course I am! what will happen will happen, all this does is drain your energy and causes you lots of unnecessary stress that you simply don't need, try not to stress about things outside of your control
- If its chucking it down or really windy on race day forget about 'going for it on the bike' focus on the run instead
- Trust in your training, if you have trained properly, you will be fine, trust in your training
- Once your race is finished sign up for another one ASAP!

**They are all fantastic Damo Thanks! One last Question, What Do you know now that you wish you knew before your first Ironman?**

I wish I would have relaxed more and not stressed about it as much, it was a big deal for me at the time but now I am far more relaxed about everything.

When you have completed your first couple at iron distance something amazing happens, remember your first sprint triathlon or your first 5k run? - how you felt about it before and how you feel about it now?

Well its the same for the longer distance....

At the end of the day we can all look back on many aspects of our life and think I wish I would have known this or I wish I would have done that, but to do so would rob us of probably the greatest gift of all

**Whats That Damo?**

The journey we go on in order to discover those things...

**With that possibly the most amazing run of my life drew to a close.....**

I couldn't let Damo go without asking for a picture, given the fact that it was still chucking it down there wasn't many people about so we went into the travel lodge to try our luck.

Here we found a lovely Australian gent over to visit family who told us how he had proudly supported the Ironmen in previous years.

With that out of the way it was time to say goodbye.

Damo had got a lift to the beehive and bear in mind we had just run almost 20k into Bolton town centre and back.

https://www.strava.com/activities/941354666

I offered him a lift home no fewer than 3 times...

Each time damo politely refused and I could tell he was absolutely in his element to get back out into the pouring rain and run all the way home....

Thanks again for agreeing to do this Damo it was a truly amazing experience for me and I am sure many visitors to this blog will no doubt appreciate your kind words for many years to come....

If I don't see you before out on the loop, I'll see you in the swim pen on July 16th!

(I might put my wetsuit on the wrong way round just for you!)

You can follow Damo's amazing journey to the 100 marathon club on his twitter feed @damonbwfc

**The Legend that Qualified for Kona but Would Rather Race IMUK Bolton**

Marc Laithwaite is a 10 x Ironman with multiple qualifications for Kona and numerous top 3 finishes within his age group.

He boasts an Ironman PB of 9:20 and regularly gives the pro's a run for their money at IMUK Bolton.

In addition to racing Ironman at a very competitive level, he is completely addicted to everything triathlon, he owns a store that sells triathlon clothing and equipment, he organises many local triathlon races throughout the year, he puts on free rides for cyclists of all abilities, runs structured open water swim sessions at three sisters and on top of all that is a Level 3 triathlon coach helping triathletes of all levels reach their goals.

This guy Eats, sleeps and breathes Triathlon!!

When he is not doing 'all of the above' he is heavily involved with a local charity, Epic Kidz, which supports volunteer groups helping children into fitness throughout the north West.

How the man is able to fit everything in is beyond me.....

I first had the pleasure of meeting Marc when he came thundering past me at a local weekly Duathlon he had organised. Yes, Marc not only organises excellent local races, he actually takes part in them himself!

This gives you a flavour of the type of guy we are dealing with here!!

That he kindly agreed to a feature on my blog blew my mind.

Here is how the interview went.....

**So Marc, 10 x Ironman, multiple qualifications for Kona, Ironman PB that begins with a 9, where did it all start!!**

I was always a good cross country runner at school but when I was 17 I came across a triathlon magazine, picked it up, looked inside and the rest is history!

**What was your first triathlon?**

The Pendle triathlon in Lancashire, 1989, it would be the equivalent of a sprint distance today, Pendle was the biggest race in the North West.

**How did you get on?**

It was a shock, I thought I could swim and cycle, then I found out I couldn't!

**Was your first triathlon Pool Based?**

Yes, and I taught myself to swim in the local pool

**What Training did you do for your first one?**

Whilst I could run, I couldn't really swim so I went down to the local swimming baths as often as I could and taught myself how to swim front crawl.

My dad gave me a Raleigh 'banana' road bike that he got from a skip and I learnt to ride on that!

**Where did you go from there?**

After the sprint I entered my first 'iron distance' race, the longest day in Wolverhampton and began to train for it

## How did you find the transition from pool to open water?

Not a problem, but bear in mind I was 17 at the time and at that age you are fearless! I think the fear creeps in as you start to get older.

## How many 'Iron' distance races have you completed now?

10

## Wow! Which Ones were they?

Ironman® Bolton 4 times, Ironman® Frankfurt Twice, Ironman® Dorest twice, Ironman® Austria, Ironman® Lanzarotte and then I also did stuff like the longest day in Wolverhampton and Ironbridge but you are going back a bit there! (These are old skool 'iron' distance)

## Out of all Those, Which One was your favourite?

Bolton

## Why?

Being a local lad Bolton is the 'big one' every year, the one we all look forward to. I have been involved in triathlons locally for 27 years and know probably 70% of the athletes that are racing at Bolton!

Not only that but I know their wives (or husbands!) their kids, their friends and their family and most of them will be in the crowd giving all the athletes fantastic support!

There's a great triathlon community in the North West and that really stands out at Bolton Ironman.

The local triathlon group 'The Triathlon HUB' make a big fuss on Hunters Hill (or Hubsters Hill as we like to call it) with a disco and fog horns etc. I really look forward to hitting that hill on each lap and then You've got Tri Preston at the Rigby Amrs, COLT (City of Lancaster Tri) on Babylon Lane and those nutters in fancy dress on sheephouse, the whole bike route is very well supported.

Once you start the run, the crowds on the marathon are just superb.

Bolton is by far my favourite race, I have loved everything about it ever since Ironman brought the organisation of the event back 'in house'!

**What is Kona Like?**

I have qualified for Kona several times but never actually been

**What? you have qualified for Kona several times but never been! WHY!?**

You know what, I would rather race Bolton. **(LEGEND!)**

**Wow! I'm loving my IMUK Bolton journey but that is one hell of a statement! Expand!!**

I Don't race Bolton to try and qualify for Kona, I race Bolton because I absolutely love racing Bolton...

Besides, Have you seen how much it costs to get to Hawaii?

Then my kids are very young so the trip would be completely wasted on them. Maybe I might do it in a few years if i'm still racing, when my kids are older. I'd like to go when I'm 50 (I'm 44 now) and make a real holiday of it. We'll see, I may not be racing when I'm 50, maybe I'll regret it.

I love the local atmosphere as I've already said, it goes past my house and it's just an amazing day for local athletes

Bolton is really special to me!

## Which of your races are you most proud of?

My top 3 finishes in my age group at Bolton. (Marc ranked just over ten hours in his last 3 at Bolton which is an unreal achievement giving some of the pro's a run for their money, you are talking top 30 finish out of over 2,000 entrants - only 20 odd places behind the likes of Lucy Gossage!)

## Which was the most difficult?

Before it came to Bolton IMUK was in Dorset and the bike course was extremely hilly, many people struggled to make the bike cut offs so I would pick that. It was in the early days, it's come a long way now and it's so much better. Lanzarote was also very tough because of the wind.

## Have you always been a competitive person?

I take part primarily because I love swimming, cycling and running. But if I'm going to race, I do want to be the best that I can be, whatever result that is.

## What Bike did you do your first Iron Distance Triathlon On?

A steel road bike, they were all the rage at the time - everyone had them!

## And What Bike Have you got now?

A Giant carbon time trial bike

**In your experience, what difference does the more expensive bike make?**

Let's put it this way, some of the guys at my first Iron distance race were riding 100 miles in well under 4 hours on steel road bikes and I still can't get anywhere near that, even on today's machines!

Without any shadow of a doubt it is the athlete not the bike!

As everyone else has said, the bike should be the cherry on the cake, but many people try to put a cherry on top of a cake that doesn't exist.

They would be better investing in themselves to become better athletes first and then upgrading to the more expensive bike.

**How Are you at punctures?**

I'm alright

**How long does it take you to change an inner rube?**

No more than a few minutes

**Have you ever had a puncture on race day?**

Yes in Germany, but it was no big deal

**If you saw a first timer broken down at the side of the road on race day would you stop to help?**

I would ask them if they were alright

**If they said 'no I need help' what would you do?**

I would stop to help them

**Really?**

Yes, why not, I would hope someone would do the same for me if I ever needed it!

**How have you got on with injuries?**

You have to push yourself to the limit to achieve great results and injuries come with the territory, there is a trail of thought that says if you aren't carrying at least a couple of niggles then you aren't training hard enough!

But I need to be careful with this, especially as I get older!

**Do you find that running is the area where injuries are most likely to happen?**

Absolutely

**Being a family man how do you balance the wife and kids with all your training?**

Support me or divorce me!

Joking aside I am lucky that I have a very supportive wife who is also into fitness herself and she completely understands.

I hope that I can be a good role model for my children and set a positive example to them as to the many benefits living such a healthy lifestyle brings. I want them to see me being active and be around other people who are doing the same. Let's face it, if they are brought up around people who do triathlon and ironman, they've got some good role models to follow.

At the end of the day your spouse and your children are everything, but you are still a person too and need to do the things that make you happy! If you sacrifice training/racing triathlon for example and that makes you very pissed off all the time then that is not going to be conducive to a happy, harmonious relationship is it?

**How do you balance working full time with all the training?**

It's tough for us all!

There are plenty of early starts and late nights not to mention all the weekends, but I am lucky in that I am my own boss so have a certain degree of flexibility as to when I train which helps, but I still need to make up the hours In the office like everybody else!

Once again it was clear that 'training' is very much a way of life for Marc and in his words it wouldn't matter if he could' never race again so long as he could still swim bike and run' - it was obvious from speaking with him that he absolutely loves all three aspects.

He went as far as to say that if he wasn't racing Ironman his life wouldn't look that much different, he just loves swimming, cycling and running!

**Do You Only Race Ironman Now?**

Marc races anything and everything, duathlons, sprints, Olympics, bike time trials, open water time trials, cross country races, run races etc. But 'Iron' distance is his preferred race distance.

## Are you a member of any triathlon or running club?

One of the big things that Marc has been involved with is the creation of The Triathlon Hub at the endurance store that he runs.

This saw the 'unification' of several local tri clubs in the area into one large 'group' of triathletes who unite to train together on a regular basis.

'Say you had 10 lads at each club that rode together, usually, 3 would be fast, 3 would be mid pack and 3 would be slow, so why not untie and create bigger groups each of the same pace? it just made perfect sense'

'I have seen in the past that clubs can be very territorial and protective. In some cases, people who leave the club can be ostracised.'

'I think in the North West, we have one of the best triathlon communities. Irrespective of your club, people get on with each other and the banter is outstanding.'

'The view of The Triathlon HUB is that we don't care what club you come from or what your ability is, everybody is welcome and we have a group to suit, from complete novice to podium contender. Yes there is banter and competition, but it's done in the right way, we train hard, have a laugh and help / support eachother.'

## What is the funniest thing you saw on your journey?

'Last year, as I started the marathon at IMUK, about 50 people shouted my name within the first ten minutes.....

I was starting to get excited as I thought everyone recognised me. It was only after about half an hour I realised that my name was written on the front of my race number in big letters and that's why they were shouting my name....

Sadly not quite as well known as I initially thought!'

## If a marathon sits above a 20k and an Iron distance tri sits above a marathon, where does an ultra sit in relation to an Iron distance triathlon?

It depends on the ultra course and the distance but ask yourself this:

How long will it take you to complete an iron distance triathlon?

Then ask yourself which would you prefer? to do the iron distance tri where you get to sit on a bike for long periods, or to run for that length of time non stop?

## Going Back To Ironman, Which One Did you PB?

Ironman Austria, where I recorded a time of 9:20.

## Wow! So what is the secret to your speed Marc?

The million dollar question eh?

The one we all want to know the answer to....

Marc went on to tell me two huge things.

One of which I had stumbled across in my training but didn't realise what I had found until Marc pointed it out and then drilled right down into the detail - this has been added to my book with Marc's kind permission.

The second is a specific way of training that Marc follows, if you want to know more about this  call  the endurance store in Wigan on 01257 251217 and ask for Marc,  tell him your 'goal time' and enrol yourself onto one of his tailored coaching programmes.

### Do you have any specific tips for IMUK Bolton?

When you start the swim do not jump off the side of the pontoon, walk to the end and jump off. Last year at least 4 people had race ending injuries by jumping off the side as it is only about a foot deep and full of bricks and rubble, don't do it!

### What would your top tips be for 1st timers?

* Race day should not be your first experience of open water swimming!

* Further, get used to swimming open water in a group

* Be aware that it can take 20-25 minutes to enter the water for the rolling swim start

* Understand what the bike cut off times are and where they are (there are several throughout the bike circuit - see 'my IMUK plan' tab for further info or check IMUK athlete guide)

* If you plan to sail close to the bike cut off times you need to factor the 'time to enter the water' into your plan as the bike cut offs are a time of day, not 'your actual race time' i.e. you need to be at David Lloyd by 14:15 on lap 2 irrespective of what time you actually started your swim.

* Don't jump off the side of the pontoon (see above)

* 'Hiding' at the back of the swim pen to avoid the 'melee' at the start is a false strategy as by the time you enter the water the pros are likely to be starting their second lap and therefore their will be a 'melee' either way - get used to swimming with others in an open water race simulation

* 40% of the field will lose drinks bottles on the bike, half of them on the speed bumps as soon as they leave penny flash - be aware of the dangers of this (in the past people have crashed into the stray drinks bottles) and consider rear mounted drinks cages to stop your own water jumping out

* Sort your nutrition out

* Get your pacing right

* Do not set off on the bike like a lion and spank all your energy In the first hour- it's a long day

* Do not beat yourself up if you are 10 minutes behind your plan on race day, do not chase the time, focus instead on your rhythm, on your technique

* Smile! Enjoy yourself! This is your day!

**Any chance of a couple of 'golden nuggets' for my book Marc?**

What do you want to know?

**What distance would you suggest 1st timers take the 'Long Slow Runs' to In training?**

Answer added to Book with Marc's kind permission!

**What would be the maximum distance you would suggest 1st timers run in brick sessions?**

Answer added to Book with Marc's kind permission!

**Questions from Twitter:**

**What tips do you have for the taper?**

Don't overdo it. Many people taper from several weeks out and they feel awful on race day. Don't go mad the weekend before then in the final week cut back by 50%. Most people only need a few days, 4 weeks leaves them lethargic and out of sorts

**Did you only ever plan to do the one Ironman?**

Didn't really have a plan first time, just wanted to have a go, then 1 wasn't enough

**What is the biggest battle when stepping up to ironman, the mental or the physical?**

Definitely physical, you can't get round on mental strength. You can only suffer for so long before you've had enough. I always aim to get to 16 miles in marathon before I start to suffer, then it's only just over an hour to finish. If you've not done enough training you'll find it hard, your mood will drop and it's tough to keep going. It's never tough mentally when you physically feel fine.

**Tips on how to deal with the mindset when it starts falling apart mid race & u know u have missed the target time so have little desire to keep going?**

The steps are as follows:

1. Your objectives need to be realistic, don't set one too high that's likely to fail from the start. If you've not done it before, don't start making up finish times

2. You need 3-4 plans. Plan A is your best time, once that fails, it's plan B. That way when you start falling apart, you just switch to the next plan and stay focused rather than losing it.

3. Your final back up plan is always to finish, never drop out, you'll always regret it.

**What is the one thing you know now that you wished you knew before your first Ironman?**

I wish I'd known about chamois cream

**When you look back on your amazing journey is there anything you would change?**

No regrets!

27 years later and i'm still loving it!

If you really had to push me I would say I wish I would have raced harder in my 20's instead of waiting until my 30's.

But triathlon has been very good to me over the years, I have met some amazing people, made many friends and built a store, events and coaching business around it so no, I wouldn't change a thing!

Marc is one of those people that you could sit and talk to all day long and not get bored, but as you can imagine, everybody wants a piece of him and his next appointment was due any second!

I managed to squeeze one final question in though...

**What keeps you going Marc? What is your motivation to keep racing at Iron distance?**

This year will be the first time that I will be in the Vet 45 category - this is my chance to put my stamp on the new age group and I can't wait!

It was obvious to me that Marc was looking forward to Bolton this year more than ever.

This way of looking at getting older - 'fantastic! -  I'm in a new age group that I can put my stamp on' absolutely summed up what an amazing individual Marc Laithwaite is.

You do realise Marc that the Ironman age groups go to 90 plus?

With that, his next appointment arrived in store so the interview drew to a close....

I watched open mouthed as the customer went on to boast 'ive done this and I've done that' yet never once did Marc mention the 10 Ironman triathlons, multiple Kona qualifications or the Ironman PB beginning with a 9.....

He just stood there smiling, without saying a single word.

You can find out more about the endurance store by visiting www.theendurancestore.com or follow Marc on twitter @endurancecoach

***Update*** – Marc went on to **win** his age group at IMUK Bolton, a truly sensational achievement.

Following some recent banter on SM about dogs not being allowed at a local tri, Marc posted a picture of his dog. When I think back, he always runs with that dog......
Laithwaite! we're onto you!

## 100+ Mara's, 14 x Iron Triathlons, 1 'Double Iron'- The Amazing Story of 'Ironman S'

In today's world it makes a refreshing change to meet someone who doesn't like selfies or instagram or shouting at the top of his voice to be heard on social media like everybody else...

Then again, it's not every day that you meet a guy who has done 14 Iron distance triathlons, 1 double iron distance and well over 100 marathons.

But Ironman 'S' is a pretty special type of guy, as you will soon find out.

He likes his privacy and he doesn't like his picture being taken, which is why i'm holding most of his 'iron' medals as proof of his remarkable achievements in the photograph to the left....(some are framed as you can imagine!)

I found huge chunks of his story beautiful and fascinating..

Ironman 'S' is one of the many runners out there that plied their trade for many years before being enticed by triathlon.

He was a runner from a very early age, first getting the bug at primary school when he entered (and won) a 50 metre 'race'.

His parents actively encouraged him to join the local running club and he went on to run at county level.

As soon as he was old enough, he entered a marathon.

He instantly became addicted to the distance and went on to run well over 100 marathons all over the world.

Yet you will not find his name mentioned in the '100' club...

"Don't get me wrong, those who are I think are fantastic & I congratulate everyone on their amazing achievement. Ok hitting 100 was a milestone & a relief to me as I'd been chasing it for sometime but I didn't make a big deal of it, **no one knew, there was no cake, no celebration or congratulations, I just got my medal, got changed behind two wheelie bins then drove home to celebrate NYE with my family."**

How humble is that?

He made sure I saw every single one of his 124 marathon medals though, 'beaming' as he showed them to me.

After he had done about 50 marathons he was looking for 'another challenge' and came across the Rossendale Sprint Distance triathlon (no way lol!!)

He entered it, loved it and immediately wanted to do another.

He set his sights on the Deva triathlon in Chester, an Olympic triathlon that included an open water swim in the river dee.

The Olympic distance felt like a 'big deal' to him at the time.

Once he conquered that he felt like he was the bees knees of triathlon.

"The next day we went on Holiday, I remember proudly wearing my Deva triathlon finishers T-shirt, strutting around the airport with my chest puffed out, thinking I was the big dog'

His Holiday destination?

Nice

As fate would have it and unbeknown to him when he booked, Ironman France was due to take place whilst he was there.

The airport lounge was filled with Ironmen and their bike boxes.

"Once I realised what the Ironman was, the 'Deva Triathlon finishers T-shirt' was quickly removed and the chest lost all of it's 'puff'!"

"When we arrived in Nice I couldn't wait to go and watch the Ironman."

"I remember being sat on the beach watching the athletes go into the water and thinking to myself....."

'What they are about to attempt' - it's impossible

"I was confused when they completed the mammoth swim and started giving people in the crowd a 'high 5'."

'Let's see if you are still doing that on the run in 10 hours time' I said to myself.

"I fully expected most of them to have withdrawn from the race by the time they got to the run with people collapsing and being taken away on a stretcher etc."

"I was really interested to see how many would still be left standing."

"As I am stood in the crowd watching the marathon ten hours later, I was astonished to see that not only did the vast majority finish, but they seemed to be having the time of their life as they did so, laughing and joking with the crowd, celebrating with all the supporters - huge smiles on their faces...."

'These people aren't wired right' I said to myself.

"I stayed watching until the final finisher crossed the line at 11pm."

"I loved every single second of it, it was one of the most fascinating things I had ever seen in my life."

"The atmosphere was electric."

"The next day I clearly remember being sat on a train with my wife with a big smile on my face."

'You are still thinking about that Ironman aren't you' she said to me.

"That was it...."

"As soon as we got back to England, I signed up to the next Ironman race in France."

"I had 12 months to train for it......"

You will soon discover How Ironman 'S' got on....

Here is how  the interview went...

**100+ mara's - Wow! which one was your Favourite ?**

Toss up between Tucson because it was in Tucson Arizona! or the NYE mara in Liverpool because it was my 100th and it was on NYE!!

**Mara PB?**

3:29 Arizona!

**Toughest Mara?**

Hell of a hill but its also one of my faves, it's 5 maras over 5 days - you can enter them individually if you want but the medal is very clever - it has 5 segments to it  (of course he has done the 'big 5')

## What got you into triathlon

After I had done about 50 marathons I was Looking for my next challenge and I got wind of the Rossendale sprint triathlon

## What training did you do for it?

I knew I had the run under my belt and I was comfortable with the bike as I was commuting to and from work on it at the time but the swim was the killer for me

## Was it Pool Based?

Yes

## What swim stroke did you use for your first tri?

Breastroke

## How did you get on?

I loved it and couldn't wait to 'go again'

## What was next?

The Deva triathlon, an Olympic distance with an open water swim in the river dee - cracking the Olympic distance was a big deal to me at the time, as was mastering front crawl!

## How did you find the transition from Pool to Open water

It was OK, I got round, but in hindsight I would have done more open water swimming as part of my training

## Where did you go from there?

Ironman France, I gave myself 12 months to train for it

**Did you follow a plan?**

I started following a very well known plan but found it very rigid so I ditched it and went my own way

**Would you agree that many people make Ironman training way more complicated than it needs to be?**

Yes!

**How many Iron distance races have you done now?**

14 and one double iron distance

**Wow! which ones were they?**

Ironman® Bolton x 6, Ironman® Wales, Ironman® France, Ironman® UK Dorset x2, Ironman® Lanzarotte, the 'Lakesman' The 'Enduroman' Single x2 and the 'Enduroman' Double (The last 3 are not Ironman branded events but are the same 'iron distance' bar the double which is double 'iron' distance!)

**Which one was your favourite?**

You will always treasure your first Ironman so I would have to say France.

I also really enjoyed my second one in Lanzarotte.

But my first IMUK when I got to carry my daughter over the finish line in my arms was really special to me - He was literally beaming when he showed me this picture (Not allowed to do this anymore - 'health and safety' see)

**Which one was the toughest?**

Without any shadow of a doubt, Ironman Wales!

## What was the 'double Iron distance' Triathlon like?

I wanted to do it for the challenge, but some weird stuff was going on during that let me tell you! (hallucinations and nearly falling asleep on the bike!)

## What was your time for your first Ironman?

13:55

## Which one did you PB?

Ironman Lanzarotte, 12:30

## How did you get your time down?

I had many tec issues for my first one so that didn't help

Second time round I had a different attitude, I was a lot more relaxed about it and  I wanted to give it  'a good go'

I did a lot more mileage on the bike, I remember booking a week off work and going for 3 century rides in 5 days!!

## You mention Tec issues - how have you got on as far as that goes on Race day?

You know what in 14 races I have only ever had one puncture.

But my first Ironman was a nightmare.

When I got to the hotel I discovered that the baggage handlers had damaged my bike so I was unable to get the back wheel on.

Thankfully it was covered by Insurance and the Insurance company allowed me to go and buy a new bike.

I went down to the local bike shop and took whatever they had available within my budget.

30 miles into the bike and my gears got stuck in the bottom ring.

I ended up riding the rest of the bike circuit in the low gear which wasn't ideal, but I got round and managed to get my hands on the medal!

**Are you a member of a Triathlon Club?**

No, I find them too rigid, I prefer to do my own thing on a day and a time to suit me

**How Do you find working full time with all your training?**

It's not easy and I work shifts too which doesn't help, but you find a way

**How do you balance the family with all your training?**

When I first got together with my wife I was already well into my fitness so it came with the package so to speak!!

But i'm not going to lie, once you have a child, it's tough.

There are  plenty of very early starts to get the training out of the way!!

I find combining an Ironman with a holiday makes it a far more appealing proposition for your other half!

**What do you love most about IMUK Bolton?**

Without doubt the supporters.

The crowds on the bike route on sheephouse and Babylon Lane and Hunters are amazing.

Once you get onto the main 'triple loop' for the marathon the atmosphere from the crowd is just electric.

**What are your top tips for first timers?**

Take advantage of your special needs bag, many people neglect it but why? You may as well fill it so it's there for you if you need it!

Don't worry about the swim, every first timer does, but you don't get to the start line of Ironman without practicing the swim distance in training - if you have already done it once then you can do it again - don't worry about it!

Try not to stress about things on race day, you will find everything just clicks into place

The man who finishes in 16:59 gets the same medal as the man who finishes in 10 hours

Focus on getting the medal not a certain time

Race times get lost in archives, medals last forever

Be disciplined with your fuel strategy

Force yourself to eat even if you are being sick, your body is like a car, it needs fuel

Don't leave anything till the last minute, prepare properly

Get the century rides in on the bike

Be aware that it can take around 15 minutes to enter the water on the rolling swim start

Be aware of your surroundings at all times, (like pros coming past you on the bike before you pull out to overtake for example - don't worry about it but be aware of it if that makes sense)

Be aware of what is going on around you (potholes etc) chillout instead of 'going for it' and give yourself chance to 'react'

The crowd will lift you more than you realise

If you have trained properly race day is easier than what you think

Sign up for another asap

Whilst you are the one racing,  your family will be going through the same emotions as you......always thank them for there continued support because they've played a huge part in your journey to the start & finish line!

**What do you know now that you wish you knew before your first Ironman?**

Don't panic everything will be OK

**Any tips on dealing with lack of sleep because of excitement on 'Race Eve'?**

The fact is you aren't going to get much sleep but you will feel more awake than ever on race day from all the adrenaline

**Why do you keep entering Ironman, what is your motivation?**

My daughter absolutely loves it when I bring another medal home for her, she puts them all in a box under her bed.

When I am long gone, those medals will still be there and I know my daughter will always treasure them and tell people 'look at what my dad did'

I would like to get her 20 Ironman medals.

**As a Father myself, part of my motivation for getting the Ironman medal is to show my daughter that 'Anything is possible in her life' - Can you relate to that?**

Absolutely!

**What was the Biggest Thing you have learnt on your Ironman journey?**

When I did my first Ironman it was a massive thing for me.

I trained really hard for 12 months for it.

Once I finally got my hands on the medal I celebrated for a few weeks.

But there comes a point when every successful first timer will inevitably ask themselves,...

'Now what?'

I have learnt that Ironman is not so much a race, but a way of living your life.

I love the person I become when I am training for an Ironman,

The way I feel.

The way I look.

The Energy I have.

Eating right,

The 'High' you get as you train.

It becomes very addictive.

Once you have experienced it, you want more.

Not only that but my family like the person I become when I train for the races too! - they much prefer him than the bloke that used to sit in the beer garden all afternoon!!

That is why I keep entering races!

**Are you always looking to chase your PB with each race?**

The answer was a very firm 'NO'.

"I did 12:30 in Lanzarotte and that will do for me"

It was clear that he now enters races with one main objective:

To get the medal.

Time is irrelevant to him.

He enters races for the love of taking part in races...

For the joy of the 'doing'

For his 'little girl'

For the person he becomes as he trains (see above)

**This enables him to enjoy each race in such a way that those constantly chasing the PB will never understand.**

I couldn't help thinking that when you spend time with people like Damo and Marc like I did recently it's difficult to not become seduced by their fantastic speed....

But to allow your 'head to be turned' would be to lose sight of the message that sits at the very core of this website....

A message beautifully illustrated by the wonderful story of 'Ironman S'

# Nick Thomas : 13 x Iron Distance, Double Iron, Triple Iron, Kona racer & Ultra champion!

For many, Nick Thomas will need no introduction.

He has completed no fewer than 13 'Iron' distance triathlons all over the world and boasts an Ironman PB of 9.36.

That PB saw him realising his ultimate dream of racing at the Ironman world championships in Kona.

He later went on to complete both a double iron distance and then a triple.

Most recently he has been racing ultra marathons  at both 50 mile, 100 mile and 24 hour races, becoming the England athletics ultra distance champion in 2013.

The man is Hardcore!

Level 3 BTF qualified, he writes bespoke training plans for athletes of all abilities and is  lead coach at Manchester triathlon club.

Here is how the interview went....

## So Nick, 13 Iron triathlons, Kona, doubles, Triples, Ultras! where did it all start?

I was always into running at school but never particularly good!

I also enjoyed riding my BMX bike!

When I was about 18 I saw an article about the Ironman in a triathlon magazine, as soon as I read it, I was hooked.

I also remember the ITU world championships coming to Manchester, I went to watch it and Loved every second, at that time all of the top athletes were British, I wanted some!

**What was your first Triathlon?**

It was a sprint distance in Wolverhampton

**How Did you get on?**

I did better than I expected, I think I finished top 10

**Where did you go from there?**

I had a lot of fun at sprint and Olympic for a while, qualifying for the ITU world championships before moving up to Ironman

**Which was your first Ironman?**

The longest day in Wolverhampton (old skool iron distance race)

**And your time for your first race?**

10:23

**How many Iron distance races have you done now?**

13

**Wow which ones were they**

Ironman® UK Dorset, Ironman® Frankfurt x2, Ironman® Lanzarotte x2, Ironman® Lake placid, Ironman® Kona, Challenge Roth x2, Longest Day x 4 (the last 2 are not Ironman® branded events but are the same 'iron' distance)

**Which one did you PB?**

Frankfurt in 9:36

**What was the secret to your speed?**

By the time I qualified for Kona I had been racing at Iron distance for 6 years so learnt what worked for me and more importantly what didn't

I learnt to become much more efficient with my training

**Which one was your favourite?**

Without any shadow of a doubt KONA!

**What was Kona like?**

Just the most amazing experience in the world with the finest athletes in the world, getting to race at Kona was an absolute dream come true for me, I had the race of my life to qualify for it and when I got there it was everything I imagined it would be and more!

**2nd Favourite?**

Roth

**Toughest?**

Lanzarotte

**What was your motivation to do the double Iron distance?**

I had done 13 Iron distance, I wanted another challenge

## And the triple?

Same again, it wasn't long after I had completed the double and wanted the next challenge - there is only one place you can go from the double!

## How were they?

More mentally challenging than anything else, the lack of sleep is the tough one.

## What bike did you do your first Ironman on?

An aluminium TT bike

## And what bike did you PB the Ironman on?

A fully carbon cervelo TT bike

## Having ridden the Ironman on both, what difference does the more expensve bike make?

The early aluminium bikes were a tough ride and you would end up getting off them considerably more fatigued than the modern bikes of today.

As far as the modern carbon road bike verus TT bike debate goes I would say that it depends on the athlete, the course, and the athletes average speed.

If you are averging 16mph lets say for a 100 mile ride, then you are not going fast enough to make the aero gains that a TT bike would give you, so in my opinion you may as well keep the £3,000 in your back pocket.

If however  you are racing Olympic distance at 22mph average on a relatively flat course, then maybe it might be worth investing.

But comfort is key.

If you are comfortable then you will go faster.

Not only on the bike, but once you get off it to start the run.

There is no point gaining ten minutes on the bike but then unable to run because your back has gone due to the position you have been sat in for the last 5/6/7 hours!

The course also plays a big part too, in my opinion most age groupers would be better off on a sportive bike at IMUK.

The bike should be fit for purpose!

Nick used the analogy of doing a paper-round on a TT bike and asked - why would you do that?

**Do you think bodyweight makes a big difference to Race Times?**

Again it depends on the course.

Flat you can get away with it, extra weight can sometimes even help.

Most of the guys at the top of the bike time trails are big lads with huge legs and big lungs, but give them a hill and they don't like it.

On hilly courses you will notice a big difference at a lower weight.

If your heart has to lug 15 stone up hunters hill then it will require a lot more effort than if it only has to carry 11 stone up there.

The key is to lose the weight but maintain your strength.

## How have you got on with injuries?

I very rarely get injured and I never become ill

## What do you put that down to?

Training right and more than anything else - Luck!

## How do you balnce the family with all your training?

My wife runs so she understands

But its about being efficient with your time

Most of my clients are very busy people with demanding jobs and families like everybody else, but they have learnt to be very effiecent with their time.

There are lots of very early starts and plenty of late finishes.

Usually, their partners will be supportive of their Ironman journey because they like the person that they become when they train for it and the many positive things that brings.

But at the end of the day if they are not supportive, something has to give and that can only be one of two things, either the training or the relationship and I have seen the latter give way many times.

## Are you a member of a triathlon club?

Nick is one of the lead coaches at Manchester Triathlon Club

## What is the funniest thing you have seen on your journey?

I have seen people racing at events with cone hats on the wrong way round

**If a marathon sits above a 20k and an Iron triathlon sits above a marathon, where does an ultra sit in relation to an Iron distance tri?**

It depends how hard you race them

**What tips do you have for first timers?**

Question why you have entered it

Question what you want to get out of it

And ask yourself is entering an Ironman the right thing to do in the first place

**What makes you say that?**

As Ironman has become more popular and more fashionable more people want to do it.

A lot of people now enter Ironman because they feel they need to prove something - their brother in law has done it or some guy at work has done it so they feel they have to do it too.

But they don't enjoy the process of becoming one.

They don't enjoy training for it.

They don't enjoy swimming, they don't enjoy cycling and they don't enjoy running.

And they don't enjoy race day.

So I would question why you would want to dedicate 6 months of your life to something that you don't enjoy doing.!

If you would rather be playing golf - go and do that instead!

life is too short!

Becoming an Ironman is not so much about the actual race day.

Becoming an Ironman is all about the training.

And you have got to enjoy it and want to do it, otherwise what's the point of entering in the first place?

Ask yourself...

Do you enjoy swimming cycling and running?

If the answer is no then go and find something that you enjoy doing instead!!

**Any other top tips for first timers?**

If you are working, you haven't got enough time to train properly for 3 sports at the same time.

If You haven't got enough time for good training, you certainly haven't got enough time for bad training.

So what you have to do, Is make the best of a bad situation.

The training that you do has to be as specific and effective as possible.

(also see tip about bike for IMUK Bolton as above)

**What Is the biggest thing you have learnt on your journey?**

You need to be excited about the event that you have entered in order to be motivated to train properly for it.

## What do you know now that you wish you knew before your first 'Iron' Distance?

Compared to the training that I was doing for my first Ironman, the training needs to be either much easier or much harder with less of the slogging away in the middle zone.

With that, it was time for us to pack up our things and make our way down to 3 sisters for the open water TT.

I had spent an hour with Nick but felt I had barely scratched the surface with him.

Nick is one of those 'proper' old skool Ironmen.

Nothing illustrates this more than our conversation on the way back to the car...

'In the old days, Ironman was a sport for people who loved training for it and were prepared to suffer, they battered themselves in training and same again on race day'

'They didn't just enter one Ironman, they entered lots, it was their chosen sport - entering just one would be like a footballer playing one football match and then quitting football, but look at the start line of an Ironman today and you will see that a large percentage will be first timers - not only that, but their first Ironman will be their only Ironman and i'm not convinced most people are there because they want to be there'

I couldn't help but detect a little hint of sadness in Nicks voice about what has happened to the sport that he adores so much as it has become more and more popular over the years.

Make no mistake, there are still thousands of hardcore Ironmen around today, exactly like the ones that Nick describes....

And, should I manage to get my hands on the sacred medal this July, you won't find anyone that has enjoyed the process of becoming an Ironman more than Iron Rookie....

But whether or not my first Ironman will be my only Ironman....

Well that is a different matter entirely!!

To your amazing journey!

## Iron Legend Dave Clamp : 'Deca Dave'

I am sure that 'Deca Dave' (or should that be Double Deca Dave?) needs no introduction.

His list of achievements is endless!

He has been racing triathlon since it first came to England over 30 years ago.

During that time he has completed the 'Iron' distance over 150 times.

Yes you heard that right - 150!

He has completed around 50 'single' iron distance races.

He qualified for Kona at IMUK.

He boasts an Iron distance PB of sub 9 Hours.

He then went on to do 6 'double iron' races and 9 x Triple iron distance races.

Not content with that he has completed the 'Deca' (10x Iron distance back to back / continuous) no fewer than 5 times.

Pretty amazing right?

You ain't heard the half of it....

He then went on to set the world record for the double deca - 20 x iron distance over 20 days back to back!

And here is me and you stressing about doing the one!

Kind of puts it all into perspective don't you think?

If this is a website about what is possible, then you won't find a better example of 'what is possible' than Deca Dave......

Period.

But make no mistake, this guy isn't just completing the races - he's bloody racing them!

Here is how the interview went:

**So Dave, 150 x Iron distance! Sub 9 IM,  Kona, Doubles, Triples, Deca's - Double Deca's! World Records!  where did it all start?**

Believe it or not I was hopeless at school, I would always come last in the 100 metre race and I was the kid who was left standing against the wall last to be picked.

I still enjoyed sport, I just wasn't very good at it and found myself going down the cross country route.

When I was 21 I spent some time in France - me and my colleague would do a little  running as a bit of fun in our spare time, nothing major just a few miles now and then, but we saw an advert for the Paris marathon and decided to enter.

**How did you get on?**

4 and a half hours and I ran in Dunlop Tennis shoes - it makes me laugh how people moan about a few cobbles at the London marathon - in paris 20 of the 26 miles were on cobbles!

**Where did you go from there?**

I got married and had kids so that and work took over but I would turn up at the odd marathon now and again with a little bit of training inbetween, just a bit of fun really.

I mananged to get my time down to about 3:30 but I used to look at those guys doing sub 3 and wonder how the hell they did that!

**How many marathons did you run before your first triathlon?**

About 20

**So you were very much a runner turned triathlete?**

Yes!

**How did you get into triathlon?**

I got wind of an event in Northampton in 1983, I am not sure if it was the first ever one in England, I think there might have been one in Darwen slightly earlier, but it was certainly one of the first ever races in this country!

We had to swim for 2.4 miles, 50 mile bike which was loops of a caravan park and then we went and joined in with the Northampton marathon!

I did it on a borrowed bike!

We all had an individual time keeper!

**How did you get on?**

I got a DNF! I kept being sick on the run!!

**What happened next?**

A circuit developed at Olympic distance in England, each race had virtually the same 300 people in it, you knew almost everyone at each race - it was great!

**Where did you go from there?**

Quite quickly I moved up to the full Iron distance doing my first
In 1988 at Roth

**How did that go?**

I did ok, 10:13

Ok? at that time Roth was part of Ironman and his time got him
a place at Kona!

They asked me if I wanted my Kona place but I declined! I
didn't really understand what it was! plus it was in October and
school teachers are not allowed to take any holidays then!

**How many iron distance have you done now?**

Dave has done the iron distance approximately 150 times.

He has done the 'single' Iron distance around 50
times including the longest day in Wolverhampton no fewer
than 9 times.

He went on to do 6 x 'double iron' and 9 x triple iron distance
races!

He then completed the 'Deca' 5 times!! (10 x iron distance back
to back or continuous!) and 1 x 'double deca' (20 x Iron
distance back to back over 20 days)!!

**Which was you favourite single?**

Roth

**Why?**

The atmpsohere and the course, the roads on the bike are like billiard tables!

**How many times have you done Botlon?**

Once

**How did you get on?**

It was quite a recent thing.

Qualifying for Kona seemed to be all the rage at my local tri-club - so I set Bolton as the target to do that.

**How did it go?**

I won my age group and I got my place in Hawai!

**What did you like most about IMUK Bolton?**

The crowds

**Which was your Toughest race?**

The one in the alps

**Which race was you most proud off?**

My PB where I went sub 9

**What is the Secret to your speed?**

Specific speed/track work

Realising that you can run faster, despite your limiting beliefs

I did a lot of fell racing which helped me get used to running at maximum heart rate for a long priod of time when your muscles and your lungs are screaming at you on the way up!

Ability to maintain it close to the red line for long periods

Willingness to suffer and tolerate the pain

**What difference do the really expensive bikes make? is it the bike or the rider?**

Its a combination of the two

I have seen some people do incredible times on 'crap bikes'

Strong legs play a huge part

That said, the bike is the cherry on the cake

It's the 'Ferrari' feeling.

I remember getting some really expensive wheels and there is a huge pyscological impact - I said to myself 'I will look a right knob if i'm not fast with these on!!' and guess what? I was fast!

**What made you move to the double iron distance?**

By this time I had done countless singles, I remember being sat round at Christmas with some friends drinking beer and someone said hey look at this.....

That was it!

Same with the triples!

## How did you get into the Deca - 10 x iron distance!

I was vaguely aware of it, I had read bobby brown's book which planted a seed but I had already done loads of singles, doubles and triples so the 'Deca' was the next challenge!

## Did you go straight from the triple to the Decca?

Yes

## How was it?

Tough, I think I finished almost last!

## Which is the harder format? 10 a day for 10 days or continuous?

It depends on your ability

The guys who are racing at the front finish each day with sufficient time to rest in the one a day format.

That is not the same for the guys at the back.

It's the lack of sleep that is the killer.

With the continuos format you have 14 days to do it so you can plan your days as you like - you can't do that with 'one a day'!

I would say the Continuous format is 'easier' for the slower athletes and one a day is 'easier' for the faster.

## How many times did you do the Deca?

5 times, 2 x continuous 3 x one a day

**What is the Secret to the Deca?**

Learning how to train for it

A bloody good support crew!

**Then what did you do Dave?**

A double Deca! 20 iron distance in 20 days!

**How did that go?**

I broke the world record!

**Wow! Congratulations!- Which distance do you prefer now?**

The Deca's, there is something incredibly special about them

**How do you balance the Family with all your training?**

All I would say is this...

It's very easy for people to become so consumed with their training that they forget about other things that are really important in their life

**How have you got on with Injuries?**

If you ask people at Bolton Tri they will tell you that I was forever getting injured, but now I hardly get injured

**Do you find it's when you are pushing the speed on the short runs that you are most likely to get injured?**

Absolutely

**Are you a member of any triathlon club?**

I was with Bolton Tri for a long time but now I live in Knutsford so I am with them

**If a marathon sits above a 20k and a iron triathlon sits above a marathon, where does an ultra sit in relation to an iron tri?**

It depends how hard you race them

**What difference does bodyweight have on your speed?**

Huge difference

One of the biggest things an old coach would repeat over and over - if you want to go faster, lose the weight

**What keeps you going?**

if I was in the middle of the pack I doubt I would continue, its the fact that im breaking world records at 57 that keeps me going

**What top tips do you have for first timers?**

It's a cliché, but understand that completing an Ironman is not impossible

When we haven't done something we are scared of it - it depends how much you want it and the only reason why it wouldn't be possible is because you don't want it enough

Ask yourself what you want to get out of the race, The difference between compete and complete is that there is one L of a difference!

The last 3rd of any race is always the toughest

People think they cant run fast but they can!

So much of it at this level is the play off between the mental and the physical

Pain tolerance - get used to hurting

Track running will help your speed no end

Fell running was some of the best training I ever did

Strong legs are very important

If you're first starting out to swim, learn to bilateral breathe from the start

The race is never easy if you want a good result

You have got to learn how to hurt

The course makes a massive difference to your time

Nutrition and hydration - start early on in the race and stick to your plan like glue

You don't realise how much you sweat during the swim, take a few seconds to top up your fluid before the bike

Practice nutrition in your training

People know they should do a mix of long slow runs, speed work and hills but what happens is people just merge the 3 so become expert plodders

Combat blisters by washing your feet in turpse 2 weeks before a race and vassaline the essential areas on race day!

Your race performace is not decided by how you react as you are gliding along on the bike, your race performance is decided by how you react when the pain comes because it will come, but its how you deal with it that makes all the difference

Everyone is looking for the magic pill....

There is no magic pill - you have to get out there and train!

People spend way too much time theorising aboiut it -just get out there!

**What do you know now that you wish you knew before your 1st ironman?**

You can push the bike and it doesn't affect the run

**I am surprised you say that, everybody else has said the opposite!**

In fairness, I am naturaly a runner, Your physical build does make a big difference and It helps no end that the run element is one of my strengths!

**What is next for you then Dave?**

Well my Personal training keeps me busy and I enter lots of races with my clients (Dave trains people and then often actually does the race with them!) but I feel another Deca coming on,

At 57, Dave told me that his 10k PB will probably go to the grave with him.

I asked if his sub 9 hour Ironman PB would do likewise.

'Not neccesarrily' he replied with a twinkle in his eye.

'Deca Dave' is without doubt one of the most amazing people I have ever met on my journey.

Already I find myself thinking about him as I struggle up Hunters Hill (It's only a 'single' Iron Rookie - what's the matter with you lad?)

I will remember him for many things, but probably the biggest one of all was when he shared this phrase.....

**"The difference between Complete and Compete is that there is one 'L' of a difference!"**

You can discover more about Dave and his tailored Personal Training  at www.daveclamp.com

## Marc Laithwaite    'Deca Dave'

## 'Damo'

## Nick Thomas

## Now What?

Now that the final chapter in my journey has come to a close, the inevitable words 'what next' appear on everybody's lips.

Writing this almost 14 days after IMUK, I have to tell you that I do not know the answer to the question.

It very much feels to me as if I have spent the last 6 months climbing up a mountain.

Having finally stuck my flag atop of it, I am now quite enjoying the view.

I do not know what will happen next, I am sure something will catch my attention sooner or later.

I would love to be involved with Ironman UK at some point…..

In terms of training, got to be honest, I have done very little since the big day, that said, my legs now feel like a couple of loaded machine guns, so I can definitely feel another run/ride coming on in the very near future!

You will be able to get updates on my website, www.iron-rookie.com please call in from time to time and have a see what I am up to! (I'm thinking of doing guided IMUK 'loop' rides if anyone fancies it!)

If you are reading this when I am long gone, then you will find my spirit roaming the Ironman race circuit, especially on race day.

Once a Wanderer, always a Wanderer.

There is a famous saying that goes 'if we are related, then we shall meet'

In closing may I borrow the words from the great Napolean Hill when he wrote;

'If we are related, then we have, through these pages, met'

To your amazing journey!

PK, the Iron Rookie

(Now please go and leave me that bloody review on Amazon!)

## Acknowlededgments

Of course none of this would be possible without the unconditional love and support of my wife and family so I must begin by paying tribute to them.

I have met so many fantastic people along my journey that it would require an entire book to list them all!

But I would like to say a special thank you to Katerina Tanti of @uktrichat on Twitter who supported me from day 1.

I need to thank every single Ironman that I ever met, the way you were with me throughout this entire process blew my mind.

I would also like to thank everybody involved with Ironman UK and Bolton council, together with all the wonderful volunteers and supporters that lined every inch of both the IMUK bike and run circuits on race day for giving me one of the most magical experiences of my life.

Huge appreciation goes to Sam, Crooky, Damo, Marc Laithwaite, Ironman S, Nick Thomas and Deca Dave who's interviews towards the rear of this book will no doubt inspire generations for years to come.

Finally, to the thousands out there that ever clicked 'like' on one of my social media posts I salute you….

To the thousands more that went on to send me messages of support and encouragement then thank you, thank you from the bottom of my heart, your kind words meant more to me than you will ever know…

To your amazing journey!

The Iron Rookie

Printed in Great
Britain
by Amazon